The world-wide distribution of David Hamilton's book, *Evolutionary Economics,* established his international reputation as a leading figure in the literature of American institutional economics. But his contributions to evolutionary institutional economics are also contained in the steady stream of articles he published over the last half of the twentieth century. This definitive collection of his publications makes that body of work immediately accessible. Hamilton's refreshingly original ideas, clothed as they are in a graceful prose that is seldom found in economic writing, are as pertinent today as they were when he wrote them. He demonstrates why mainstream economics is generally irrelevant to the world in which we live and how a reorientation of the discipline to an evolutionary perspective would correct this deficiency.

(Paul D. Bush, Professor Emeritus of Economics, California State University, Fresno, USA; 2009 Veblen-Commons Award Recipient)

David Hamilton emerged in the 1950s as one of the most important American figures in the original tradition of institutional economics. Among his many forceful and enduring themes is his emphasis on the evolutionary and Darwinian character of Veblenian institutionalism. This is a very useful collection of his writings.

(Geoff Hodgson, Research Professor in Business Studies, Business School, University of Hertfordshire, UK)

Cultural Economics and Theory by David Hamilton and edited by Glen Atkinson, Bill Dugger and Bill Waller, is a remarkable book. It is about how to practice institutional economics as a science of culture and change, written by one of the greatest practitioners in the field. It analyses the culture of capitalism, dealing with practices and policies associated with money, consumption, fashion, factors of production, technology and ceremony. Hamilton has done nothing less than surveyed the problems and prospects of advanced capitalism in the modern world. It is brilliant in its penetrating scrutiny of poverty amid plenty, technology and institutions, making goods and making money, as well as engaging in war or cooperating together. All students of social and institutional economics must read this book, and all good libraries should have it in stock.

(Phillip Anthony O'Hara, Professor of Global Political Economy and Governance, Global Political Economy Research Unit, Curtin University, Perth, Australia)

T0382729

Cultural Economics and Theory

David Hamilton is a leader in the American institutionalist school of heterodox economics that emerged after World War II. This volume includes twenty-five articles written by Hamilton over a period of nearly half a century. In these articles he examines the philosophical foundations and practical problems of economics. The result of this is a unique institutionalist view of how economies evolve and how economics itself has evolved with them. Hamilton applies insight gained from his study of culture to send the message that human actions situated in culture determine our economic situation.

David Hamilton has advanced heterodox economics by replacing intellectual concepts from orthodox economics that hinder us with concepts that help us. In particular, Hamilton has helped replace equilibrium with evolution, make-believe with reality, ideological distortion of government with practical use of government, the economy as a product of natural law with the economy as a product of human law, and, last, he has helped us replace the entrepreneur as a hero with the entrepreneur as a real person.

These articles provide an alternative to the self-adjusting market. They provide an explanation of how the interaction of cultural patterns and technology determines the evolutionary path of the economic development of a nation. This is not a simple materialist depiction of economic history of the type some Marxists have advocated; instead, Hamilton treats technology and culture as endogenous forces, embedded and inseparable from each other, and therefore from economic development. This volume will be of most interest and value to professional economists and graduate students who are looking for an in-depth explanation of the origins and significance of institutional economics.

David Hamilton is currently Emeritus Professor at the University of New Mexico. **Glen Atkinson** is Emeritus Professor of Economics at University of Nevada, Reno. **William M. Dugger** is Professor of Economics at the University of Tulsa. **William T. Waller Jr.** is Professor of Economics at Hobart and William Smith Colleges.

Routledge advances in heterodox economics
Edited by Frederic S. Lee
University of Missouri–Kansas City

Over the past two decades, the intellectual agendas of heterodox economists have taken a decidedly pluralist turn. Leading thinkers have begun to move beyond the established paradigms of Austrian, feminist, institutional-evolutionary, Marxian, post-Keynesian, radical, social, and Sraffian economics – opening up new lines of analysis, criticism, and dialogue among dissenting schools of thought. This cross-fertilization of ideas is creating a new generation of scholarship in which novel combinations of heterodox ideas are being brought to bear on important contemporary and historical problems.

Routledge Advances in Heterodox Economics aims to promote this new scholarship by publishing innovative books in heterodox economic theory, policy, philosophy, intellectual history, institutional history, and pedagogy. Syntheses or critical engagement of two or more heterodox traditions are especially encouraged.

1 **Ontology and Economics**
Tony Lawson and his critics
Edited by Edward Fullbrook

2 **Currencies, Capital Flows and Crises**
A post-Keynesian analysis of exchange rate determination
John T. Harvey

3 **Radical Economics and Labor**
Frederic Lee and Jon Bekken

4 **A History of Heterodox Economics**
Challenging the mainstream in the twentieth century
Frederic Lee

5 **Heterodox Macroeconomics**
Edited by Jonathan P. Goldstein and Michael G. Hillard

This series was previously published by the University of Michigan Press and the following books are available (please contact UMP for more information):

Cultural Economics and Theory

The evolutionary economics of
David Hamilton

**David Hamilton, Glen Atkinson,
William M. Dugger, and
William T. Waller Jr.**

 Routledge
Taylor & Francis Group

LONDON AND NEW YORK

First published 2010
by Routledge
2 Park Square, Milton Park, Abingdon, Oxfordshire OX14 4RN

Simultaneously published in the USA and Canada
by Routledge
711 Third Avenue, New York, NY 10017
First issued in paperback 2014
Routledge is an imprint of the Taylor & Francis Group, an informa business

© 2010 David Hamilton, Glen Atkinson, William M. Dugger, and William T. Waller Jr.

Typeset in Times by Wearset Ltd, Boldon, Tyne and Wear

British Library Cataloguing in Publication Data
A catalogue record for this book is available from the British Library

Library of Congress Cataloging in Publication Data
A catalog record for this book has been requested

ISBN 978-0-415-49091-7 (hbk)
ISBN 978-1-138-80302-2 (pbk)
ISBN 978-0-203-86984-0 (ebk)

Contents

PART II
Structural policy and economic theory   93

Poverty

Consumption

Critique of orthodoxy

Elements of institutionalism

Preface

David Hamilton constructs his heterodox economic theory out of his study of culture. He replaces orthodox concepts that cloud our vision with heterodox concepts that shed light on economic problems. He replaces equilibrium with evolution, make-believe with reality, the ideological ban on government with the practical study of government, the economy as a product of natural law with the economy as a product of human law, and, last, he replaces the entrepreneur as a hero with the entrepreneur as a real person. Let us look at each replacement in turn.

Hamilton replaces equilibrium with evolution. The social world is not necessarily one of stability and beneficence but rather one of change and whatever beneficence or malevolence we have built into it. Hamilton's evolutionary economics is not a biologicalization of economics. He does not make the same kind of mistake as that made by neoclassical economists in their attempt to make economics into physics. Economics is not physics. Economics is not biology either. Economies do evolve, however. They evolve through a cumulative sequence of cause and effect that results from endogenous change (Darwinian evolution), not from divine intervention. Furthermore, the resulting economic trajectory is not a jerky movement from one point of static equilibrium to another. It is not changeless change; a temporary deviation from the norm. It is a change in the norm; it is cumulative and structural change.

Hamilton replaces the make-believe economy of neoclassical economics with the cultural economy of social science. (If one looks at it simply, culture is an evolving body of beliefs, meanings, and values.) Hamilton's cultural theory is enriched by but significantly different from Karl Polanyi's. While Polanyi argues that the market economy has become disembedded from its culture, Hamilton argues that the market economy has become obscured by make-believe. The economy has not necessarily been torn loose from its cultural moorings. Rather, Hamilton emphasizes, it has been lost in the fog of myth. The power and status relations within it are camouflaged by cultural make-believe, not disembedded from culture. Hamilton, more than Polanyi, emphasizes that neoclassical economics is the religion of the market economy.

Hamilton replaces the make-believe view of government from neoclassical economics with a balanced view of government derived from experience. He is free from a logical need to defend or attack government control of the economy. Thus, Hamilton can praise or denounce specific aspects of government and specific government programs because of how they work or fail to work, without getting caught up in his own ideological underpinnings. He does not agree that government is inherently incompetent or corrupt, leaving us with no choice but to follow the lazy fairy (laissez-faire). Hamilton explains that we have real choices. However, in keeping with his evolutionary view, Hamilton is not an eclectic on government. To him, government is potential. It becomes what we can make it through our collective action.

Hamilton replaces the factors of production as fundamental elements of the natural order with the factors of production as social constructs. He explains that the factors of production are grounded in the legal order, not the natural order. Trobriand Islanders did not work with the same factors of production we work with. Products of the legal order readily change when humans change the laws (formal or informal) under which they live in society. Not so with products of the natural order. In Hamilton's formulation, it is the legal order that moves to the fore. In Hamilton's formulation it is possible to reconstruct the economy – to try to make it evolve in different ways than it is doing now.

Hamilton shows that the entrepreneur is a mythological hero, not a real person. This makes Hamiltonian heterodoxy fundamentally different from Schumpeterian. The Schumpeterian line of thought on the entrepreneur becomes celebratory. The Hamiltonian remains critical. The Hamiltonian line represents advance in heterodox economics because it allows us to examine what actual businesspeople do and how their actions affect economic relations.

Hamilton develops a unique voice and role in economics, analogous to the voice and the role of Mark Twain in literature. Mark Twain was an American who loved America but who also criticized it in its own vernacular. David Hamilton is an economist who loves economics, but is quite critical of its religious faith in laissez-faire.

David Hamilton's audience stretches from the man or woman in the street to the professional, academic economist. His voice is a middle-brow one because it intermediates between the high-brow syntax of the groves of academe and the low-brow conversation of the streets of your hometown. He does not talk up to the former or down to the latter. His voice is that of a public intellectual who can explain clearly and convincingly why we should be critical of the economic policies supported by the economic manuals. He has coined some wonderful phrases, just as Thorstein Veblen and John Kenneth Galbraith have done. My favorite is his parody of laissez-faire ideology as "the lazy fairy."

In equilibrium economics, government policy interferes with the free market system, making us worse off. In David Hamilton's evolutionary economics, government policy pushes the evolution of society in a direction that could make us better or worse off; it is not predetermined. David Hamilton pushes hard against the predetermination of laissez-faire ideology. He is not unique in this regard. But he is uniquely effective. His steadfast resistance to the ideology of the free market is an important contribution to heterodoxy. He coined the phrase "lazy fairy" to demonstrate his disapproval of the pro-market, anti-government bias in orthodox economics. Since he understands change to be non-teleological and endogenous, it follows to Hamilton that if the government were to leave the present economy alone, the economy would not naturally evolve in an increasingly benign direction, but would evolve in the direction it was pushed by whoever had the power to push it. Hamilton goes beyond both Clarence Ayres and Thorstein Veblen. Veblen was an anarchist. He believed that modern democratic states were dominated by business. Veblen did not look to the modern state as a way of saving ourselves alive out of a precarious institutional situation. Hamilton, though quite critical of misguided state action, does look to the modern democratic process as a way out. He is not held in thrall by Veblenian pessimism with regard to the state and the business regime. Ayres criticized past-binding traditions that slowed the advance of knowledge. Hamilton is in agreement with this thrust in Ayres. Hamilton is rich in anthropological lore. However, Hamilton shifts his critical focus away from the Ayresian past and moves it forward to the Keynesian present, to the problems of the modern economy in need of the guidance provided by enlightened public policy. Hamilton criticizes the myths of our time that hinder the intelligent application of public policy to the public's problems. In particular, Hamilton criticizes the mythology of the entrepreneur not because it is a past-binding tradition but because it interferes with government policies that can improve the social provisioning process. Hamilton criticizes laissez-faire not because it is a tradition from the past but because it is a myth of the present. The lazy fairy interferes with public policies that stabilize the economy and widely distribute the real income it generates. Hamilton has been an advocate for the poor and the dispossessed, not the rich and the possessors. His support for but critical assessment of the war on poverty will make government action more effective in helping the poor – when we finally decide to try again.

Four mavericks edited this volume. Each did his graduate work at a southwestern university where institutional economics lived in exile from the center of academic power in the United States. Glen Atkinson studied at the University of Oklahoma, William Waller at the University of New Mexico, William M. Dugger, and David Hamilton himself at the University of Texas. The editors have wandered far beyond the cultural confines of the American Southwest and the theoretical constraints of orthodox economics.

Atkinson works on economic problems at the state, municipal, and county levels of Nevada. He applies insights from John R. Commons to the problems he encounters. For several years he edited the *Journal of Economic Issues* at the University of Nevada, Reno. Waller has written extensively on institutionalism, feminism, methodology, and philosophy. He wrote his dissertation under Hamilton at the University of New Mexico. Dugger came of age during the Vietnam War. He has written extensively on radical institutionalism. Hamilton forged his own line of heterodox economics and has generously shared it.

Each chapter is accompanied by an editorial commentary. Thus, the volume contains the central contributions of David Hamilton and a running editorial analysis of the significance of his thought. We believe that the volume sheds light on the central problem of our age: How to get back on the path of an efficient economy and just society after being pushed off it during a period of ideologically supported greed?

William M. Dugger
The University of Tulsa

Reflections from a student

This selection of essays by David Hamilton is not just a collection of assorted works of a noted scholar. Instead they were selected because we believe they constitute a unique approach to original institutional economics. David Hamilton's cultural institutional economics is a variant of the Thorstein Veblen–C. E. Ayres tradition of original institutionalism with considerable incorporation of the work of Karl Polanyi and John R. Commons. Hamilton's cultural approach to institutional economics is greatly influenced by his reading of the work of Emile Durkheim, Bronislaw Malinowski, V. Gordon Childe, and Lynn White. Hamilton's scholarship also demonstrates a continuing appreciation for the contributions to economic thought of John Maynard Keynes, John Hobson, and Barbara Wootton. The breadth of Hamilton's project, a systematic incorporation of cultural anthropology into evolutionary economics, both as a method to critique neoclassical orthodoxy and as a focus to strengthen, augment, and focus institutional economics, is so ambitious as to provide an agenda for considerable future research.

I have professionally benefited from this expansive view of institutional economics characteristic of David Hamilton's scholarly vision. As a graduate student more than a few years ago casting about for a dissertation topic, concerned that there was no guarantee that a genuinely new research question would present itself just because I happened to need one, I was greatly relieved to discover that David was a font of suggestions. Indeed, my work with him seemed designed to lead me to an intriguing topic that I fruitfully pursued for many years and continues to inform my own scholarly work. He had me read his article "The Great Wheel of Wealth" and had me read an unpublished doctoral dissertation by Walter Wagner (1953) exploring the theoretical relationship between general equilibrium and social reciprocity. David suggested that this was an area that warranted further investigation. From there my own dissertation (1984) was written and my own research program launched.

Hamilton's work is replete with such potential and possibilities. His article on the entrepreneur as a cultural hero suggests ways to explore the Schumpeterian concept and connect it with the modern scholarship on entrepreneurship. His many observations regarding the relevance of the work of Barbara Wootton suggest a continuing thread in her incredibly broad body of scholarship that connects methodologically and substantively with the original institutional economics. These two examples show that Hamilton's work, in terms of his selections of problems for consideration, areas of theoretical development of institutional theory, methodological influences on the elements of sound cultural inquiry, and his incisive evaluation of the elements of value within the contribution of many diverse economic, historical, anthropological, and sociological scholars, provides many entry points for expanding upon the cultural institutional foundations he has provided.

As a student I found all this a little intimidating. Charles Whalen once described, jokingly, Thorstein Veblen as the last scholar who knew everything. As a student I was extremely fortunate to study with two outstanding institutional economists: Louis Junker and David Hamilton. To my naïve eyes, both seemed to have been scholars who had read everything (I have since learned that this characteristic is typical of a great many excellent scholars). While helping David move some books I inquired whether I would have to read all of these books. He responded, with a wry smile, that I would not. He said, "I read them all so that you would only have to read the good ones." It is both an honor and a pleasure to work with Glen Atkinson and William Dugger in being able to add this volume of David Hamilton's scholarship on cultural institutional economics to the list of "the good ones."

William Waller
Hobart and William Smith Colleges

References

Walter Charles Wagner (1953) "The Theory of Economic Equilibrium: A Reflection of Social Reciprocity." Unpublished Ph.D. dissertation, University of Texas, Austin.
William T. Waller, Jr. (1984) "Social Reciprocity in Market Economies." Unpublished Ph.D. dissertation, University of New Mexico, Albuquerque.

Reflections from a colleague

My first encounter with David Hamilton was in 1965 when the graduate students at the University of Oklahoma invited him to speak at our annual banquet. He gave an erudite but down-to-earth talk on an institutional theory of consumption. He spent considerable time afterwards in relaxed conversation with students and faculty. I have since learned that his style is scholarly and conversational.

David turned 90 in August 2008. He still teaches a course at the University of New Mexico, and the students regularly rate him as the outstanding teacher in the department.

David grew up in Pittsburgh, Pennsylvania, that famous industrial city known for its steel mills. He came of age during the Great Depression, when unemployment in Pittsburgh hovered between 14 percent and 19 percent. He earned his BA at the University of Pittsburgh, which was followed by an MA in 1941. He was able to study heterodox economics at Pittsburgh and was introduced to some work of Clarence Ayres. Following graduation he served in the South Pacific during World War II. David was hired as an instructor at Pittsburgh when he returned from his military service. During the years after his graduation he was able to read more of Ayres' work, including *The Theory of Economic Progress*, which was published in 1944.

The University of Texas offered him a position as an instructor while he pursued his Ph.D. in economics. At Texas, Clarence Ayres offered an opinion in a conversation with David that two of the major gaps in orthodox economic theory are the conception of price and the conception of change. David realized that an institutional theory of change was a promising dissertation topic. He wrote his dissertation on this topic under the direction of Ayres and received his degree in 1951.

After graduation, David took a position at the University of New Mexico, where he has remained. The University of New Mexico Press published his dissertation in 1953 with the title *From Newtonian Classicism to Darwinian Institutionalism*. The title was changed for subsequent editions to *Evolutionary Economics: A Study of Change in Economic Thought*. That book is still in print fifty-five years later. When I was the editor of the *Journal of Economic Issues* (JEI), I noticed that the book would reach its fiftieth anniversary in 2003. In recognition of that landmark, I invited fifteen scholars to take a fresh reading of

Hamilton's book and comment on the treatment of the evolution of the economy at the beginning of the twenty-first century. Those essays were published in March 2003 in the JEI.

The origins of David's thought on the nature of economic inquiry can be found in that book. A look at the bibliography makes it clear that Hamilton begins with economic theory but ranges well beyond the discipline's classics. He includes anthropological, sociological, political, psychological, and natural scientific literature in his work. These other disciplines are not treated superficially, but are basic to his conception of economic change. They form the theoretical foundation of Hamilton's evolutionary economics.

Economic change, according to Hamilton, cannot be understood without an appreciation of all aspects of human nature. He built his economic theory from this holistic view that he learned from his study of culture. One of David's favorite references is a book by the anthropologist V. Gordon Childe, *Man Makes Himself* (1948). This holistic foundation for economic theory is a far cry from Bentham's passive hedonism. Economic theory built on a cultural foundation becomes evolutionary economics because cultures themselves continue to evolve. The articles in this collection will confirm that David's scholarship has continued to be wide in scope and deep in content as it evolved.

David continues to contribute articles and reviews for publication. He has always been eager to engage in conversations with younger economists and share his personal insights about the development of institutional economics. In addition to his formal teaching, he has been an informal teacher and inspiration to many of us. For half a century now, he has contributed to the evolving community of scholars who share his interests. The publication of these articles will extend his influence even further.

Glen Atkinson
University of Nevada, Reno

References

Ayres, C. E. (1944) *The Theory of Economic Progress*. Chapel Hill: University of North Carolina Press.

Childe, V. Gordon (1948) *Man Makes Himself*. London: Thinkers' Library Edition.

Hamilton, David B. (1999) *Evolutionary Economics: A Study of Change in Economic Thought*. New Brunswick, N.J.: Transaction Publishers.

Introduction

David Hamilton

It seems to me, after reviewing these papers written over a period of fifty years, that a common thread running through them is the distinction long ago made by Veblen between economic affairs that might be labeled matter-of-fact and those labeled ceremonial. The first of these two distinguishing marks refers to all of those prosaic technological processes by virtue of which human beings secure a livelihood and by virtue of which they improve their lot. The second refers to the fanciful assignment to individuals playing varied cultural roles personal credit for the accomplishment. In other words, a social process, technology, is personalized and attributed to great feats of individual prowess. And this social phenomenon is to be found in all cultures to which the anthropologist has turned attention.

In the conventional mind of all peoples, heroic figures gave to them sometime in the past a life way. And today's world is similarly beholden to such heroes whether they be priests, soldiers, kings, inventors, entrepreneurs, or CEOs – to use a contemporary referent. Today's heroes in their dramatic roles are reenacting the heroics of those ancestors to whom we are allegedly beholden for our current life way. The mores as well as the taboos assure such a replication. It is by such reference to the past that the power of today's cultural leaders is authenticated.

We might metaphorically refer to the rise of human beings to today's technological level as the long march from Olduvai Wash to Silicon Valley. Until recently, much of our history was the parade of cultural heroes who, by virtue of heroic cultural feats, led us out of the Wash. The attention of historians was focused on the dramatic aspect of the human enterprise that Veblen categorized as ceremonial. This myopia is no longer excusable in light of what now is known about the long course of technology through Paleolithic, Neolithic, and industrial culture, and now, perhaps, post-industrial culture. These categories are based on tool development, not on heroic individuals. As a matter of fact, the potential abilities of all who participated in this long march cannot be so differentiated. It is not for lack of intelligence that late-Paleolithic peoples lacked the airplane or the computer. Nor was it for lack of some vague thing called intelligence that the denizens of Greek and Roman classic civilization lacked the automobile and offset printing.

As the student of technological history would respond, times were not "ripe" for those inventions. The technology for the creation of the automobile or the offset printing process was not yet available. The technological process is one of invention by virtue of the combination of pre-existing traits. Discovery also plays a role, as often noted, but it should also be noted that discovery also depends upon pre-existing traits. Without the microscope and the power of magnification, the discovery of the human cell would still be awaiting its discoverer.

With the long march of science and technology now rather well known, it is interesting how it remains so elusive to the economist, especially when one considers the course of economic development in the short-term past as well as the present. The economist remains enamored with the accumulation of capital in its monetary formulation. The conventional economic mind remains fascinated with the savings rate, whether in the United States, the United Kingdom, or Japan. The post-World War II rapid growth of Japan relative to that of the United States was attributed largely to a high propensity to save in Japan relative to that which prevailed in the United States. In one sense this obsession with money accumulation does not differ from that of the early mercantilists known as the bullionists. And although it is found in its most virulent form among the high priests of Wall Street, economists of the conventional persuasion are by no means immune from the same obsession.

At the opening of industrial culture, ownership of the new technology fell into the hands of the medieval town merchants, not into the hands of the feudal rural aristocracy. And as the flow of new technology went into the hands of these town merchants and craftsmen, they displaced the primary power-holding landed aristocracy.

This displacement took place by virtue of money power. Control of the new productive technology was exercised through ownership, the latter being a function of alienable property. How easy it was to attribute the occurrence of that which was owned to the process by virtue of which it was owned: buying and selling took on the same significance in the eyes of the participants that bullroaring took in the manufacture of sailing canoes in the eyes of the Trobriand Islanders of Malinowski's time in those islands.

The confusion of two separate social processes as one continues today in the confusion over the meaning of the term "capital." In one sense it is money funds used to secure ownership of some part of the tool process. In another sense it is used to refer to "produced means for further production." And to the native as well as the economist it is quite easy to slip from one meaning to the other because they are both supposedly forwarding the onward march out of Olduvai Wash.

The term "investment," closely allied with that of capital, suffers from the same kind of inherent confusion. Economists belabor the point that the personal use of investment refers to ownership and an exchange of ownership while in the truly meaningful sense economically it refers to the creation of real "capital" assets. From the social sense, the first meaning is trivial while in that same social sense the second meaning is highly significant for general economic well-being.

What is at stake is what long ago John R. Commons referred to as engineering efficiency in contrast to business efficiency. The first meaning is fraught with significance for social and group well-being; in the second sense it has only an invidious meaning.

The same phenomenon was noted long ago by the eminent English economist Edwin Canaan when he defined the study of economics as analyzing how all of us taken collectively fare as well as we do and how some of us fare much better than others.

I suppose some readers might well yawn and say, "So what?" But it seems to me that this basic distinction within institutional economics is the essence of what institutionalism is all about. If one lets the illusion of money becloud one's view of what is going on, it does make a lot of difference just how one approaches real economic problems.

This point was never clearer than during the Age of the New Deal. Problems were addressed directly in their technological dimension. If farmers were without electricity because the profit system controlling central station power distribution saw no way within the bounds of conventional wisdom to get the farmer out of the darkness, then do it directly by such a device as the REA [Rural Electrification Commission]. If the profit system pitted each farmer against the other, worsening a general condition of abject depression, then take care of matters by limiting acreage, the AAA [Agricultural Adjustment Commission]. If freight could not be moved on the roadbeds of railroads largely federally financed in the past, then open up a set of waterways constructed by the Army Corps of Engineers. And if we had idle labor and hungry families, then construct public buildings, courthouses, post offices, children's hospitals, college campus buildings, hiking trails in the national forests, Adirondack huts for wayward campers, and a symphony in Newark composed of formerly unemployed musicians, WPA [Works Progress Administration], PWA [Public Works Administration], CCC [Civilian Conservation Corps], etc. If old age could only be financially provided for by individual retirement accounts (individual savings accounts) which never seemed to do the job, then Social Security for all.

That institutional economists of some variety influenced much of this was largely because they were not blinded by the money illusion.

If these papers have any meaning, it is because they point in this experimental direction. That outlook comes from recognition that technology is primary and money is secondary. It comes from recognition that if something is technologically possible it is socially fundable, a point made forcefully long ago by Stuart Chase in his *Money to Grow On* (1964). It should be noted that Chase was often considered to be some kind of institutionalist, and was most certainly influenced in his economic thinking by Veblen.

These papers, from the earliest, dating from 1953, make use of this cultural distinction that characterizes and differentiates institutionalism from the conventional mind. The distinction does make a difference, as the 1930s and the New Deal testify. While the conventional wisdom had nothing to offer save "the lazy fairy," the New Deal and its intellectual authors were out to save a people from a precarious situation that was of human origin and resolvable by the application of human intelligence. Faith in the market or what have you is of little help under such conditions. Giving the public weekly assurances that prosperity is "just around the corner" is equivalent to blowing into a strong wind in expectation of changing its direction. In a way, that is what these papers are all about.

Reference

Chase, Stuart (1964) *Money to Grow On*. New York: Harper & Row.

Part I

Economic thought and cultural economics

David Boyce Hamilton was born on August 31, 1918 in Pittsburgh, Pennsylvania. Trained as an economist, with degrees from the University of Pittsburgh (MA, 1941) and the University of Texas (Ph.D., 1951), Hamilton taught at both these universities before moving to the University of New Mexico in 1949, from which he retired in 1988. He is currently teaching as professor emeritus.

Hamilton first encountered the work of Thorstein Veblen when he read *The Theory of the Leisure Class* (1953 [1899]) as an undergraduate at Pittsburgh. This early encounter with Veblen has been a continuous influence on Hamilton's scholarly works, especially his continuing interest in the theory of consumption. He continued his study of institutional economics at the University of Texas, writing a doctoral dissertation comparing the influence of Newtonian mechanics with the Darwinian-inspired evolutionary approach of institutional economics, under the direction of C. E. Ayres. This dissertation evolved into his now classic *Evolutionary Economics* (1991), which has been in print continuously for the past fifty years.

Hamilton's contributions to institutional thought occur in four interrelated areas: institutional method, consumption theory, the problem of poverty, and explorations of the cultural significance of orthodox economic theory. Hamilton's scholarship refocuses and recovers the anthropological roots of institutional economics. His emphasis is on careful description and analysis of social processes. Employing his unique version of the Ayresian framework (with a distinctly Polanyian influence), Hamilton's work recaptures both the cultural emphasis and the playful cynicism of Veblen, though always managing to avoid the dark edge that characterized Veblen's commentary. In his most recent work, Hamilton has emphasized technology as a cultural process, rejecting the common misconceptualization of technology as tools and techniques. His work contextualizes technology as an integral and inseparable (except analytically) part of culture. Hamilton's emphasis on the interrelated and inseparable character of cultural processes led to his defining technology as socially organized intelligence in action.

Treating economic behavior as only an analytically separable part of continuous interconnected cultural processes also shaped Hamilton's work on consumption and poverty. In his book *The Consumer in Our Economy* (1962), Hamilton updated and extended Veblen's analysis in *The Theory of the Leisure Class*. He combined Veblen's treatment of consumption of goods as both symbols of status and instruments to achieve ends-in-view with the Keynesian insight of the importance of aggregate consumption for the well-being of the entire society. In his analysis of poverty (1968), Hamilton emphasized its cultural character meaning that the problems of people with inadequate real income were related to larger cultural processes which distributed income and legitimized that distribution.

The overall anthropological thrusts of Hamilton's insights into institutional economics, and those insights' applications to consumption and the problems of poverty, are intimately related to his evaluation of orthodox economics. Hamilton has analyzed the role neoclassical economics plays in our culture in terms of legitimizing certain behavior and delegitimizing other behavior. For example, the concept of the entrepreneur is treated by Hamilton (1957) not as a description of actual behavior, but as a hero myth legitimizing, though not accurately describing, the economic behavior of businesspersons. He analyzes the corporation as a social structure that is only indirectly concerned with production and is primarily involved in maintaining and legitimizing the rights and status of contributors of capital. He argues that the marginal productivity theory is not a theory of production, but rather a myth that legitimizes the distribution of income. He also argues that the great wheel of wealth used to describe the market economy is a reflection of the role of social reciprocity in legitimizing market exchange, and that money is a formal method for satisfying reciprocity. Underlying all of these analyses is the collective representation of market society – an idealized self-perception used to legitimize the status quo, rather than a theory of economic activity and behavior. For Hamilton, neoclassical economics is the religion of market society.

Hamilton's emphasis on cultural processes allows him to reintegrate both methodologically and theoretically institutional thought into a coherent whole. By refocusing on Veblen's emphasis on the evolutionary character of both particular cultural processes and society generally, he is able effectively to use and stress the essential continuity among the works of Veblen, Commons, Mitchell, Polanyi, and Ayres. Hamilton's emphasis on cultural processes brings continuity to institutional thought, while simultaneously embracing its eclectic tendency. This same emphasis on cultural processes also makes apparent the interdisciplinary character of institutional thought.

This first part of David Hamilton's work covers his articles from the 1950s into the 1960s. They are the core of his construction of his cultural institutional economics.

William Waller
Hobart and William Smith Colleges

References

David Hamilton (1955) "The Social Origins of the Factors of Production." *American Journal of Economics and Sociology* 15 (1), pp. 73–82.

—— (1957). "The Entrepreneur as a Cultural Hero." *Southwestern Social Science Quarterly* 38, pp. 248–56.

—— (1962) *The Consumer in Our Economy*. Boston, Houghton Mifflin.

—— (1968) *A Primer on the Economics of Poverty*. New York: Random House.

—— (1991) *Evolutionary Economics,*. New Brunswick, N.J.: Transactions Press.

Veblen, Thorstein (1953 [1899]) *The Theory of the Leisure Class*. New York: New American Library.

1   Veblen and Commons

A case of theoretical convergence

Southwestern Social Science Quarterly, vol. 34 (September 1953), pp. 43–50

COMMENTARY BY WILLIAM WALLER

In this article, Hamilton draws our attention to an area of theoretical convergence between the two founding theorists of institutional economics: Thorstein Veblen and John R. Commons. Hamilton argues that this convergence became more apparent after the posthumous publication of Commons' *The Economics of Collective Action* (1951). Hamilton notes that in his last book Commons' analysis is more explicitly cultural than in earlier theoretical work, primarily his two-volume *Institutional Economics* (1934), in which Commons focused on fitting his particular analyses into the history of economic thought and explicating his theory of reasonable value. Hamilton locates the theoretical convergence in the case of the cultural distinctions characterized by C. E. Ayres as ceremony and technology. The particular distinction between business enterprise and industrial efficiency employed by Veblen in *The Theory of Business Enterprise* (1904) is compared to Commons' distinction between man-hour efficiency and dollar-value efficiency in his analysis of business activity.

Hamilton balances his case for theoretical convergence when he observes that Commons' conception of the transaction, including bargaining, managerial, and rationing transactions, does not fit quite so nicely into Veblen's framework.

This article illustrates Hamilton's approach to his exploration of the history of economic thought. His focus is not on the methodological similarity of overarching concepts such as "holism" or "coercion." Instead he focuses on substantive similarities and complementarities in the work of economists seriously considering actual economic issues.

VEBLEN AND COMMONS: A CASE OF THEORETICAL CONVERGENCE

The impression that institutional economics is a hodge-podge of unrelated hypotheses and descriptive monographs is of long standing among orthodox economists. Yet of late it is becoming increasingly apparent that this is not the case. There is emerging a body of identifiably institutionalist theory and work that is closely associated. The posthumous publication of *The Economics of Collective Action*[1] by John R. Commons brings further evidence of the cohesive nature of institutional theory.

For many years, orthodox economists have contended that there were certain institutional economists such as Veblen, Commons, and Hamilton, but no body of institutional theory. Each was an entity unto himself and outside of some vague similarities; there were no general areas of agreement. This thesis has been challenged recently by several institutional economists. In a comprehensive volume on institutional economics and economists which covered the contributions of Veblen, Commons, Mitchell, J. M. Clark, S. N. Patten, Rexford G. Tugwell, and Gardiner Means, Allan Gruchy found a connecting thread in what he calls "holism" after the philosophy of Jan Smuts. As he states the case:

> The post-Darwinian type of scientific thought which Smuts describes as "holistic" takes the physical world to be an evolving, dynamic whole or synthesis, which is not only greater than the sum of its parts, but which also so relates the parts that their functioning is conditioned by their interrelations. The holistic viewpoint which has proven so fruitful in the biological and physical sciences is precisely the viewpoint of the heterodox economists whose work is the primary interest of this study. These economists all have the same holistic orientation or intellectual approach which Smuts finds to be so characteristic of modern scientific and philosophic thought.[2]

In another post-World War II volume, John Gambs claims that the "hidden premise" that runs through the work of institutionalists is that of coercion. As he writes:

> Monopoly, unfair competition, exploitation of weaker groups – all are recognized by standard theory. On the whole, however, such phenomena are deemed to be atypical, occasional, and relatively unimportant. Institutional theory erects the occasional into the general. Coercion is deemed to be as pervasive as the air we breathe and, normally, equally unnoticed, except when we are confronted with cruel or shocking or criminal instances of exploitation, monopoly, or unfair competition.[3]

Although some institutionalists might take issue with both authors over the emphasis on holism or coercion as the unifying thread, it can hardly be said that they fail to prove that there is some degree of unity among institutionalists along these grounds. Certainly more can be said for these efforts at finding a common ground among institutionalists than can be said about earlier attempts to find a concert of opinion.[4]

Nevertheless, further evidence of a uniform body of institutional thought is to be found by a comparison of the theory of Commons as found in his last published work with that of Veblen. In a sense, Commons and Veblen have been looked upon as establishing two schools of institutional economics with not too much similarity in thought. This may have been due partially to the nature of Commons' earlier theoretical works. Because he used his theory as a basis for studying the legal aspects of economic activity, his theory is not as sharply drawn in the *Legal Foundations of Capitalism*[5] as it is in *The Economics of Collective Action*. Nor is it as clear in his *Institutional Economics*,[6] which included a mass of extraneous material which seemed to hide his theory. There is a sense in which his *Institutional Economics* is an examination of the history of economic thought from his own theoretical position. With his theory obscured by these other aims, the similarity to that of Veblen was obscured. Yet upon a closer examination of the economic thought of Commons there is evident a remarkable similarity to that of Veblen.

Both Veblen and Commons put great emphasis on collective action, rather than individual action. In fact, the title of Commons' book should be evidence enough of this emphasis in his latest work. The subject of this study is collective, rather than individual action. As he states: "This is an age of collective action. Most Americans must work collectively as participants in organized concerns in order to earn a living."[7] Commons defined an institution as "collective action in control of individual action."[8] He gives to custom an important role in shaping human behavior, stating that "individuals must adjust themselves to what others are doing (custom), regardless of logic, reason, or self-interest."[9] Although custom has a compulsory character, it varies in the degree of compulsion with which it falls upon individuals.

This position is similar to that of Veblen, who in all of his work emphasized the compulsive role of institutions. These institutions were so compulsive that "history records more frequent and more spectacular instances of the triumph of imbecile institutions over life and culture than of peoples who have by force of instinctive insight saved themselves alive out of a desperately precarious institutional situation."[10] In all of his work Veblen looked upon human behavior as cultural behavior and, like Commons, took the orthodox economists to task for laying a science of behavior on a physiological basis, hedonism.[11] Both Veblen and Commons viewed the individual as an active agent, a doer rather than a passive agent being acted upon.[12] This was in contrast with the hedonist psychology of orthodox economics. Differences of terminology aside, both Commons and Veblen looked upon human behavior as culturally conditioned behavior and as understandable only on that premise. Both dismissed without much ceremony the hedonist explanation of human behavior. In fact, Commons went so far as to call the incremental economics of Gossen, Jevons, Menger, *et alii* "Home Economics."[13]

As a consequence of the rejection of hedonism, both writers criticized individualistic economics based on hedonism as Newtonian. Commons stated:

> The early nineteenth century economists patterned their work upon the
> materialistic sciences of physics and chemistry, instead of on a volitional

science of the human will as developed by the courts. According to the materialists, the human individual acted somewhat like an atom, or like a natural law, and only in the one direction of overcoming the resistance of nature's forces in the production of wealth.[14]

Although Commons does not refer to Newton in this context, it was this aspect of classical doctrine that led Veblen to call it pre-Darwinian in contrast to an evolutionary science largely influenced by Darwinian evolution.[15] In another context Commons is more explicit in condemning classicism for its Newtonian outlook. He says:

> False analogies have arisen in the history of economic thought by transferring to economics the meanings derived from the physical sciences, as we have seen in Locke's derivations from the astronomy and optics of Sir Isaac Newton, or from the more recent biological sciences of organisms, or even from the human will itself.[16]

This at first might appear to conflict with Veblen's Darwinian approach, but it should be remembered that Veblen was drawing on the evolutionary aspect of Darwin and not drawing organismic analyses. In still another context, Commons claims that "individualistic economics" is static and "institutional economics" is dynamic.[17] These positions are identical with those taken by Veblen, which are explicitly stated in the critical essays on classicism contained in *The Place of Science in Modern Civilization* and particularly so in "The Preconceptions of Economic Science."

Although it could hardly be sustained that either Veblen or Commons placed primary emphasis on coercion, both gave it a prominent place in their theories that the classicists did not give it. Of course it is not implied that either one used it in the sense of crude brute force. Coercion is a subtle thing, the product of culture and of status, of the relationship between superior and inferior. Commons states that coercion is used to insure conformance with what he calls the "working rules."[18] In Commons' theory the managerial transaction is a coercive relationship between superior and inferior.[19] In discussing "holism," Commons brings out the fact that coercion of the individual is a product of collective action.[20] Veblen expounds a similar idea throughout his work, but nowhere more concretely than in *The Theory of the Leisure Class.*[21] Here the coercive nature of society is revealed in Veblen's usual brilliant satire.

But all of these similarities are probably well known. The significant upshot of the latest Commons volume is the similarity revealed between Commons and Veblen in their larger systems of theory.

Probably the most outstanding contribution of Veblen to economic theory is the distinction he detected in cultural behavior between "technological" and "ceremonial" behavior. All of those who evaluate Veblen point out the distinction he made between making goods and making money. Not all have understood the general significance of this distinction. It was part of a larger distinction in which Veblen held that man engaged in activities, some of which result in the furtherance of human welfare and others in the drawing of invidious distinctions. Professor C. E. Ayres, in his latest volume, contends that this distinction may "prove to be as fundamental for economics (and perhaps for the social sciences generally) as the idea of elemental substances was for chemistry."[22] Veblen made much of this distinction in all of his work. In some, it took the form of workmanship and exploit, in others the form of industrial efficiency and business enterprise, in others matter-of-fact knowledge and myth. Veblen began *The Theory of Business Enterprise* with the statement that "the material framework of modern civilization is the industrial system, and the directing force which animates this framework is business enterprise."[23] Throughout the book he showed how business enterprise and exploit work at cross-purposes to the full utilization of the industrial system. Money was made and prestige acquired by "throwing sand in the wheels" of the industrial system. In *The Engineers and the Price System*[24] he compares business activity to sabotage working to thwart the industrial system. In his essay entitled "The Place of Science in Modern Civilization"[25] he contrasts matter-of-fact knowledge with the dramatized myth and legend. The matter-of-fact knowledge is the basis of the instrumental or technological behavior and the dramatic myth is that set of sentiment and belief which sustains the ceremonial behavior.

According to Veblen, all culture is characterized by these two aspects. In technological behavior, activity proceeds on a matter-of-fact reasoning from means to end, subject to continued empirical verification of efficacy in the long-run life process. In the technological area, valuation is in matter-of-fact terms – concerned with reasoning from means to end and the further consequences. It is identifiable with the scientific process. In contrast to this is the ceremonial aspect of culture. Here myth reigns supreme as the ultimate test of validity. All behavior must conform to myth. It is the area of coercion, of superior and inferior. In institutions the valuation process is concerned mainly in making invidious distinctions – matters of status and prerogative.

These two aspects of cultural behavior have been noted by others such as the anthropologist Bronislaw Malinowski,[26] as well as by John Dewey.[27] And although Veblen has become well known for his effective utilization of this cultural dichotomy, not much has been said about Commons' glimmerings of the same thing. Yet in his latest volume there is clear evidence that Commons had a grasp of the same ideas. Throughout the volume he demonstrates an awareness of technological and ceremonial patterns of culture.

Commons makes much of the distinction between transfer of commodities and transfer of ownership.[28] In other words, he sees a distinction between the flow of goods and the flow of ownership. This is essentially the distinction which Veblen makes between business and industry, the form the dichotomy assumes in contemporary society. There is a pattern of ongoing industrial activity accompanied by the ceremonial of business transactions transferring ownership status to the usufruct of the industrial process.

The basic unit of economic investigation according to Commons is the transaction. This is in contrast to classical political economy, which took the exchange as the basic unit of investigation. Commons claims that the exchange of classical political economy was one-sided. It encompassed the transfer of ownership only; it ignored the pattern of relationships involved in the exchange of commodities. He finds three types of transactions, the bargaining, the managerial, and the rationing transaction.[29] Within his system the bargaining transaction involves a legal transfer of ownership, while the physical transfer of the good is encompassed in the managerial transaction. The rationing transaction has to do with the apportionment of the wealth of production among the subordinates by the sovereignty. He states that the most frequent form this takes is a tax. As Commons puts it, "The physical and labor transfers have come to be comprehended in modern economics under the name of managerial transactions, while the legal transfers are the bargaining transactions and the rationing transactions."[30] Since the bargaining and rationing transactions involve transfers of ownership, this area of activity is comparable to what Veblen calls "business" while the managerial transactions concerned with the flow of goods are comparable to what Veblen calls "industry." In another way the bargaining and rationing transactions in Commons' system are similar to the ceremonial area in Veblen's system while the managerial transaction in Commons is similar to the technological in Veblen.

There is one point of difference, however. The managerial transaction has several facets. It is a relationship between two persons, a superior and inferior. In this sense it is a coercive relationship. Veblen confined coercion to the ceremonial area of activity, to the status hierarchy of "graded men." But the managerial transaction has as its purpose the production of wealth. "The universal principle of bargaining transactions is scarcity, while that of managerial transactions is efficiency."[31] Since the managerial transaction is a pattern of organization or social relationship that has as its purpose the efficient production of wealth, it is a technological pattern of behavior. That aspect of superior–inferior which smacks of coercion would be ceremonial behavior in Veblen. But this difference notwithstanding, there is a close similarity here also between Veblen and Commons.

In his distinction between assets and wealth, Commons is even closer to the fundamental distinction Veblen makes between business and industry. Commodities have a double meaning: one as assets possessing a proprietary character, and the other, a technological meaning as wealth. The populace at large has an interest in increasing wealth. Business has an interest in maintaining scarcity, so as to maintain the asset value of wealth.[32] Although Commons does not draw the sharp conclusion that Veblen does that business thwarts the full realization of the fruits of modern science and technology, he comes precariously close to this position when he says:

> Modern business is conducted on the basis of assets, that is, scarcity of wealth, and not on the abundance of wealth according to Smith. With assets one can give security for loans of money, but the security is worthless if the supply of "wealth" is increased so greatly that assets have little or no scarcity value when sold upon the markets for money. This paradox of wealth

and assets is confusing to common sense. But common sense has previously injected unconsciously something that restricts the supply and maintains scarcity value.[33]

In this statement Commons would appear to be on the same ground as Veblen when he states that business restricts and thwarts output in order to maintain pecuniary values. This is contrary to classical doctrine, which held to the identity between public and private interest guided "as if by an invisible hand."

To carry this distinction further, in dealing with efficiency Commons distinguishes between man-hour or engineering efficiency and dollar efficiency. As he states it:

> Efficiency itself can be measured, as Taylor had demonstrated. It is a ratio of output to input, which I name man-hour efficiency, to distinguish it from the dollar efficiency, which is not efficiency, but is the relative scarcity of bargaining transactions.[34]

The classicist maintained that dollar efficiency was synonymous with engineering efficiency. In fact, it was held to be the measure of engineering efficiency.

In showing that dollar efficiency hangs on scarcity and restriction of output, Commons shows that it jeopardizes engineering efficiency.[35] In doing this he aligns himself with Veblen in such works as his *Engineers and the Price System* and puts his finger on an aspect of our culture that Veblen found to be true of all culture.

Although Commons has been called an "institutionalist of a sort"[36] and has been said to have a theory personal to himself, it is apparent that his theory was not in many respects too different from that of Veblen. The difference between the two is largely one of approach. Commons came to his theory through long years of research among labor unions, cooperatives, and government agencies. Veblen approaches the economic problem from anthropology and a long study of culture. Commons, coming without the advantage of anthropology, but arriving at a similar position to that of Veblen, is further verification of the existence of the "ceremonial-technological" aspect of culture, which would seem to be the chief contribution of institutionalism to modern economic thought.

Notes

1 New York, Macmillan, 1951. Cited hereafter as *Collective Action*.
2 Allan Gruchy, *Modern Economic Thought: The American Contribution* (New York, Prentice-Hall, 1947), 3–4.
3 John Gambs, *Beyond Supply and Demand* (New York, Columbia University Press, 1946), 13.
4 "Economic Theory – Institutionalism: What It Is and What It Hopes to Become," *American Economic Review*, vol. 21, no. 1, Supplement (March 1931), 131–41; "Round-Table Conference on Institutional Economics," *American Economic Review*, vol. 22, no. 1, Supplement (March 1932), 105 f. 45.

5 New York, Macmillan, 1924.

6 New York, Macmillan, 1934. Cited hereafter as *Institutional Economics*.

7 Commons, *Collective Action*, 23.

8 Ibid., 26.

9 Ibid., 111.

10 Thorstein Veblen, *The Instinct of Workmanship* (New York, B. W. Heubsch, 1922), 25.

11 Thorstein Veblen, "Why Is Economics Not an Evolutionary Science?" in *The Place of Science in Modern Civilization* (New York, Viking, 1942), 56–81, cited hereafter as Veblen, *Place of Science*; Commons, *Collective Action*, 109, 113.

12 Veblen, *Place of Science*, 74; Commons, *Collective Action*, 154–5.

13 Commons, *Institutional Economics*, 85.

14 Commons, *Collective Action*, 36.

15 Veblen, *Place of Science*, 32–55.

16 Commons, *Institutional Economics*, 96.

17 Commons, *Collective Action*, 52.

18 Ibid., 40.

19 Commons, *Institutional Economics*, 64f.

20 Commons, *Collective Action*, 135.

21 New York, Macmillan, 1912.

22 C. E. Ayres, *The Industrial Economy* (Boston, Houghton Mifflin, 1952), 25.

23 Thorstein Veblen, *Theory of Business Enterprise* (New York, Charles Scribner's Sons, 1935), 1.

24 New York, B. W. Huebsch, 1921.

25 In Veblen, *The Place of Science*.

26 See his *Magic, Science, and Religion* (Boston, Beacon Press, 1948), 1–71.

27 See the opening passages of *The Quest for Certainty* (New York, Minton, Balch, 1929).

28 Commons, *Collective Action*, 43–57.

29 Ibid., 48–56.

30 Ibid., 48.

31 Commons, *Institutional Economics*, 64.

32 Ibid., 94–5.

33 Ibid.

34 Ibid., 100.

35 Ibid., 100–1.

36 Lewis H. Haney, *History of Economic Thought* (New York, Macmillan, 1936), 743.

2   Hobson with a Keynesian twist

American Journal of Economics and Sociology, vol. 13 (3) (April 1954), pp. 273–82

COMMENTARY BY WILLIAM WALLER

In this article, Hamilton notes that while John Maynard Keynes respectfully referred to John A. Hobson's contributions to economic thought, subsequent post-Keynesians have largely ignored his contribution. Hamilton ascribes this neglect to two major factors. The first is Hobson's supposed theoretical inelegance. This Hamilton dismisses as a result of the second factor, which is that Hobson's underconsumption theory is best understood when it is put into Hobson's entire theoretical system. Hamilton argues that Hobson's theory of unearned surplus which leads to excess savings and overinvestment leads directly to his theory of underconsumption and his theory of imperialism.

The article then undertakes an even-handed assessment of the strengths and weaknesses of Hobson's argument. Especially important here is Hobson's continued adherence to the classical position on the relationship between savings and investment. Hamilton also clearly articulated the differences between Hobson's and Keynes's views on consumption and investment, and notes the policy differences that emerge from their respective positions.

HOBSON WITH A KEYNESIAN TWIST

It may seem like dealing in antiquities to discuss John A. Hobson in relation to Lord Keynes at a time when Keynesianism of some variety has seemingly swept before it all economic thought. After all, Keynes paid his respects to Hobson as one who had "preferred to see the truth obscurely and imperfectly rather than to maintain error" when the more reputable economic pundits chose to remain in utter darkness. Reasonable men would be presumed to allow things to lie in such a rectified state. Hobson has had his day in court! But things are not in a finished state for there is more to be said. The theoretical affinity between Hobson and Keynes is closer than appears at first glance.

Although Keynes recognized the Herculean efforts of Hobson, Keynesians have not been any kinder to Hobson than they were before conversion. Alvin Hansen in 1927 wrote that Hobson had "restated the argument of his predecessors, but has contributed little, if any, to their work."[1] In a more recent and post-Keynesian work his evaluation of Hobson remains unchanged.[2] Others have found Hobson lacking in theoretical elegance and have dismissed him on this ground.[3] Presumably this criticism rests on the assumption that one mark of theoretical adequacy is a proliferation of erudition. The first of these criticisms can best be answered by looking into the second. As to the second, it can be said that unfamiliarity with all of Hobson's work leads to such a statement. Hobson was a prolific writer and, as with Veblen, one must read comprehensively to get a view of the whole system. Any one volume is related to the whole, but, as in the case of an iceberg, there remains much that is not immediately apparent. Hobson did have a well-worked-out system of economic theory in the traditional sense of what is taken to be a well-worked-out system. He did have a theory of value and distribution which made use of the usual factor analysis in terms of increments, decrements, and margins.

In justice it must be said that he did not work within the traditional framework, but he certainly did work with a framework. Although he accepts the factor analysis, it is not to the same end that the neo-classicist did. The end-result of Hobson's manipulation of increments and decrements of the factors is to demonstrate the disharmony of what had been used, at least since the Austrians had "saved the day," to demonstrate an essentially harmonious economic universe. On cursory examination his use of the accepted terminology appears to make Hobson orthodox in theory. There have been those who have intimated that Hobson was orthodox in everything but his underconsumptionism.[4]

To hold that he was orthodox in all but his underconsumption apostasy may be true, but true only in the same sense that Marx was orthodox in everything but his concept of surplus value. Hobson's underconsumption position rests on his distribution theory and his concept of the unearned surplus.[5] Hobson had a rather tight system as systems go. Details of his distribution theory may come under attack by those who are predisposed toward the more orthodox marginalist version. But there is little gained by such attacks, for in these matters of recondite speculation the only ones convinced are those who desire conviction. One theory may serve the purpose as well as another, the only difference being to the particular status group in whose favor the theory may be turned to account. No marginalist has yet convinced a Marxist, and no Marxist has yet convinced a marginalist! Hobson, in so far as theoretical elegance is concerned, comes out as well as can be expected from this sort of endeavor. But from his theory of the unearned surplus, Hobson worked out his underconsumption theory and his theory of imperialism. These three are the cornerstones of Hobson's whole system of economic theory and none stands alone. The unearned surplus results in a maldistribution of income. The maldistribution of income means excess saving. Excess saving leads to overinvestment. Overinvestment, the product of excess saving, means inadequate purchasing power. This leads to economic breakdowns. The latter are temporarily staved off by imperialist freebooting which for a while provides both an outlet for excess saving in foreign investment and for surplus product in foreign markets.

This is all too brief an account, but it does serve to show the interconnectedness of Hobson's system of economics. In a sense he had a much more integrated scheme of economic theory than that of the more reputable economists. Certainly his breakdown theory flows more clearly from the rest of his theory than what is now called macro-economics flows from micro-economics. Thus, to accuse Hobson of theoretical inelegance in cycle theory is to fail to see the role his underconsumption theory plays in his complete system of economic thought.

This very failure to see the whole of Hobson has led cycle theorists to treat his underconsumption doctrine distinct from his unearned surplus theory. Yet there is a significant connection between these two theories that puts Hobson closer to Keynes than has usually been conceded. Outside of a passing mention by R. F. Harrod[6] on the interconnection between them, little reference has been made to the complementary nature of the two theories.[7] In fact the theory of the unproductive surplus is not even mentioned in the standard manuals on business cycles.[8] Hobson's underconsumptionism is discussed without linking it in any way with his theory of the economic surplus.

Like Malthus, Hobson contends that saving takes place on such a large scale that effective demand is unable to take the goods produced as a result of the invested savings at a profitable price. This brings on a breakdown, a decrease in investment, income, and employment. The glut (as he calls it) of unsold goods must be eliminated before prosperity can once again be realized. This glut is removed as people, conservative in spending habits, attempt to maintain an earlier-established standard of living despite diminished income. Some live beyond current incomes by dipping into past savings. Eventually the glut is removed, profits begin to rise, investment increases, wages lag, making profits seem even higher, and a return to prosperity is negotiated. There is one difficulty, however. The very factors that have given rise to the prosperity are the cause of its downfall. Rising profits accompanied by the wage lag once again lead to over-saving and a glut.

Hobson puts much store in what he calls the right proportion between savings and consumption expenditure. There is a correct proportion which is equated with continued prosperity. That correct proportion is one at which the current consumption expenditure will be sufficient to take off the goods produced at a profit. In the long run, consumption outlay and savings must rise proportionately so that increased production can be matched by increased consumer spending. This condition maintained, there is no reason for a breakdown.

Unlike Keynes, Hobson clings to the classical role of savings for the most part. All saving is realized in the form of new investment. In fact, saving is essential to economic growth, and elimination of all saving would bring economic progress to a halt. For, as he says:

> Indeed, it must be admitted that upon this natural conservatism of present consumption, strengthened and directed by reasonable regard for future

consumption, the economic progress of mankind depends. It is this conservatism that is expressed in saving. The real economic function of saving must be clearly kept in mind. It does not consist in not spending, i.e. in putting money income in a bank, or even making an investment. It consists in paying producers to make more non-consumable goods for use as capital, instead of paying them to make more consumable goods and consuming them. This is the vital distinction between spending and saving, so often obscured by dwelling on the merely monetary aspect.[9]

The cause of economic fluctuations in the Hobsonian system is the disproportionality between savings and capital formation and consumer spending. His is, then, an over-saving or overinvestment theory. Although Hobson does not specifically tie together his over-saving theory with his theory of unearned surplus incomes in all of his discussions of unemployment, the two are complementary and the latter is important to understand fully Hobson's position.[10] The neglect of the latter can only be ascribed to the more general neglect of Hobson by the orthodox sect of economists. The mild "inspected and approved" endorsement of Hobson's underconsumption position by Keynes enabled it to slip through the main gate, but his unearned surplus position still awaits without. Nevertheless, it is a vital part of Hobson's analysis.

In brief, he contends that productive payment to the factors of production consists of the cost of maintenance (subsistence and replacement) and the cost of growth. This latter may provide for growth in two ways: (1) by a more intensive use of the factor, and (2) "by calling into use supplies of these factors."[11] Anything paid over these costs he calls unproductive surplus. Hobson claims that this unproductive surplus may be received by any of the factors, but is mainly found in the rent of land and in monopoly earnings of capital.

As has been seen in his underconsumption argument, Hobson contends that over-saving results from a disproportion between consumption and saving which causes failure of effective demand. The relation of his "unproductive surplus" to his over-saving doctrine is revealed in the following passage:

> But as regards cost of growth there is no such security for adequate provision. The surplus of wealth remaining after costs of maintenance are defrayed does not automatically distribute itself among the owners of the several factors of production in such proportions as to stimulate the new productive energies required to promote the maximum growth of production. Instead of disposing itself in these proper proportions, the surplus may be so divided as to furnish excessive stimuli to some factors and defective stimuli to others, thus retarding that full progress of industry which requires a proportionate growth of all the factors.[12]

The real difficulty would appear to lie in the unproductive surplus and primarily in that paid to capital. In a period of business expansion, profits rise, wages lag, and the unproductive surplus paid to capital increases. This condition results in a rise in capital investment disproportionate to the rise in wages. The disproportionality is aggravated by credit expansion. The result is the deluge. In the contraction, the proportionality is changed, wage decreases continue to lag, profit declines, and distribution of the unproductive surplus shifts from capital to labor. However, labor spends it for consumer goods, which reduces the time-period necessary to remove the glut. Thus, ultimately in the Hobson system the causes of fluctuation are to be found in shifts in income proportionality and the distribution of the unearned surplus. Now, at the time Hobson was writing, the classical concept of saving was still held in much esteem. All savings were realized in some form of investment. The only difference between Hobson and the classicist was over the matter of savings being excessive. Since the classicist was a true believer in Say's law of markets, savings could never be excessive.

But no real violence is done to Hobson's system by a slight modernization in that part which pertains to the identity of saving and investing. Since Hobson developed his system at a time when no one questioned the identity of the saving operation with the investment operation, it would seem nothing more than charitable to allow Hobson's system to undergo renovation on this point.[13] It should be kept in mind that Hobson did not have the advantage of Keynes as Keynes did of Hobson.

The results of revising Hobson's concept of saving are startling in their effect. If one is allowed to inject the idea of saving as a residual of income rather than as automatic investment, the result is an underconsumption argument with a Keynesian twist. Using Hobson's unproductive surplus argument in conjunction with the Keynesian concept of the passive role of savings, it becomes apparent that all wage costs represent largely consumption expenditure, while cost of subsistence and the cost of growth of capital represent depreciation expenditure and new investment outlays, while unearned surplus income represents saving not realized or abortive attempts to save not offset by investment expenditure. By this revision Hobson becomes Keynesian, but Keynesian with an underconsumption accent.

According to Hobson, then, shifts in the distribution of income or in the ratio between capital and labor have different effects on the economy. An increase in the unproductive surplus to capital results in abortive attempts to save and a decline in income. A shift in the unproductive surplus to labor leads to an increased consumption expenditure with a multiplier effect on investment. In the first case a shift in the unproductive surplus results in a failure to close the savings gap by investment expenditure. In the second case a large increase in consumer spending has a multiplier effect on investment and income.

In the cycle, it would follow that as profits rise from an increase in consumer spending, and wages lag, a shift in the distribution of the unproductive surplus from labor to capital takes place. The result is a rise in savings, which, not being offset by increased investment, results in a fall in income. The result is a shift of the unproductive surplus from capital to labor, which provides income to remove the glut and bring on the conditions that lead to recovery.

The result of such a transformation in Hobson is to make his system compatible with present-day concepts of saving and investment without doing any major damage to his system. In this way the main advance on underemployment would seem to call for a frontal assault via underconsumption rather than a flanking attack via underinvestment.

Keynes states that Hobson's error was in assuming that all saving did result in investment outlay.

> In the last sentence of this passage there appears the root of Hobson's mistake, namely, his supposing that it is a case of excessive saving causing the actual accumulation of capital in excess of what is required, which is, in fact, a secondary evil which only occurs through mistakes of foresight; whereas the primary evil is a propensity to save in conditions of full employment more than the equivalent of the capital which is required, thus preventing full employment except when there is a mistake of foresight.[14]

By making the substitution of passive savings for active savings in Hobson's system, this "root of Hobson's mistake" would appear to have been successfully grubbed. By such grubbing it would also appear that underconsumption theory and underinvestment theory are brought more closely together. The main problem in either case is what is now notorious as the savings gap. Vow to close the gap! The major difference between Keynesians and underconsumptionists would appear not to be in theory, but in predilections about how to close the breach. Nevertheless, it would be fatuous to assume that this rapprochement would satisfy Keynesians even though it might have satisfied Keynes.

Keynesians are confirmed underinvestment advocates. The more timid variety favor this approach because it indicates to them an indirect approach to the problem of stability that will leave the status quo untouched. As with monetary theorists such as Hawtrey, chief reliance would be placed on bank rate manipulation. Through low interest rates, in periods of a low marginal efficiency of capital, investment would be encouraged. Resort to more direct methods would be had only on the occasion of what Hawtrey has called a "credit deadlock." Even in this eventuality, public investment would be on a moderate scale in line with what has been called traditionally a public works program. Greater reliance would be put on moral exhortation and blandishment of the reluctant captains of industry.

To this group of Keynesians any suggestion of underconsumption is morally repugnant. Underconsumption is correctable by alteration of the pattern of income distribution. But this also means an alteration in a system of status and reputable expenditure that would reduce the standard of living from that level to which the more reputable elements have become accustomed and raise that to which the less worthy elements would have to become accustomed. To gentlemen of sensibility it is noxious to view simultaneously decayed gentlefolk and splurging on the part of the common run of man. It is this precise state of affairs in England at the present time that is the source of so much alarm in the United States about the wretched condition to which the English have been reduced. The upgrading of the standard of living of the lowest third of the population is viewed in silence.

To the more venturesome variety of Keynesians, underinvestment is compatible with their habitual way of viewing things. Traditional economic theories, the classical and neo-classical as well as Marxian, have been theories of capital accumulation. By doing without today, the lot of the common man will be raised tomorrow when there will be more to go around. When this argument is used again tomorrow to justify further sacrifice by the common run of man, the argument begins to get a little threadbare. All too frequently the argument has also been turned to an account of the accumulation of money funds which by some mystic process are identified with machines and means of production.[15] But putting all of this aside, the penchant for underinvestment on the part of Keynesians of this stripe stems largely from predilections on the source of human welfare and its enlargement on the morrow. To this way of thinking, the enlargement of consumption would encroach on the rate of growth of capital and reduce the speed of economic development.

Further, Keynesians of all variety put much stock in what is called autonomous investment. Keynes himself does not give to consumption much of a role as a determinant of investment. It is notorious that Keynes put little emphasis on the accelerator.[16] But he does in his discussion of Hobson give strong intimation that there is some connection between consumption outlay and investment outlay. In commenting on Hobson's argument he states:

> The subsequent argument is, admittedly, incomplete. But it is the first explicit statement of the fact that capital is brought into existence not by the propensity to save but in response to the demand resulting from actual and prospective consumption.[17]

But Keynesians, in letting so-called autonomous investment rest on technological innovation, population growth, frontiers, and wars as independent variables, are leaving much to be answered.[18] Technological innovations replace some other technology for which there is already consumption outlay. Certainly it is true that the railroad into the west made possible cash crop agriculture, which meant demand for the railroad. But to look at it in this fashion only is to ignore that the movement west had been under way on foot, on horseback, and in the covered wagon long before the rails were laid across the prairie.[19] Likewise, man was quite a mobile creature before the automobile. The Studebaker wagons were a cause of consumer outlay for many years before the Studebaker automobile was such. Similarly, people were habituated to gathering in their homes in front of a box designed to pick up and amplify radio sound waves before television came into vogue.

As to population growth, there is no other way this can manifest itself on investment except through increased consumer outlay. Malthus was as astute in pointing this out as he was in seeing the weakness in the argument of J. B. Say.[20] New frontiers as a source of investment outlay find Keynesians and Hobson on common ground. Keynesians are more discreet in naming what Hobson bluntly called imperialism.[21] This source of closing the savings gap can take the form of investment and consumption outlay. In calling it foreign investment its consumption aspect is obscured. But foreign markets for the domestic surplus are a long-tried if not true means of closing the gap. As for wars, there is no more rapid means of consumption. Autonomous investment may be independent to those who do not care to look beyond it, but its consumption roots are apparent to those who care to grub a little further. Keynes may have noted this and thus it may account for his more charitable treatment of Hobson.

Underconsumptionists, however, approach the problem of economic stability from the consumption side because of other predilections just as strong as those of the Keynesians. Underconsumption has largely been the stock in trade of trade unionists, social reformers, and heretics with a strong penchant for elevating the lot of the common man. With these leanings, the answer to the savings gap would also seem to be cut out for solving the problem of abject poverty. From the standpoint of economic stability, blessed are the poor, for they shall have their reward on earth instead of heaven!

When all is said and done, whether Hobson is held to possess an advantage over Keynes or Keynes an advantage over Hobson would seem to rest on the value placed on a more or less permanent closing of the savings gap. An underinvestment approach would call for an almost permanent anticyclical policy. An underconsumption approach would get at the "root of the error" and close the gap once and for all. The answer one takes rests on predilections which in turn rest upon background training and experience. Theoretical elegance would appear to have little to do with the issue.

Whether it can be said that Hobson failed to add anything to what had already been said by Malthus depends upon how narrowly one looks at Hobson. If one looks only at the disproportion between savings and consumption argument, the contention that nothing new has been added is valid. If one looks at Hobson's explanation of the origin of the disproportion, its consequences, and its correction, then it must be concluded that something has been added. But in so adding, Hobson becomes compatible with Keynes more so than is Malthus.

Notes

1 Alvin Hansen, *Business-Cycle Theory*, Boston, Ginn, 1927, p. 15.
2 Alvin Hansen, *Business Cycles and National Income*, New York, Norton, 1951, p. 255.
3 Robert A. Gordon, *Business Fluctuations*, New York, Harper, 1952, p. 344; Gottfried Haberler, *Prosperity and Depression*, New York, United Nations, 1946, p. 119.
4 See for instance Joseph Dorfman, *Thorstein Veblen and His America*, New York, Viking, 1934, p. 211.
5 Paul T. Homan, *Contemporary Economic Thought*, New York, Harper, 1927, p. 336.
6 R. F. Harrod, preface to fourth edition of J. A. Hobson, *The Science of Wealth*, Home University Library, Oxford University Press, 1950, p. vii.
7 Paul T. Homan in an essay on Hobson in his *Contemporary Economic Thought*, op. cit., does discuss Hobson's theory of the unproductive surplus and his underconsumption theory. He states that the latter arises out of the first, but since he is "not particularly concerned with cycle theories," he does not elaborate the point.

8 See for example A. H. Hansen, *Business Cycles and National Income,* pp. 254–8; R. A. Gordon, *Business Fluctuations*, pp. 342–4; J. A. Estey, *Business Cycles*, New York, Prentice-Hall, 1942, pp. 274–80; Asher Achinstein, *Introduction to Business Cycles*, New York, Crowell, 1950, pp. 38–40.
9 J. A. Hobson, *The Economics of Unemployment*, London, Allen & Unwin, 1922, p. 34.
10 He does have a short note on some aspects of the subject in *The Science of Wealth* in Chapter VII, "Other Surpluses." This is the note Harrod refers to. He also alludes to the unearned surplus in his discussion of the business cycle, as for instance when in discussing public policy he advocates full taxation of the unearned surplus and redistribution of this to low income receivers. In his *Economics of Unemployment* he mentions the unearned surplus in reference to taxation only. He does definitely join the two in *The Industrial System* in Chapter 18, "Unemployment."
11 Hobson, *The Science of Wealth*, p. 59.
12 Ibid., p. 60.
13 There is all the more reason for this in the light of R. G. Hawtrey's slight revisions of his works on this score. See for instance the fourth edition of Hawtrey's *Currency and Credit*, London, Longmans Green, 1950. "In the previous edition I took for granted too readily that money saved would be invested and that money invested would be spent.... That was still accepted doctrine when I wrote" (p. vi). In a long footnote in his *Confessions of an Economic Heretic*, London, Allen & Unwin, 1938, pp. 192–3, Hobson apparently came around to this point of view, which would put him in the under- instead of over-investment category. Unfortunately he never got around to amending any of his works on this front.
14 J. M. Keynes, *The General Theory of Employment, Interest and Money*, London, Macmillan, 1936, pp. 367–8.
15 For discussion of this point see C. E. Ayres, *The Divine Right of Capital*, New York, Houghton Mifflin, 1946, part 1.
16 This is not to ignore the fact that latter-day Keynesians seem singularly bent on rectifying this neglect. They have found the accelerator of great advantage in building what they rather euphoniously call models of the trade cycle. See for instance J. R. Hicks, *The Trade Cycle*, London, Oxford University Press, 1950; Alvin Hansen, *Business Cycles and National Income*, op. cit.
17 Keynes, op. cit., p. 368.
18 For a more complete discussion of the relationship between consumption and investment outlay see H. G. Moulton, *The Formation of Capital*, Washington, D.C., Brookings, 1935, chap. IV.
19 Francis Parkinson, *The Oregon Trail*, New York, New American Library edition, 1950.
20 T. R. Malthus, *Principles of Political Economy*, New York, Kelley, 1951, pp. 311–14.
21 J. A. Hobson, *Imperialism*, London, Allen & Unwin, 1948, chaps. VI, VII.

3 Keynes, cooperation, and economic stability

American Journal of Economics and Sociology, vol. 14 (1) (October 1954), pp. 59–70

COMMENTARY BY WILLIAM WALLER

In this article, David Hamilton addresses the paucity of economic theorizing with regard to cooperative organizations. He notes that the neoclassical framework is unsuitable for any person or organization that does not maximize net returns either to consumption or to production. He notes that theorizing about cooperatives was largely left to heterodox economists such as Sidney and Beatrice Webb in their book *The Consumer Cooperative Movement* (1921). But he notes that the macroeconomics of John Maynard Keynes is not inherently hostile to cooperative organizations and that a case can be made for cooperative organizations contributing to macroeconomic stability.

Hamilton's argument is based on the fundamental difference between profit-making firms and cooperative organizations. Profit-making firms pay dividends to stockholders or profits to owners. These individuals tend to be relatively affluent and consequently have a low propensity to consume. Cooperative enterprises pay patronage dividends to their members. Cooperative members have historically developed as alternative institutions serving farming and working-class families who tend to have a high propensity to consume. Cooperative enterprises have also avoided the excessive managerial salaries and compensation packages typical of private firms. This, too, contributes to affect the distribution of income in such a way as to support a higher propensity to consume.

Hamilton notes the tendency of cooperative organizations to engage in vertical integration in response to the unwillingness of the business community to supply goods to cooperative retail operations, thus forcing the cooperatives to move into wholesaling and production.

Hamilton concludes his paper by noting some objections to his argument. It is interesting that he anticipates many of the issues explored by Jaraslov Vanek's *The General Theory of Labor-Managed Economies* (1970) fifteen years later.

KEYNES, COOPERATION, AND ECONOMIC STABILITY

Among the orthodox economic theorists, cooperation as a way of economic organization has never been accorded more than passing acknowledgment. In fact the treatment of this modern phenomenon in the standard manuals has been such as to lend the impression that it is an eccentric and insignificant aspect of the western economy. Such an outlook on the part of the American theorist is in no way astonishing. The cooperative movement on the North American continent and especially in the United States has been, when all is said and done, a rather feeble one, noted more for a large volume of well-meant enthusiasm than for a large role in the economy. But that is not the case in Great Britain or the few Scandinavian countries. In fact, in Great Britain the cooperative movement encompasses well over ten million members and does a large volume of the retail and wholesale trade in the British Isles. In size and scale there is no single private enterprise that can touch it and the only endeavor on a larger scale is that of the government.

Despite the large role played by the cooperative movement in the seedbed of orthodox political economy, the leading lights of British economics have been hardly less receptive than their North American colleagues. Not Marshall, Pigou, Keynes, or even Harrod has deigned to acknowledge cooperation in theoretical discourse.[1] Despite the inattention of the economists there has been no want of partisans and the cooperative movement has not gone begging for champions. But the champions have been better known in the "economic underworld" than in accepted circles. No one could ask for more able partisans than the Webbs. Yet their advocacy could hardly be said to have smoothed the way and opened doors for the entrance of cooperation into the charmed circle of things accepted in traditional economic thought.

Yet such a state of affairs is to be looked upon as the normal run of events and only what one could have expected under the circumstances. The major premise of the cooperative movement stands at cross purposes to the basic premise with which the standard theorist works. Standard economic theory has been constructed on a conception of human nature that for want of a better designation is called individualism. This concept of human behavior runs through all the accepted theory from the time of Adam Smith to the present. Although not all have stated bluntly that man is differentiated from the other mammals by a natural penchant to "truck, barter, and exchange one thing for another," all have leaned heavily on the myth of profit motivation. In the present-day manuals the idea is more apt to take the form of a claim that all economic endeavor is aimed at "profit maximization" through successful trucking and bartering. Although not exactly a "dog-eat-dog" affair, the economic aspects of human behavior take on all the earmarks of enterprise in civilized predation. The business enterprise is looked upon as the fighting formation in which this natural human penchant works itself out. Free enterprise is looked upon as more than an accident of economic order; it is the product of human nature.

To the orthodox economist the claims of the advocate of the "cooperative commonwealth" have little to recommend them. In fact they appear to be on the far side of utopianism. For the cooperator rests his case on a diametrically opposed theory of human action. To him the process of cooperation takes precedence over that of competition. And of course there is much in western culture to recommend such an outlook.[2] Not only is there evidence of such cooperative behavior in western culture, but appreciable evidence is available that cooperation is as typical of behavior in other cultures as is exploitation.[3] It would appear on the basis of the evidence that the cooperator has as much to substantiate his basic premise as has the keeper of received economic theory.

Nevertheless, the economic theorist, even when favorably disposed toward the aims of the cooperative movement, has been extremely skeptical of the chances for success. Self-interest or the combative instinct is held to be so strong in man that a concept of order based on some other aspect of human behavior is looked upon as utter self-delusion. Enterprise, looked upon as the source of efficiency by the economist, can only be stimulated by giving full rein to combativeness and pugnacity. The cooperative movement, despite its successes against odds never faced by private enterprise,[4] is viewed as having little chance to arouse sufficient enterprise essential to efficiency. It is usually with reluctance that the sympathetic economic theorist draws the conclusion that until the moral rejuvenation of human nature, cooperation must remain among things hoped for. Since human nature is looked upon as something fixed, there is little chance for cooperation despite well-meaning enthusiasts.

Cooperation and economic theory

But if the economist has paid little attention to cooperation, the cooperator has paid little attention to economic theory. The arguments for cooperation have been on other grounds than those of accepted economic theory. Some of the milder cooperative theorists have justified cooperation as a yardstick in an essentially competitive economy. According to this view, cooperators serve as a counter-balance against the excesses of unbridled enterprise.[5] Others see cooperation as a way of economic order that will eventually come to prevail over the entire ecoomy.[6] To this school of thought, cooperation is the "third force." There is still a third group who view cooperation as a part of an economy which has been socialized in all those areas now operating under private enterprise.[7] Here the cooperative movement would be confined largely to the wholesale and retail distribution of consumer goods. In fact G. D. H. Cole contemplates the existence of competing cooperative societies within the socialist commonwealth.

All of these theoretical formulations have something of the vagueness of all theory that has to do with things to come rather than things of the here and now. The question might well be asked, what about the theory of the cooperative movement now? Is there nothing that can be said for it? Certainly nothing can be said in so far as the metaphysical speculations of marginalist economics are concerned. As stated above, these schemes of theoretical gymnastics rest on premises remote from those on which rests cooperative theory. But that is not the case in so far as what is now popularly called "macro-economics" is concerned. In fact what formerly could not be brought into the main stream can now, thanks to the contributions of Keynes, be brought into that well-patrolled course. And it is this possibility that can be considered Keynes's contribution to the cooperative movement.

Although the opportunity is at hand to utilize the Keynesian tools to domicile cooperative theory in respectable quarters, the cooperators to date have been tardy in doing so. This reluctance may be a product of the long years of dwelling on the margin of organized economic theory. An intellectual existence on the husks of economic thought is not conducive to a ready recognition of the opportunity that lies at hand in Keynes. Yet just such an opportunity has presented itself and the cooperators would be well advised to make the most of it.

The major tenets of the Keynesian thesis are widely known and no purpose would be served by going into them at this point. It would appear sufficient to point to the means by which cooperative theory may be accommodated to Keynes.

Patronage dividends and stability

The main distinguishing mark of the cooperative movement is the principle of dividends on patronage rather than on ownership. Although cooperators tend to stress all of the principles of the Rochdale Pioneers, such as market price pricing, one vote per member, small and fixed dividends, all business on a cash basis, open membership, etc., the principle of dividends on patronage is what marks off the cooperative from the various types of private enterprise. In fact it is this latter principle that would appear to be the key to the intense opposition to cooperation in business quarters. Carried out on a full scale as contemplated by the advocates of the cooperative commonwealth, this feature would spell the "euthanasia of the rentier" more effectively than any reduction of the rate of interest contemplated by Keynes.

But it is not with these long-run social implications of this distribution principle that the present argument has to do. What is of more immediate importance is the bearing that the patronage-dividend principle has on the problem of economic stability. Although the cooperator has argued that cooperation would bring greater economic stability, the reasons put forward have been pre-Keynesian. One argument has been to the effect that cooperation would "minimize industrial fluctuations through the adjustment of output to current demand."[8] It is contended that the cooperative would confine its operations to stable lines for which there is a fairly predictable demand. In this way temporary market gluts would be avoided. But this argument has meaning only in the case of one individual enterprise and not to the economy as a whole. Such gluts are mistakes of ordering of no serious consequence during high levels of income and employment. The effect on one enterprise is a lower rate of turnover than had been anticipated. During a depression when aggregate stocks are found to be more than sufficient to meet an already ineffective demand, it cannot be said that such a state was brought on by over-stocking. What appears to be over-stocking is only such in light of the general ineffective demand which remains unexplained.

The belief has also been asserted that cooperative employment is more stable than that in private enterprise. The argument has been based on the fact that cooperatives in the depression of the 1930s experienced in most countries a net increase in employment.[9] This empirical evidence, however, is indicative only of the fact that in times of crises even the most cherished habits of thought are apt to suffer some erosion. In the depths of the depression the climate of opinion was such that the general antipathy to cooperation was less intense. Those who had been disillusioned by the chaos in private enterprise were willing to experiment with the economic order. Under these circumstances, cooperatives were bound to expand. The effect was a decrease in private enterprise employment and an increase in cooperative employment with probably no net increase in aggregate employment.

A further argument has been put forth largely by the British cooperatives. They contended that the policy of building up a large reserve by maintaining a low patronage dividend no matter the size of actual earnings enabled them to have a volume of employment in the depression that would not otherwise have been possible.[10] This issue will be dealt with later. At this point, suffice it to say that such a policy is deflationary in prosperity and does at least as much to unstabilize employment in the prosperity phase of the cycle as it does to stabilize it during the depression phase.

Of more importance to the problem of economic stabilization is the effect of the patronage dividend on general economic stability.[11] In accordance with Keynesian theory the major problem in maintaining economic stability would appear to be the savings gap. With a given propensity to consume and a rising national income the savings gap becomes a more intense problem. For at the higher levels of national income, increasing volumes of investment expenditure are called for to offset the increasing volume of savings. Yet it is hardly likely that, with a falling proportion of consumer outlay, the marginal efficiency of capital will be sufficiently high to call forth the requisite investment. The faith that investment alone would be sufficient to close the gap rests on the assumption that expectations are independent of rates of consumption. However, if the propensity to consume could be shifted upwards, the savings gap at higher levels of income would be less burdensome. It would appear that this is precisely what the patronage-dividend principle portends.

Patronage dividends and income shares

At the crux of the problem of the propensity to consume would appear to be the pattern of income distribution. As a general proposition it is reasonable to state that a more even distribution of income would mean a higher propensity to consume; a less even distribution of income a lower propensity to consume. One of the factors contributing to the greater unevenness of income distribution is the receipt of property income. In the United States for the years 1919–38, 1 percent of the population received 65 percent of the dividends paid and 5 percent received 77 percent of the dividends paid.[12] As a general rule, receivers of property income are in the upper income brackets. Or more precisely, the largest proportion of property income goes to those in the upper income brackets. Thus any reduction in the receipt of property income reduces the proportion of the aggregate income going to upper income groups. If this reduction is shifted to lower income groups, the effect is to raise the propensity to consume and reduce the size of the savings gap at any level of income and employment. The patronage-dividend principle works precisely in this direction.

The patronage dividend means that what would normally go out as profit income to holders of stock certificates goes to the multitude of consumers in the form of patronage dividends. The full effect of this so far as the consumption function is concerned is apparent when the percentage return is compared with that on invested capital. Frequently the success of cooperative undertakings is judged in the light of patronage percentages. On this basis the returns do not seem startling. In the grocery business, patronage dividends rarely run over 5 percent and most frequently they are below this figure. However, this is a return on patronage or on sales. The earnings of cooperatives when looked at as a return on invested capital are quite often startling. It is not unusual for earnings rates computed on share capital to run over 100 percent.[13] Under private ownership such earnings are engrossed by the proprietors in the form of enhanced personal income or in the form of stock dividends. The latter is more frequently the case as the retail chain brings increasing weight to bear in distribution. The effect of such a scheme of income disbursement is to transfer income from the mass of purchasers to the smaller group of stockholders. Such a transfer of income aids and abets the uneven distribution of income, which perpetuates a relatively low propensity to consume.

But not so with the cooperative patronage dividend. The distribution is to the mass of purchasers from whom it has already been collected. There is no shift of income. More than this can be said for the patronage dividend as a stabilizer. As it has worked itself out in western culture the cooperative movement by and large has been a farm and working-class movement. As such, its supporters have been preponderantly in the low income groups. In the ordinary course of events, income would be transferred through profit distribution from these groups to the proprietors or to the stockholders of the privately owned establishments. Since these latter are generally more advantageously placed in the structure of income distribution, this results in a shift of income from low to higher income receivers, the result being a reduction of the propensity to consume.

Income and consumption effects of cooperation

The reverse is the case when such activity comes in for cooperative organization. For since cooperatives have been formed under the auspices of financially less favorably placed groups of the population who otherwise would be in the hands of the private trader, the effect has been to reduce the flow of income from low to high income receivers. In fact, the establishment of the "cooperative commonwealth" would disestablish the high income receiver. Thus it would appear that the cooperative movement introduces a stabilizing factor into the economy indirect proportion to the extent that aggregate economic activity is engrossed by cooperative organization.

On the basis of this latter proposition it can be argued that the vertical extension of cooperation is in the interest of greater economic stability. In nations such as England and Sweden in which the cooperative movement has pursued a course of vertical integration, the ostensible reason has been to protect the integrity of the consumer societies. These latter have of course been buffeted about by the hostility of the private trading community. One of the common difficulties has been the reluctance of wholesalers to service cooperatives. Even those wholesalers with no congenital hostility to cooperation have frequently been intimidated by the threats and cajoleries of the private retailers into refusing service to cooperatives. The effect of such action has been to push the retail cooperatives into wholesale activity. The cooperative wholesales then experienced the same difficulties on the production level, so that they were forced into production. This was the course of events in England which gave rise to the Cooperative Wholesale Society, which now operates, among other things, wheat farms in Canada and tea plantations in Ceylon. In the mid-continent area of the United States the extension of cooperation from retailing of gasoline to that of the production and bulk distribution of oil and gas has been a result of the same pattern of organized resistance on the part of private enterprise. To date this vertical integration has been defended as a defensive measure by many cooperators, although some have seen it as the beginnings of the cooperative commonwealth. But the fact remains that it has been dictated by the situation and has been a successful piece of strategy in meeting the hostility of the corporate-enterprise fraternity.

But such a process need not be defended only as a piece of strategy in economic warfare. Profits and thus dividends are paid at the production and bulk-distribution levels as well as at the retail. In fact these two areas of activity are a larger source of such property incomes than is retailing. The extension of cooperatives into these areas means a shift of profits from owners of stock shares to patronage dividends. Of course cooperative wholesaling and cooperative production are not owned by a mass of individual cooperators. The usual procedure is for the cooperative retail societies to own the wholesales, which in turn own the production cooperatives. The effect is for patronage dividends to flow from production to wholesaling to retailing, where the cooperative member receives the savings either in a lower price or enhanced patronage dividend. In either case the effect is a rise in the propensity to consume. For the contribution of profits to a steeply pyramided income at these earlier economic stages is eliminated. Thus cooperators may argue that vertical integration is also in the interest of a greater economic stability.

Some objections to the argument

Objections may be raised to the above arguments on three major grounds. First, it may be claimed that there is no reason to assume that under the "cooperative commonwealth" the same wide income disparities might not come to prevail as now prevail. If, for instance, cooperative management should find it possible through control of the direction of cooperatives to provide for themselves inordinately large incomes and bonuses, as is commonly the practice among corporate managers and directors, this could represent an appreciable flow of income from low to newly established high income receivers. This is certainly not beyond the realms of possibility. In some of the British cooperatives especially, the membership has grown to such proportions that much of the affairs of the cooperative is conducted by a relatively small group. Although not exactly the case, as this small group of ardent members are owners to as great an extent as any other group selected at random from the membership, there is a sense in which ownership has become separated from control just as has occurred in the large corporation.

Yet this is not likely to be the course of events. In the cooperative movement to date, wage and salary incomes have been modest and disparities in income of a size long accepted in private enterprise would not be tolerated by cooperators. Although cooperatives have been faced with the same numbers problem that has effectively scotched any semblance of democracy in the modern corporation, the cooperators, unlike corporate owners, are still firmly in control of the organization. Management has not acceded to control of the directive body as it has in the modern corporation; the cooperative movement is not in the position of having managers in the capacity of directors passing on their own pecuniary worth. This has a tendency to hold incomes in check.

In the modern corporation the manager has acceded to the status position once held by the entrepreneur. In the hurly-burly of an earlier capitalism, this economic buccaneer was in a position to engross for himself all that the traffic would bear. The populace at large looked upon this as only right and good, for each of these entrepreneurs was viewed as a public benefactor working for "an end which was no part of his intention." In fact munificence in remuneration was essential to continued acts of creation. This same public solicitousness has been carried over to the corporate manager. His enterprise, initiative, and foresight are looked upon as a frail growth which needs constant pecuniary rejuvenation. There is a certain parallel in the public sentiments and attitudes toward the welfare of corporate managers and that of the public sentiments and attitudes that once prevailed toward the well-being of royalty. Such sentiments and attitudes toward the pecuniary well-being of cooperative managers have never developed. Cooperative managers have never been esteemed as creators or public benefactors or patrons of industry. They have been viewed as good and faithful workmen who should be paid as such. This attitude has held down the extremes of income distribution within cooperative endeavors.

A second objection to the stabilizing effect of the patronage-dividend principle may be raised. Cooperatives do have share capital on which dividends are paid. If this share capital should become highly concentrated, there could be a minor shift in income distribution and the establishment of a new group of high income receivers, patronage dividends notwithstanding. But that is not likely to be the course of events. The returns on cooperative share capital are fixed at a relatively low rate of return rarely higher than 4 per cent. But this source of income disparity is most effectively limited by the fact that share-holdings are generally limited either as to financial amount or number. With such a limitation, stock concentration is not possible.

One further, and more serious, objection may be raised. As is well known, corporate savings in excess of new corporate investment can be a most serious deflationary factor. In fact some students of the problem of economic stability are inclined to emphasize this source of savings as a more serious threat than the level of individual savings. Cooperatives too are in the habit of cutting out of current earnings certain sums for reserves. The British cooperatives have accumulated extremely large reserves which some students have contended have been in excess of any possible need. The fund has been on such a large scale that it has been a serious deflationary force.[14]

This aspect of cooperative policy must not be ignored. Such action in reducing the circuit flow of funds is serious whether done in the spirit of cooperation or the name of corporate strategy. Yet it would appear to be a passing thing among cooperatives. Cooperation has grown up in an extremely unstable economy not of its own making. The cooperative movement has been buffeted by the economic storms largely generated in the private enterprise sector of the economy. All of the many depressions through which the cooperative movement has come have taken their toll in individual cooperative societies. But as the cooperative movement becomes a larger element in western economic life, the intensity of these storms should be appreciably reduced for the reasons recited above. With such a reduction there would no longer be the necessity for reserve accumulations on the scale characteristic of the past. But even without such a reserve reduction, with the reduction in personal income disparity through the patronage dividend, there would be a net gain in favor of greater economic stability. In fact the large role played by the British cooperative movement in the British economy was probably a factor in the more rapid recovery of the British economy from the worldwide depression of the 1930s.

Saving and investment under stability

Cooperators could reasonably argue that in the world of things hoped for, the cooperative commonwealth, there would be no savings problem. With the elimination of the economic storm-generating areas, there would be no reason for such excess saving as has sometimes characterized cooperation in the present-day world. Current excess cooperatives savings are in the nature of a protective device to assure continuity of the corporate body through a general economic recession. In the cooperative commonwealth, savings would be made only to take care of planned investment.

In the jargon of the economic trade, ex ante savings would always equal ex ante investment and thus ex post saving and investment would be equal. Increases in saving would never be a problem for they would be equal to increased investment. The only reason for a divergence between ex ante saving and ex post investment would be technical problems encountered in accomplishing an investment program. These should be easily corrected for and localized in nature. At worst, they would only extend the time period over which an equality between savings and investment would be worked out. At best, investment program lags would be balanced off by investment program leads. But in any event, such slight discrepancies as could conceivably occur would not be likely to precipitate a general economic recession.

From the preceding argument it is apparent that the cooperators can rest their case for cooperation in the immediate present on other than sentimental grounds. The cooperative movement can be urged as a part of a general program of economic stability perfectly compatible with Keynesian economics. Of course strict Keynesians would not be receptive toward such a use of Keynes. Keynes's *General Theory* can be construed as an underconsumption argument and it can even be argued that he would not have minded such a reading.[15] But the keepers of Keynes have not been in the tradition of the denizens of Keynes's "economic underworld." The keepers of Keynes are the inheritors of the classical tradition in which investment is the thing. Keynes's admonition to advance on both fronts at once has often been overlooked by those who insist on corralling Keynes into the underinvestment school. Nevertheless, the cooperative movement would appear to have a case compatible with contemporary economic thought and should no longer have to remain as a sport in the history of the evolution of economic order.

Notes

1 John Stuart Mill of course became enamored of cooperation, mainly of the producer variety. But his enthusiasm in no way led him to play fast and loose with the received doctrine and it was handed down from the ancients unsullied. See his *Principles of Political Economy*, book IV, chap. VII. Of course Pigou in his *Economics of Welfare* devotes some time to what he calls Purchaser's Associations, which he likens to joint stock companies. After itemizing their economic advantages over privately owned enterprise, he relegates them to a small role in economic affairs. "Even, however, in departments of work where experience gives good hope of efficiency and success, it does not follow that Purchaser's Associations will always come into being. Very poor people may lack the initiative and understanding needed to form one.... Better-to-do persons, while fully competent to develop Purchaser's Associations, if they had the wish, may, in fact, not have the wish.... British tenant farmers ... are slow to overcome their native individualism for the (to them) relatively small advantages of cooperation with their neighbors." Op. cit., London, Macmillan, 1924, p. 295. See also Marshall's similar dismissal in *Principles of Economics*, London, Macmillan, 1930, 8th ed., p. 307.
2 The usual examples cited are the family, fraternal, and religious organizations. But, although most frequently ignored by the economic observer, there is a large volume of economic endeavor of a cooperative nature not labeled as such. See for example

Findley Mackenzie, *The Development of Collective Enterprise*, Lawrence, University of Kansas Press, 1943. Much of what passes under the name monopolistic competition in standard theory could be called cooperation, albeit the ultimate aim being successful completion of predatory pecuniary ventures at the expense of the commonwealth. But notwithstanding the ulterior aims of such endeavor, monopolistic cooperation as a designation of such action has in many ways more to recommend it than monopolistic competition.

3 Margaret Mead (ed.), *Cooperation and Competition among Primitive Peoples*, New York, McGraw-Hill, 1937.

4 In the popular mind it is often held that the cooperative has it all one way. This most frequently rests on the erroneous belief that "cooperatives pay no taxes." But the cooperative not only pays all dues, but has to buck the hostility of the private trading community. In addition, the general sentiment of the community at large is not usually favorably inclined toward cooperation. This mental hostility is the reverse of the mental climate faced by the private trader, who is looked upon as a public benefactor. In activity in which community "good will" is an item bought and sold at handsome prices, the lack of it at any price may spell the doom of an otherwise well-founded endeavor.

5 Paul Hubert Casselman, *The Cooperative Movement and Some of Its Problems*, New York, Philosophical Library, 1952, chap. II, pp. 11–13; chap. X.

6 J. P. Warbasse, *Cooperative Democracy*, New York, Macmillan, 1927.

7 G. D. H. Cole, *The British Cooperative Movement in a Socialist Society*, London, Allen & Unwin, 1951.

8 Colston E. Warne, *The Consumer Cooperative Movement in Illinois*, Chicago, University of Chicago Press, 1926, p. 286.

9 J. P. Warbasse, *Cooperative Peace*, Superior, Wis., Cooperative Publishing Association, 1950, p. 202.

10 Inquiry on Cooperative Enterprise, Report on Cooperative Enterprise in Europe, Washington, U.S. Government Printing Office, 1937, p. 62.

11 Some cooperators have had glimmerings of this aspect of the issue. See for example E. R. Bowen, *The Cooperative Road to Abundance*, New York, Henry Schuman, 1953, pp. 63–4. But none have seen the full implications in terms of modern income and employment theory.

12 Simon Kumets, *Share of Upper Income Groups in Income and Savings*, New York, National Bureau of Economic Research, 1953, p. xxxvi.

13 H. H. Turner, *Case Studies of Consumers' Cooperatives*, New York, Columbia University Press, 1941, pp. 98–9; Warne, op. cit., p. 272.

14 A. M. Carr-Saunders, P. Sargent Florence, and Robert Peers, *Consumers' Cooperation in Great Britain*, London, Allen & Unwin, 1938.

15 See for instance Chapter 23, pp. 358ff., in *The General Theory of Employment, Interest and Money*, London, Macmillan, 1936. See also H. Gordon Hayes, "Keynesism and Public Policy," in Glenn Hoover (ed.), *Twentieth Century Economics*, New York, Philosophical Library, 1950.

4   A theory of the social origins of the factors of production

American Journal of Economics and Sociology, vol. 15 (1) (October 1955), pp. 73–82

COMMENTARY BY WILLIAM WALLER

This is my personal favorite for introducing students to institutional economists' critique of neoclassical economics. It also demonstrates the analytic power of having a cultural approach to understanding and constructing economic theories.

Hamilton begins by noting that the categories of land, labor, and capital as factors of production in neoclassical production theory are historical artifacts that developed along with market capitalism in the industrial revolution. He points out that the manorial economy which preceded capitalism in Western Europe cannot be explained by the analytic concepts that emerged along with capitalism. He further notes that the categories themselves in fact represent social status groups in capitalism where individuals belong in a group based upon the source of their income. If they receive interest or profits from owner-ship of capital, they are capitalists; if they receive rent from ownership of land, they are landlords; and if they receive wages from work, they are laborers.

Using Durkheim's method in *The Elementary Forms of the Religious Life* (1947), Hamilton argues that disparate items employed in productive processes entitle their owners to a share of the income generated by the enterprise based on social relations; the only similarity these items have is their characterization as one of the factors that is entitled to an income. The actual categories of land, labor, and capital are the totemic status groups that determine rights and obliga-tions in capitalism – all things, in all circumstances, must be placed in one such category; or a new, similar type category must be generated such as management or entrepreneurship.

Hamilton simultaneously argues that in fact neoclassical production theory is incapable of actually telling us anything about actual production processes in our own modern industrial culture; much less does it have any use in understanding production in any non-industrial society. The real purpose of the factors of pro-duction is to provide a framework for justifying the distribution of income shares in capitalism.

This is the first article in which Hamilton suggests an important theme in his later work, namely that neoclassical economic theory is the religion of modern industrial culture.

A THEORY OF THE SOCIAL ORIGINS OF THE FACTORS OF PRODUCTION

Within recent times the contributions of Emile Durkheim to an understanding of social structure have become increasingly apparent.[1] Yet his service to a clearer understanding of the origin of current economic conceptualizations remains to be appreciated. Outside of his *Division of Labor*, little attention has been paid by the student of economic thought to the contribution of Durkheim to an understanding of social phenomena. The student of standard economic theory has not been one to wander far afield into what to him appear to be the byways of social inquiry. As a result, economic inquiry in its underlying social preconceptions remains essentially where Adam Smith delivered it. Unfortunately the vast progress in the other social sciences, especially anthropology and sociology, has had little influence on the speculative peregrinations of the economic theorist.[2] Yet by turning to the work of the ethnologist and the sociologist, a better understanding may be gained of the background of economic thought. In short, it is to that area of inquiry now designated the "sociology of knowledge" that the modern student of economic thought must turn for a full appreciation and understanding of the background of economic thought. Durkheim is of extreme value as a contributor of new vistas in this area of inquiry.

One of Durkheim's major contributions was his demonstration that the idea of class arises from society itself.[3] Members of societies are arranged and graded on a basis peculiar to that particular society. The system of grades and ratings may have its authentication in kinship, feudal fealty, contract, force and fraud, sex, or what have you. Nevertheless, all societies with which the ethnologist is familiar have been found to be so graded. The character and intensity of the system varies, but it is just as much a status system whether among the Trobriand Islanders, the Coorgs of India, the Maori, or the feudal society of medieval Europe.

Durkheim also noted that these societies project this social stratification into a classification of the universe. All things of experience are so classified. Items of the universe take on the same complexion of grades and ratings that are peculiar to the social organization.[4] According to Durkheim, there is nothing in the universe itself to suggest such a system of classification. In the case of the Australian totemic society he demonstrated that the scheme of classification of the universe was a projection of the totemic classification. It was because society itself was divided into clans, phratries, and tribes that the overall schemes of classification were derived. Although Durkheim seemed to err in attributing the origin of the concept class to a common totemic origin of all societies, he did have a concept that was useful to an understanding of classification systems in all cultures. Frequently those schemes of classification, which are resorted to whether in a totemically divided society or not, are themselves reflections of a system of social grades and ratings, of a myth-authenticated system of invidious distinctions. Although the abstract concept of classification as resorted to in many areas of inquiry, such as the biological sciences, is now reasonably free of immediate social origin, it is by no means true that all schemes of classification are so freed or uninfluenced by current social organization. There is reason to believe that classifications ostensibly drawn on a matter-of-fact basis in some areas of social inquiry are in fact projections of a preexisting social order. Precisely this can be shown in the case of what are called, in economic thought, the factors of production.

Within the realm of established economic discourse the factors of production have a long and honored place.[5] In fact both traditional production and distribution theory work from a basic classification of things into land, labor, and capital and sometimes management. (The latter is an addition recently made as a result of a cleavage in the cultural matrix that goes by the name of the separation of ownership from control. Within the main stream of economic thought, these factors have been looked upon as agents of production. They have been in existence prior to theory and in fact can be found in all cultures. It remains only for someone to claim them for there to be landlords, laborers, and capitalists. At least, that would appear to be the gist of the following statement from John Stuart Mill, a position from which latter-day economists have not been known to dissent:

> The three requisites of production, as has been so often repeated, are labour, capital, and land: understanding by capital, the means and appliances which are the accumulated results of previous labour, and by land, the materials and instruments supplied by nature, whether contained in the interior of the earth, or constituting its surface. Since each of these elements of production may be separately appropriated the industrial community may be considered as divided into landowners, capitalists, and productive labourers.[6]

Among economists of the present day it is fair to say that the factors of production are conceptualizations which to them seem to have a substantive meaning. The factors have a real existence and it is because they may be "separately appropriated" that there are landlords, laborers, and capitalists. In fact, so fixed is this concept in the habits of thought of western man that frequently even the affairs of primitive cultures obviously far remote from such a state of organizations as western culture, are viewed as ventures in the combination of land, labor, and capital.[7] As Veblen stated the case in regard to distribution:

> e.g., a gang of Aleutian Islanders slushing about in the wrack and surf with rakes and magical incantations for the capture of shellfish are held, in point of taxonomic reality, to be engaged on a feat of hedonistic equilibration in rent, wages, and interest. And that is all there is to it. Indeed, for economic theory of this kind, that is all there is to any economic situation.[8]

In short, the productive factors are held to be universal social constructs. But such is not the case.

The origin of the factors of production is to be found in those cataclysmic industrial events that long ago were dubbed "the industrial revolution" by an earlier Arnold Toynbee.[9] To analyze medieval handicraft or manorial agriculture in terms of land, labor, and capital, if not seeming absurd today, would have seemed so at the time. Medieval culture was one characterized by a social organization composed of lords of the land, knights, freemen, serfs, and slaves. The system of status as to categories was quite remote from that of present-day western culture. There is to be found nowhere in medieval economic thought an allusion to the factors of production.[10] To describe the economic affairs of a manorial unit in terms of varying dosages of land, labor, and capital would be to miss the mark by a wide margin.

As the manorial organization disintegrated in the face of a rising industrialism, so did that status system demarcated by landlord, knight, freeman, serf, and slave. In its place arose the business enterprise, the corporate form of which has come to predominate in more recent times. Although the status system of the medieval culture disintegrated, status as a differential ordering of mankind did not disappear. Under the suzerainty of business enterprise, society came to be demarcated by the status groups which had come to the front in the business unit. In short, the industrial revolution broke down the feudal relations of social reciprocity which had been the core of the feudal status system. But relations of social reciprocity were not forgone. New ones were established in the way of landlord-capitalist and capitalist laborer.[11]

It is a piece of popular conceit that status in contemporary western culture is of no significance and that western culture differs from its feudal predecessor by the substitution of contract for status.[12] This, however, fails to see that status exists in contemporary western culture just as it did in medieval culture. What has changed is the basis of the status system and the status categories. Fealty was the basis of the feudal status system whereas contract is the basis of the business status system. The capitalist–laborer relationship can be defined in terms of rights and duties just as the lord–serf relationship could be defined. In the latter case the rights and duties were defined by long-established use and wont reinforced by ecclesiastical fiat. In the former case these relationships are defined by contract reinforced by the use and wont defined by the common law. But in either case the end product is a well-defined system of status.

What is of significance to the present discussion is the fact that as the last vestige of manorialism disappeared, this newer status system came to pervade the entire society. Men were graded and rated in an overall status system bounded by landlord, capitalist, and laborer. The whole of western culture came to be so divided. It is true that individuals might have relationships that placed them in more than one category. But it can be said without too much stretching of a point that the major source of one's income, in most cases, did define rather clearly the major category into which one would fall. On this issue of division into landlords, laborers, and capitalists the Marxian theorists would appear to be on safer ground than the fuzzy popular division into upper, middle, and lower class. Although this latter, at least at one time, corresponded to the landlord–capitalist–laborer division, it has come to mean very little except as a statistical division based on the place of one's income in an array of all incomes by size. As an interpretation of the normal distribution of income it has more to recommend it than as a description of status. Division on an income basis means very little so far as status is concerned. A laborer may earn more than a capitalist if the latter be an entrepreneur of some small affair, yet the latter position would fall higher on the social scale. Members of trade unions who in their workday affairs wear the traditional garb of the laboring man are not good material for the private country club no matter how financially solvent they are. Yet the creditor-harried proprietor of a shaky business enterprise is usually an acceptable candidate for membership.

In short, western culture has come to be divided into landlords, capitalists, and laborers to an extent which the society itself is reluctant to recognize. There have been and are variations in this set of arrangements. It is truer of western European peoples to include landlords as a division than it would be of those areas to which the economic arrangements of western Europe were carried. In these latter areas, such as North America, Australia, and New Zealand, the vestiges of the feudal hierarchy are carried along only in some of the more archaic habits of thought which diffused with the social arrangements. But feudalism never had an opportunity in these new areas, not because of the free land available, but because such an organization of things was already on the wane in western culture. Likewise, in more recent times it would be more correct to include management as a category to the extent that this group has been successfully demarcated from that of capitalist and from that of labor. Such a separation has taken place in the modern corporation.

Such variations in the pattern are evidence for the major thesis of the present paper. These changes have been reflected in what was held to compose the factors of production. At one time little question was raised on the inclusion of land as a factor of production. However, in recent times land has been more frequently subsumed under capital.[13] This is nothing to cause any great amount of surprise, for except in a few limited areas in England and in that area until recently presided over by the Junkers in Germany, the landlord has become a vestigial appendage from an older order of things. In the newer areas of European settlement the ownership of land distinct from the capital appurtenances is not a common arrangement. Under these circumstances it has become common practice for capital to engross land in a factorial merger. The rise of a new social group distinct from both capital and labor in the form of business management has also given rise to a change in what are recognized as factors of production. As a result of management usurping the traditional rights, prerogatives, and appurtenances of capital in corporate direction and control, a new factor has been found on the economic horizon.[14]

At this point the question of Durkheim's contribution is in order. It is all well and good to point out that the factors of production are derived from society itself. After all, it may be contended, economics is a social science and the productive factors are nothing more than a part of that social organization to which the inquiry is directed. They are the agents out of which flow goods and services, and such would be apparent to any impartial observer. But such is not the case. As one critic has put it recently:

> What are the factors that affect production most decisively? If we could imagine ourselves attacking such a question today for the first time, there can be no doubt that our attention would be directed to such matters as the state of our knowledge, the prevalence of essential skills, the physical availability of essential equipment, the state of public order and social conditions generally, and all that sort of thing. As everyone knows today, these are the decisive conditions.... But according to the classical tradition of economics the factors of production are very different. They are: land, labor, capital and management. It may be true that these rubrics can be conceived in such a way as to include considerations of science and technology, and even those of social institutions. But in that case the difference of expression is still very striking. "Land, labor, capital, and management" is an odd way to summarize the blessings of civilization.[15]

This "odd way" of summarizing "the blessings of civilization" is a product of the conceptualizing process to an explanation of which Durkheim contributed so much. Economics in its classical form, just as systems of religion, is a conceptualization of the universe. The early formulators of economic thought did precisely what man has done time out of hand. To the explanation of this view of the universe they projected the status structure of the western European business culture. Everything to which ownership could be extended – and there is little remaining to which some enterprising free-booter has not extended ownership – fell under one of these categories. Each of the multitude of items which make up the universe as experienced by western man was subsumed under some one of the factorial heads.

It might well be argued that all scientific endeavor is taxonomic to some extent and that chemists and biologists have systems of classification which cover the universe similar in nature to those of the economist. There is, however, a significant difference between the taxonomic schemes of the chemist and biologist and that of the economist. The former classify on the grounds of some matter-of-fact demonstrable identity, i.e. on distinctions that can be readily recognized by people of diverse cultures. The classifications of economic belief are based on some feeling of spiritual unity and participation.[16]

The multiplicity of things included under each of the factors of production should make this clear. Land includes a diversity of items under what is euphoniously referred to, at least since Ricardo, as the "indestructible powers of the soil." Herein are such diverse things as mere space itself, soil, flora and fauna established and domiciled by nature, coal, iron ore, oil, copper, lead, gravel, water, and a multitude of other things. To the untrained eye there is no seeming identity among these items. Yet they have a spiritual identity in the sense that they participate in those mysterious powers that beget classification as the "indestructible powers of the soil."[17]

Capital items are of the same diverse nature. Included under this head are such things as "factories clustered here and there over the country," "farms, retail and wholesale stores, barbershops, mines, office buildings, banks," "highways, post offices, schoolhouses, and power dams," "tractors and barber chairs, blast furnaces and display windows, derricks and typewriters generators and electric motors," "stocks of raw materials, ... goods on the assembly line, and finished goods waiting to be shipped," "canned peas, soap, radio tubes, tires, tin cans, and baby bottles," "shoes and shirts and food and toothpaste." These items of equipment ... and these stocks of goods in the possession of business firms, are known collectively as "capital goods."[18] Other, more inclusive classifications have been known to include techniques and ideas of manufacture (patented) under this head as well. Furthermore, bonds, stocks of gold, stock certificates, and good will are capital items of some sort and participate in some manner in the mystic force that ties together the items listed above under capital goods. All are of the essence of capital.

Labor is no better. Labor is held not to be the person of the laborer. Labor is an abstract thing called labor power, or rather a multitude of identifiable skills acknowledged as manifestations of labor power. Included in this category are such diverse skills as medical, machinist, printing, janitoring, scavenging, horse bookmaking, gambling, lawyering, teaching, scienceing, and all the rest of the multitude of complex skills found in a modern industrial culture. Again the only identity would appear to be a spiritual participation in what is called "labor power."

The absurdities of such a scheme of classification have frequently been pointed out. In fact it is this basic factorial analysis that led Veblen to call traditional economic thought "taxonomy." The results of such taxonomic endeavor are fraught with absurdities and difficulties. A slave, for instance, engaged in the production of cotton is a capital item while the freeman beside him engaged in the same activity is classified as labor. A housewife, although performing the same tasks as an innkeeper and dietitian, remains a housewife outside the charmed circle of productive labor.

Difficulties multiply. A croupier in Nevada is a productive laborer; a croupier in New York is a fugitive from free room and board at state expense. Capital can only be defined as something which yields a pecuniary return called interest, which is that type of pecuniary return received by the owner of capital, who in turn is differentiated as one who receives a pecuniary return from just such a source. The absurdities of applying such a tautological definition become apparent in practice. Automobiles become either capital or consumer goods. If they serve as the basis for an imputation of pecuniary return in the form of interest, they are capital goods. If no such return can be imputed, they are not. If owned by a capitalist or a capital-possessing enterprise, they will have some pecuniary return in the form of interest imputed to them, for a capital item is one to which can be imputed a pecuniary return called interest. Items to which such an imputation has been made take on all of the trappings of capital by common usage.[19]

But this "odd way" of viewing things is revealed for what it is by these absurdities and difficulties. Although factors make no sense in an analysis of production, they do have a meaning as establishing claims in distribution, based on an imputation of productive efficacy. There are people receiving wages who are labor, those receiving profits who represent owners of capital, and those receiving rents who represent owners of land. All members of western culture fall roughly into such income categories, each of which is defined by custom-prescribed rights and duties or reciprocal obligations. All are related through the culturally defined practices of business enterprise as the larger caste groups of India are tied together by relations of reciprocity.[20]

In summary, there arose out of the industrial revolution new social relationships. An all-inclusive social hierarchy was established which graded and rated all income receivers into one of the various productive categories in accordance with the type of income to which it was entitled – rent, wages, interest or profits. In analyzing the economy, the early formulators of classical political economy projected these social classes into a view of the entire economic universe. All items of economic significance were fitted into one of these categories even if violence was done to reason.

Durkheim is significant, for he demonstrated the existence of such a conceptualizing process. It also appears, once this process as it worked itself out in western economic thought becomes clear, that the analysis of production in terms of productive factors served some larger social purpose. By elaborate schemes of reasoning such as that of marginal productivity, the returns or rights of each one of these status groups was made to seem equivalent to the obligation or duties of each.[21] In this way a status system was rationalized and a "scientific" legend has been provided as attestation of the authenticity of the status system.

Notes

1 Claude Lévi-Strauss, "French Sociology," in Georges Gurvitch and Wilbert E. Moore, *Twentieth Century Sociology*, New York, Philosophical Library, 1945, pp. 503ff.
2 An exception has been the institutional school in America and some continental scholars. See for instance W. Stark, *The Ideal Foundations of Economic Thought*, New York, Oxford, 1944.
3 Emile Durkheim, *The Elementary Forms of the Religious Life*, Glencoe, Ill., Free Press, 1947, book II, chap. 3.
4 Durkheim, op. cit., pp. 141–4; see also Sir Baldwin Spencer and F. J. Gillen, *The Arunta*, London, Macmillan, 1927, vol. 1, chap. 5.
5 See Edwin Cannan, *Theories of Production and Distribution*, London, King, 1924, chap. 2.
6 John Stuart Mill, *Principles of Political Economy*, London, Longmans Green, 1909, W. J. Ashley ed., p. 238.
7 See J. B. Clark, *Essentials of Economic Theory*, pp. 4–5. Some ethnologists have attempted to utilize these standardized conceptualizations in analyses of other cultures with rather indifferent results. See for example Melville J. Herskovits, *Economic Anthropology*, New York, Knopf, 1952; Raymond Firth, *Primitive Economics of the*

New Zealand Maori, New York, Dutton, 1929; also *Malay Fishermen: Their Peasant Economy*, London, Kegan Paul, Trench, Trubner, 1946.

8 Thorstein Veblen, "Professor Clark's Economics," reprinted in *The Place of Science in Modern Civilization,* New York, Viking, 1942, p. 193.

9 Arnold Toynbee, *The Industrial Revolution of the Eighteenth Century in England,* London, Longmans Green, 1908, especially chaps. 2–8; see also J. L. and B. Hammond, *The Rise of Modern Industry*, London, Methuen, 1925, especially Parts I and II. See also Edward Heimann, *History of Economic Doctrines*, New York, Oxford, 1945, chap. 2, for an excellent presentation of the influence of the social background on the theories of the "predecessors of Adam Smith."

10 Certainly there were earlier formulations of what were considered to be "factors" of production. But these too were reflections of a social structure. What is referred to in the above statement is the latter-day conceptual scheme of land, labor, and capital. See Edwin Cannan, op. cit.: "This triad of productive requisites did not very early become an integral part of English political economy. Its origin is apparently to be found in Adam Smith's division of the component parts of prices into wages, profit and rent" (p. 40). Also Max Beer, *Early British Economics*, London, George Allen & Unwin, 1938, p. 112.

11 For a general discussion of reciprocity as a function of social organization see Bronislaw Malinowski, *Crime and Custom in Savage Society*, New York, Harcourt Brace, 1926.

12 For the classic presentation of this argument see Henry Maine, *Ancient Law*, London, Routledge, 1905 ed., chap. 5.

13 For the standard treatment of this see Bruce Knight and Earl Hines, *Economics*, New York, Knopf, 1952, chap. 2.

14 See James Burnham's *The Managerial Revolution*, New York, John Day, 1941, which says in a popular and somewhat superficial manner what Adolf A. Berle and Gardiner C. Means, *The Modern Corporation and Private Property*, New York, Macmillan, 1932, lead up to in a meticulous and scholarly manner.

15 C. E. Ayres, *The Industrial Economy*, Boston, Houghton Mifflin, 1952, p. 354.

16 For a discussion of this subject see Lucien Levy-Bruhl, *How Natives Think*, London, Allen & Unwin, 1926. Levy-Bruhl assumed that the principle of association by participation gave way in contemporary society to the law of contradiction. This difference in logic divides the pre-logical from the contemporary logical period. This aspect of Levy-Bruhl's analysis is faulty, for no such clear-cut distinction between man in "earlier" and "later" societies can be made. The fact of the matter is that the "law of participation" and the law of contradiction are characteristic of thought in all societies. But we owe to Levy-Bruhl a debt of gratitude for having pointed out these phenomena of the thought process.

17 In observing the actual universe in which production takes place, George Geiger in *The Theory of the Land Question*, New York, Macmillan, 1935, demonstrates quite clearly that in fact there is not too much to distinguish capital from land except the secondary position of capital in the general production process. This argument seems to point further in the direction of the social origin of the three factors of production. See especially Chapter III, "Land and Capital."

18 Lorie Tarshis, *The Elements of Economics*, Boston, Houghton Mifflin, 1947, pp. 11–12.

19 W. W. Carlile, "The Language of Economics," *Journal of Political Economy*, vol. 17 (1919), pp. 434–47.

20 M. N. Srinivas, *Religion and Society among the Coorgs of South India*, London, Oxford, 1952, chap. 2.

21 For a revelation of the metaphysical grounds on which this argument rests see C. E. Ayres, *The Problem of Economic Order*, New York, Farrar & Rinehart, 1938, Part II.

5   Ceremonial aspects of corporate organization

American Journal of Economics and Sociology, vol. 16 (1) (October 1956), pp. 11–23

COMMENTARY BY WILLIAM WALLER

This article is notable for two reasons: one methodological, the other substantive. The methodological contribution consists of Hamilton's effective use of the often-mentioned but seldom employed Ayresian version of the Veblenian dichotomy – namely, the distinction between ceremonial aspects of behavior and technological (or instrumental) aspects of behavior. The substantive contribution of the article is an extension of his exploration of economic categories as collective representations of modern industrial culture's belief system.

In this article, Hamilton notes that the corporate organizational form of the firm ascribes productive activity to corporate organization while primarily articulating and facilitating the assigned reciprocal rights and obligations to the various status groups, defined by either the particular form of capital contributed or the contribution of other so-called factors of production, in differing circumstances. The corporation does not cause productive activity; instead, it is permissive of such activity, given the traditional and legal private ownership rules of modern industrial capitalism. He goes on to note that the primary role of the corporation is to exercise power over the status groups that make up the corporation with regard to: (1) rights to proceeds; (2) residual rights; and (3) coercive rights.

Not surprisingly, Hamilton finds the activities of the modern corporation almost wholly ceremonial in character. Yet he notes the power of the belief that only private enterprise, including corporations, can produce real goods and services efficiently and effectively in the minds of members of modern industrial culture. This belief even creates deep suspicions that something is not quite right when non-corporate, non-private enterprises such as the U.S. Postal Service and the Tennessee Valley Authority regularly manage to make productive contributions of goods and services daily to that same culture.

The overwhelming assessment of corporate activity as ceremonial, or at least not substantially interacting with the actual production activities of the enterprise, might have something to do with the efficacy of the ceremonial–instrumental distinction's efficacy, or at least its clarity, in this analysis.

CEREMONIAL ASPECTS OF CORPORATE ORGANIZATION

In current economic theory the business organization – sole proprietorship, partnership, or corporation – is usually accorded an important place. A description of each of these modes of organization generally suffices to cover the subject of the organization of an economic enterprise and presumably the principal modes of economic organization. The reader is usually left with the inference that the end all of such organization is productive activity. In fact in standard economic theory a discussion of the structure and legal rights and prerogatives of all parties in such a business endeavor usually precedes the more direct discussion of what comes under the head Production. It becomes clear that these forms of business organization are held to contribute to production, if not directly, at least in some fashion but once removed.

This sentiment and habitual point of view toward a prominent piece of institutional furniture is not peculiar to western culture although business organizations are peculiar to it. All cultures can be divided for analytical purposes into what have been called ceremonial and instrumental patterns of behavior.[1] The first are generally associated with the establishment of rights and differential status, the making of individual distinctions among individuals in accordance with habitual modes of drawing social precedence that, culturally, are long-established. The latter, or instrumental patterns, are drawn on a more matter-of-fact basis to fit the needs of the task in hand. Matters of social precedence and differential social esteem are irrelevant in social organization along instrumental lines. Tools and instruments become the foci of patterns of social organization, in the one case as means of establishing rights and claims that have in most cases a distributive significance and in the other of establishing social relationships in conformance with technological sequence. The first involves coercive relationships such as employer–employee while the latter involves functional or technological relationships such as compositor–pressman. In all activity both of these aspects of social organization are to be found. Among the Trobriand Island peoples the garden magician heads the ceremonial patterns accompanying all taro raising as well as performing as planner in the instrumental endeavor essential to taro raising. Within the totality of this activity there are both ceremonial and instrumental aspects.[2]

This dichotomy of social organization is peculiar to all cultures and to all aspects of culture. Tools are used both as instruments to achieve some end-in-view and ceremonially as means of establishing claims and drawing invidious distinctions. Among the western peoples the latter is achieved through vestiture of ownership.

In current economic theory, previously noted, the business organization is looked upon as a productive form of organization. It is the aim of the present inquiry to show that the corporation is ceremonial in nature and only indirectly is concerned with the advancement of production. The inquiry is restricted to the corporation, because of its overriding significance in the western economies.[3] But the same distinction could be made in all forms of business enterprise.

The corporation is a culture complex peculiar to the western culture, to those cultures in other parts of the world which themselves are transplantations of western culture, and to those cultures which have come into continued and direct contact with western culture. The corporation as it is now found is a comparatively new culture phenomenon. Although it existed in an earlier form in what is commonly alluded to as a joint stock company (which in turn was preceded by what is called a joint venture), among the members of western culture, the corporation is looked upon as a latecomer as cultural phenomena go.

Although the corporation is generally viewed as a vital part of social organization directed primarily at the furtherance of productive activity and is much esteemed by the general members of western culture, the facts appear to be at variance with this widely held opinion. Not only does a comparative study with other cultures expose the fatuousness of this belief, but a careful examination of the corporation in western culture tends further to reveal the bankruptcy of the fiction. As stated earlier, the corporation as a form of social organization is peculiar to western culture. In those other cultures unaffected to any intense degree by western culture, such as the Bantu,[4] the Bemba,[5] or the Maori in its purer form,[6] no evidences of the corporate phenomenon, and those related phenomena such as stock jobbing and brokerage, are to be found. In well-known general surveys of primitive economics, any discussion of the phenomenon of the corporation is not to be found.[7] Nor is it to be found in those cultures over which the Communist power-system or scheme of differential personal advantage has come to prevail – in neither Russia nor those consanguineous cultures into which the Russian has been rapidly diffusing either by forced imposition or domestic cupidity. In fact, in many of these latter areas and in the cultural center itself, Russia, the corporation was once a familiar piece of culture. But under the present power system the corporation as a culture complex is being forcibly eradicated. In fact it is allowed no place in the Communist culture.

It might be contended, by those unfamiliar with viewing social phenomena from the vantage point of culture, that the absence of the corporation in more primitive cultures, i.e. on a technological level, was to be accounted for by the primitive state of the industrial arts. But certainly this could not be said about its absence in the Communist cultures Although not as widely proliferated as in some of the centers of western culture, modern technology is at home in Communist centers. If the corporation were essential to productive activity on an elaborated technological scale, it should be found in these latter-day cultures even if not found in others in the technological backwaters.

Even more convincing is the fact that not all productive activity in the western culture takes place under corporate auspices. Although a great fetish has been made of the essentiality of "business enterprise" to successful productive undertakings, there is much in western culture that has not been brought under the sway of corporate business principles and organization. In fact there is much more not under the sway than the members of the culture are readily willing to admit. As in most cultures, the daily comings and goings of the tribe deviate considerably from the ideals as expounded in the tribal legends. Despite the general suspicion that activity not coming under business sway is lacking in authenticity, there is much that is without. Some is organized in the cooperative form and much under some kind of government auspices. Productive units operate in the same type of economic activity with all types of ceremonial overlay and with no apparent disadvantage to those units outside the business system proper.

In short, the belief that the business unit – and, in the present instance, the corporation – is of essential productive nature remains unverified. In fact, there is much evidence that one of the major incidences of the corporation is a "conscientious withdrawal of efficiency."[8]

As further evidence of the non-productive nature of the corporate complex, not only is much instrumental activity not ceremonially authenticated by corporate formation, but much corporate formation takes place with only an imputed relation to productive activity. One need but refer to the more remote holding companies to bring home the point. Of course the connection between many other types of corporate forms such as investment trusts and productive activity might justifiably be brought into question. These types of business enterprise have as a major endeavor the expansion of ownership claims without any necessary concomitant expansion of productive apparatus. Nevertheless, in the view of those deeply saturated in the sentiments of western culture, all corporate activity has some productive efficacy. But this faith has the same validity as the belief among the Trobriand Islanders that garden magic has some demonstrable efficacy in the production of taros. That is, it has a cultural validity in the eyes of those deeply imbued with the eternal verities of western culture, and that is all the validity it has. It has in fact some putative spiritual efficacy that remains unproved and unprovable.

But if the corporation cannot be held to be a productive form of organization, the question might well be asked what role does it play in western culture? Certainly it would be folly to deny any connection between technological activity and the corporation; but the true connection is not the one usually assumed by the members of that culture. Corporate formation is looked upon as essential to industrial activity and without it no industrial activity will transpire. In times of pecuniary stress when the omens which indicate the degree of financial propitiousness, such as the relationship between the marginal efficiency of capital and the rate of interest, are read as unfavorable, corporate activity comes to a halt. With the halt of the formation of corporations, no new industrial undertakings will be permitted and many old ones are either halted or obstructed. That is, even in the face of desperate need for expanded technological activity, none will be allowed unless the prospects for pecuniary gain are looked upon as favorable. Thus the observer of western culture is treated to the spectacle of periodic obstruction of the technological apparatus causing physical want and hardship because the opportunity for solvent corporate activity is at a low ebb. This is the business depression, a phenomenon peculiar to western culture.

But it is one thing to state that corporate or business activity is an efficient cause of such technological disruption and another to say that it is a sufficient cause of such disruption. In western culture the role of the corporation is fraught with significance because of the emotional conditioning of the members of that culture to look upon all "business enterprise" as peculiarly fraught with significance. That production is augmented and made effective by virtue of financial activity in general and corporate activity in particular is deeply imbedded among the collective representations of the western peoples. In view of this fact, it can be stated that corporate formation is a permissive or rather an efficient cause of industrial activity only. All industrial activity must be solemnized or sanctified by the establishment of a power structure aimed at the classification of all those looked upon as in some way engaged in the productive venture. It is this latter activity which a corporation carries out. The acquisition and utilization of technological apparatus in any culture without vestiture of entitlement to utilization is disallowed as a criminal act. The corporation serves the purpose of vestiture of entitlement of capital as well as labor. That is, through the wage contract within the corporate framework, labor is entitled to utilization of technological apparatus. This is the function of a corporation – it gives ceremonial entitlement or adequacy.

More light is thrown on this aspect of this general cultural phenomenon by a comparison with canoe ownership and canoe construction and operation in the Trobriand Islands. All canoe building is overlaid with a large amount of ceremonial and power claims. In canoe construction the Trobrianders are well aware of the instrumental relationship between the size of the outrigger and the canoe proper, on the shaping and digging out of a log, on proper selection of a tree for a canoe, and the mass of matter-of-fact knowledge essential to the successful construction and later sailing of a canoe. The organization for canoe building reflects this aspect of the matter. Certain individuals possess the expertise and thus engage in canoe construction on these grounds.

But this is not all that is involved in canoe building. The instrumental work is punctuated periodically by magical ceremonies and incantations directed toward propitiation of those spiritual elements with which the Trobrianders see fit to contend. This latter endeavor has largely to do with the establishment of *toli* or ownership and concomitant claims associated with ownership. Canoes are vested with the spiritual worth of the *toliwaga* (canoe owner), and likewise that spiritual stuff of which all canoes are possessed diffuses to the owner. On the basis of such spiritual identity the suzerainty of the owner is established over the canoe. But this ownership likewise establishes a system of discretionary control over the use of the canoe and the distribution of the usufruct from canoe ventures, be they fishing ventures or Kula expeditions. In all sailing ventures, coercive control is vested in the owner, who is also the village chief. It is by virtue of the adequacy of his spiritual personality that success or failure may be looked for in sailing ventures. But there is in existence, in kind of a cultural symbiosis with the discretionary control, an instrumental organization for sailing. Those aboard the sailing canoe include experts in each phase of sailing – navigation, handling of the sail, and steering or handling of the tiller. The interdependent relationships of these functions make up an instrumental social complex – but one in which the members are related by technological consanguinity rather than by some differential possession of a common spiritual essence.

Some students of western culture have readily identified the general business system for what it is in fact, a power system.[9] This position can best be shown by an analysis of the corporation in western culture. For the business unit is at the base of this whole power structure. It has to do with the aggrandizement of personal and corporate prestige and pecuniary power rather than enhancement of technological efficiency.

All of this becomes apparent when what is called the "capital structure" of the corporation is subjected to analysis as a cultural phenomenon. The capital suppliers are made up of stockholders and bondholders, the difference being held to be based on the degree of permanence of the contribution of "capital." But the contribution of such "capital" establishes a complex of status which is authenticated by a network of reciprocal rights and obligations.[10] These latter can be ascertained in any specific case by reference to the capital status of the individuals concerned. By the same means a hierarchy is established with the common stockholders at the apex. Final ownership is vested in them.

Each class of capital contributor is distinguished from each of the others by differential rights and prerogatives pertaining to ownership, pecuniary control, pecuniary dissolution, division of the pecuniary fruits of the endeavor, etc.

For example, a common stockholder has usually the right of electing to the board of directors and is therefore held to have control of the corporation. He also has a right to all of the remaining fruits of the venture after the fixed obligation to other capital contributors has been met. In turn he has obligations which are presumably of a degree of onerousness exactly equivalent to the pleasures enjoyed from the rights of common stockholdership. He has but a residual claim on the fruits of the venture, all the rest of the capital contributors preceding him in the division of the earnings. In event of a financial disaster, he again is the last individual to share in the pecuniary remains. In fact among those who have a certain amount of expertise in the governance of such matters, these latter obligations are generally held to justify the prior rights. As in all cultural systems, all rights are held to be exactly balanced off by equivalent obligations.

Preferred stockholders usually are held to have forgone certain privileges of pure ownership, such as the right to control by means of the vote, for the acquisition of new rights of equivalent value such as the right to precede the "pure" owners in the division of the usufruct. Right to share to an unlimited amount in the fruits of the venture has been relinquished for prior rights to the "pure" owners in the rites of dissolution. Although it cannot be said that each of these rights has been forgone for some specific newly acquired right, there is considerable feeling among those in the populace-at-large familiar with such matters that there is some vague but rather precise equivalence between the total rights forgone and rights gained.[11] Likewise, the preferred position or claims of the preferred stockholder are held to rest on obligations equivalent in onerousness. His degree of participation in the earnings is limited, but he has a prior claim; his right of control is restricted or eliminated, but he fares better in distribution of the pecuniary fruits, etc.

All of this goes by way of illustration of the fact that the corporation is a distributive and not a productive organization. The suppliers of capital can be graded and divided as follows in Figure 5.1.

The distinction upon which this classification rests is the rights and prerogatives of each role. These are all defined as contractual relationships among the several financial participants in the corporate venture. The rights of any one role are balanced off by what is considered to be an equivalence in obligatory commitments. But this structural hierarchy has nothing whatever to do with productive activity. This defines who shall control the division of the usufruct, the proportion to go to each, ownership, and like questions of a ceremonial character.

But this hierarchy of status can be extended even further. The roles above are those occupied by the suppliers of capital, and may be said to be the corporation proper. Yet there are a whole mass of reciprocal contractual relationships that tie together other roles related to the corporation. There are suppliers of land, labor, and materials. In the usual economic conceptualization the significance of the latter would disappear in considerations of the entire economy. That is, the suppliers of materials in the aggregate economy would be subsumed under each of the factorial heads. In general it can be stated that there are suppliers of capital, of land, and of labor, and that the status of these is defined by contractually established prerogatives and duties. In this fashion the hierarchy of ranks is further extended. In western culture, where capitalism is supreme, and is the collective representation par excellence, the corporate structure is headed by the owners among the suppliers of capital, and the suppliers of land and labor fall in line somewhat tardily behind capital. This differential status is embodied in legal use and wont which defines the reciprocal obligations of all parties.

As in all ceremonial arrangements the status of individuals is conferred by rite. This is no less true of corporate activity than of Trobriand canoe construction. It is a part of common conceit in western culture to play down the existence

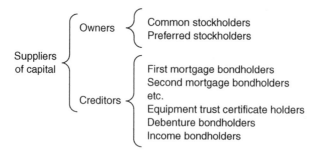

Figure 5.1 Suppliers of capital.

of status and differential ratings based on putative spiritual worth. Many of those engaged in social science are no less prone to accept this bit of glibness than the populace at large. Part of the reason for its free passage is the fact that grades and ratings are not as rigid in western culture as in some others, nor as rigid as they once were in medieval culture. But also giving currency to the belief is the failure to recognize contract as a means of establishing status. Sir Henry Maine's position that modern western culture is differentiated from medieval culture by a passage from status to contract is only half the truth. The establishment of contract does not disestablish status. Contract rather than birth is the means by which status is conferred. A contract confers rights and duties on the two parties to the contract. It vests in them certain legal status. The marriage contract confers upon each of the two parties all the rights and prerogatives of a husband in one case and of a wife in the other. A property deed duly solemnized vests in an individual all of the rights and prerogatives and mysterious powers of a property-holder. The former owner acquires the reciprocal rights and duties of a seller of property and is thereby divested of property ownership. In one case there is an investiture and in the other a divestiture.

In western culture, status is by contract-right rather than right-of-birth. The corporate structure, being a complex series of reciprocal rights and obligations, is a reflection of the conferring of status on the various participants by legal rite. Stockholders acquire status as owners by the legal ceremony in which some object of pecuniary value, tangible or intangible, is exchanged for shares of stock. In this ceremony the individual who reciprocates by contributing an object of value has duly conferred on him the status of common stockholder with all of the rights, prerogatives, and duties which pertain thereto. In the act of acquiring bonds the individual has vested in him the status of a bondholder and creditor of the corporation. In the wage contract the laborer has conferred on him the status of a wage worker with the limited rights and prerogatives which pertain thereto. So be it with the landlord, who acquires the status as such through the ceremonial of a lease duly signed, sealed, and authenticated. In this manner a status hierarchy is established which rests on claims to the usufruct of the venture. Tools become not only the means to achieving an end-in-view as productive instruments, but also through ownership serve as the source of power claims in the distributive process.

In fact three distinct sets of rights are established by means of the establishment of such a corporate hierarchy: (1) rights to proceeds, (2) residual rights, and (3) coercive rights.

1   Status sets the amount and the character of the proceeds to which one is entitled. Although in effect the outward character is identical for all parties, i.e. pecuniary income, it is looked upon as of different nature in the case of each status group. Corporate pecuniary payments are broken into what are called interest, dividends, rents, and wages. The status of an individual in the corporate hierarchy will determine the type of income payment to which he is entitled. Likewise the amount will be fixed in the contractual

conferment of status. In the case of the final owners the amount is not fixed in absolute amount but is an entitlement to all that has been adventitiously gained. Nevertheless, the major endeavor of corporate activity is the engrossment of such adventitious gains, and the whole structure is aimed at an engrossment of these by the final owners. That is the meaning of trading on the equity by which the final owners enlarge what may be called the adventitious earnings of the endeavor.

2   But the rites of status creation also establish residual rights. In the event of pecuniary failure of the endeavor instead of pecuniary success, a process of distribution is provided. In this case the order of priority is identical with that followed in distribution of the usufruct. The major difference between dissolution and a routine distribution of earnings is that in dissolution, assets instead of earnings on assets are being distributed. But under these circumstances the rights of each party involved in the dissolution are readily determined by a reference to the status of each. A residual right inheres in the final owners, although supreme coercive right shifts from them to some one class of creditors, usually a bond-holding group.

3   Within the corporate power structure there also exists a coercive system based on status. Nominally the supreme coercive role rests in the common stockholders. The word "nominally" is used advisedly, for within the modern-day large corporation the supreme coercive power has been involuntarily lifted by the legal representatives of the common stockholders – directors and management. Nevertheless, at least in the corporate complex within the culture and within the legal fiction which serves as a formal version of these beliefs, the supreme coercive role is reserved for the holder of common stockownership status. The holder of this coercive role has final authority in all corporate matters and may interject that authority in productive matters as well as in questions of pecuniary protocol. But with the acquisition of status the coercive rights of all corporate participants are determined. At times of pecuniary stringency, provisions are frequently made for the preferred stockholder to assume some coercive rights which he does not normally have.[12] In all events in case of dissolution, supreme coercive authority shifts to the bondholders (usually mortgage only). But overall coercive authority for all intents and purposes and in the normal run of events rests in common stockholdership. This latter status gives coercive rights not only over other contributors of capital, but over the contributors of land and labor as well. In fact one of the most heated questions of the day is the one involving the coercive relationship between the delegated agents of the common stockholders and the delegated agents of the contributors of labor. The activities of the latter are looked upon as an infringement of the coercive rights of the common-stockholders. The usual form of the question is "what are management's prerogatives?" The occasion for its asking is the existence of a large and concerted drive by labor's representatives to enlarge their own prerogatives at the expense of long-established use and wont enjoyed by management.

All of this goes by way of demonstrating the power nature of the corporation.[13] In short, the corporation is a ceremonial pattern of organization which touches on productive as well as pecuniary matters. But as with all ceremonial behavior, there is a well-established set of beliefs or collective representations which sustain the system of use and wont. Basic to this whole set of beliefs is one in the instrumental efficacy of pecuniary activity.

In the eyes of those deeply imbued with western cultural beliefs, the process of pecuniary manipulation is identical with productive activity. That is, pecuniary activity is taken as part and parcel of instrumental activity and no distinction is made between ceremonial and matter-of-fact endeavor.[14] Pecuniary incentive is held to be essential to all endeavor, for man is by nature a creature who loves to truck, barter, and exchange one thing for another. This popular and widely diffused belief has little to sustain it, in fact, other than that reciprocal obligations in western culture have generally a pecuniary value imputed to them. Western man does in a sense look to the main chance, reciprocity being what it is, and pecuniary obligations being what they are. But all that this states is that western man does as western culture prescribes.[15]

In actual practice, pecuniary activity as represented by the corporation is run contrary to productive activity. Corporate solvency, which means maintenance of the integrity of the corporate status system, is dependent on pecuniary earnings sufficient to meet all obligations of the corporation and satisfy the rights of all participants. This means in the cultural vernacular that a "reasonable profit on the investment" must be earned. Less than such a reasonable profit impairs the entire status system, for some status positions have the right to alter the whole scheme of things should their obligations not be met. It is the prevention of this event toward which most corporate activity is directed. Certainly no one is worried about the impairment of the tangible means of production, but merely the system of status which rests upon claims of ownership in this technological apparatus.

But it is this potential hiatus in pecuniary affairs that leads corporate activity to impinge on the efficiency of technological activity. Frequently in order to prevent such a disruption of the status system, it may be necessary to resort to what Thorstein Veblen called "conscientious withdrawal of efficiency." Thus, there is no necessary relationship between pecuniary success and productive efficiency.

Then, in summary, what can be said concerning the role the corporation does play in western culture? The corporation gives to instrumental activity its "ceremonial adequacy." It is a system of rights and duties which gives to productive activity a dramatic turn. Production from the corporate viewpoint becomes a system of dramatic combination of units of land, labor and capital which are owned and in which the owners play a dramatic role full of uncertainties and risk – uncertainties of tenure and risks of dispossession. These latter are purely pecuniary in origin, for there is nothing with less uncertainty and risk than modern production. But put in this light the corporation is new in form only. Its major role as a ceremonial piece of cultural apparatus is found in all cultures.

The fact that it plays such a role in western culture is verified by the existence of a large body of instrumental activity in western culture not so ceremonially overlaid – or at least not to the same depth. This of course was pointed out early in the paper. But what is of significance is the attitude of the members of western culture toward such ceremonially inadequate endeavor. It is viewed with a skepticism that is not to be found around "business-managed activity." The postal system in western culture is one of the most dependable operations carried on. But it is viewed skeptically because it is not overlaid by a profit and loss system upon which the existence of those in the responsible positions depends. Likewise, much other endeavor comes in for this same skeptical eye, and concerted efforts are made from time to time to establish some of these activities on a business footing by setting up an overlay of ownership claims. This is what is represented by the present-day move to sell off to private enterprise such a technological complex as the Tennessee Valley Authority. It now exists without ceremonial adequacy, which leaves it with some doubt as to its efficacy and authenticity. By establishing private enterprise in the guise of a corporation the needs of such ceremonial adequacy would be met. At least in the eyes of the proponents, all would be well.

Notes

1 C. E. Ayres, *The Theory of Economic Progress*, Chapel Hill, University of North Carolina Press, 1944, chaps. V–IX; Thorstein Veblen, *The Place of Science in Modern Civilization*, New York, Viking, 1942, pp. 1–31; *The Theory of Business Enterprise*, New York, Charles Scribner's Sons, 1904, chaps. I–III.
2 Bronislaw Malinowski, *Coral Gardens and Their Magic*, New York, American Book Co., 1935.
3 A. A. Berle and Gardiner Means, *The Modern Corporation and Private Property*, New York, Macmillan, 1932, especially the concluding statement on the role of the modern corporation.
4 D. M. Goodfellow, *Principles of Economic Sociology*, London, Routledge, 1939.
5 A. I. Richards, *Land, Labour and Capital in Northern Rhodesia*, London, Oxford University Press, 1939.
6 Raymond Firth, *The Primitive Economics of the New Zealand Maori*, New York, E. P. Dutton, 1929.
7 Richard Thurnwald, *Economics in Primitive Communities*, London, Oxford University Press 1932; Melville Herskovits, *Primitive Economics*, New York, Alfred Knopf, 1952.
8 Thorstein Veblen, *The Engineers and the Price System*, New York, Viking, 1947 (ninth printing); Wendell Berg, *Cartels: Challenge to the Free World*, Public Affairs Press, Washington, D.C., 1944; George W. Stocking and Myron W. Watkins, *Cartels in Action*, New York, Twentieth Century Fund, 1947; Thurman W. Arnold, *The Bottlenecks of Business*, New York, Reynal & Hitchcock, 1940; Hearings of the Temporary National Economic Committee, 1938–40.
9 Thorstein Veblen, *The Theory of Business Enterprise*, op. cit., chaps. IX and X; Robert A. Brady, *Business as a System of Power*, New York, Columbia University Press, 1943, chap. IX.
10 For those unfamiliar with reciprocity as a process of social structure, reference is made to Bronislaw Malinowski, *Crime and Custom in Savage Society*, New York, Harcourt, Brace, 1926; H. I. Hogban, *Law and Order in Polynesian Society*, New

York, Harcourt, Brace, 1934; Raymond Firth, *We the Tikopia: A Sociological Study of Kinship in Primitive Polynesia*, London, George Allen & Unwin, 1936.

11 For a formal presentation of this view see A. S. Dewing, *The Financial Policy of Corporations*, New York, Ronald Press, 1941 edition, chaps. 5, 7, 8.

12 Ibid., pp. 93–5.

13 For a general discussion of this cultural phenomenon see C. E. Ayres, op. cit., chap. VIII.

14 For a knowledge of this in the modern economy a debt is owed Veblen. Commons also had more than glimmerings of the same thing. See especially his *Economics of Collective Action*, New York, Macmillan, 1951. But to the anthropologist goes full credit for identifying this aspect of all culture. See for instance Bronislaw Malinowski, *Magic, Science and Religion,* Boston, Beacon Press, 1948, pp. 1–71.

15 Walton Hamilton, "The Price System and Social Policy," *Journal of Political Economy*, vol. 26 (1918), p. 31.

6   The entrepreneur as a cultural hero

Southwestern Social Science Quarterly, vol. 38 (December 1957), pp. 248–56

COMMENTARY BY WILLIAM WALLER

In this article, Hamilton explores the concept of the entrepreneur. He notes that the entrepreneur in economic analysis is the author of innovation, invention, and development in the folklore of capitalism. While noting that Joseph Schumpeter ascribed the qualities of foresight, initiative, and enterprise to these innovative individuals, Hamilton believes that this persona is appropriated by run-of-the-mill corporate managers.

Using Lord Raglan's (*The Hero*, 1956) analysis of the hero's role in an origin myth, Hamilton describes the entrepreneur as a dramatic persona in the mythology of modern industrial production which serves to justify the system of mores and status system of capitalist society.

Hamilton notes that few of the corporate managers of today have the technical ability to understand normal industrial processes, much less the ability to innovate or invent. Instead, the actual role of the modern-day entrepreneur is to engage in the rite of the market transaction where property rights are simultaneously destroyed and recreated as goods and services move from one individual to another as the socially appropriate monetary compensation changes hands. By controlling the rites of market transactions, the creation and extinguishing of property rights, corporate managers at best serve a permissive role in any processes of innovation or invention. But they have a determinate role in the rites that distribute income, assign status, and define rights and privileges in our society.

It is the widespread acceptance of this creation myth in modern industrial culture that allows pecuniary linkages to be understood as the primary element of social cohesion rather than the underlying technological linkages. Additionally, this myth provides us with a cultural hero in the person of the entrepreneur and others who appropriate this title.

This article, combined with "Keynes, Cooperation, and Economic Stability," "A Theory of the Social Origins of the Factors of Production," and "Ceremonial

Aspects of Corporate Organization," provides a thorough critique of the neoclassical theory of production and the neoclassical theory of the firm.

THE ENTREPRENEUR AS A CULTURAL HERO

Much controversy once raged over the role of myth in culture. Today there appears to be some general agreement that myths are associated with rites. Claims that myths are valid but vague recollections of a heroic past are not to be taken too seriously. Nor are they any longer held to be rather crude first approximations toward a scientific explanation of natural phenomena.[1]

As the anthropologist has probed into cultures all over the world, he has found an elaborate mass of myths and associated ceremonial rites. These myths purport to explain the status–mores complex and are re-enacted in the rites through which status and mystic properties are conferred on things as well as individuals. In all these myths, much prominence is given to a recounting of the doings of the fabulous tribal ancestors. By virtue of the chicane, deceit, cunning, stealth, and wisdom of these heroes the tribe came to have its "way of life." By exercising creative genius these original cultural heroes gave to the community its peculiar set of mores and differential gradings and ratings which the mores define. The rites performed are supposedly dramatic re-enactments of the doings of the tribal founders. As it was in the beginning, it is now, and ever shall be ...

Within the cultural framework, an individual acquires stature and virtue in accordance with how closely he adheres to the mores which prescribe proper behavior for one of his stations in life. He who adheres rigorously to the mores defining his role is said to be "virtuous"; he who is neglectful of the mores is said to be "unworthy." As sociological and anthropological inquiry advances our knowledge of social structure, it is becoming clearer that each institutional structure is made up of a complex of roles. Each individual plays, of course, several of these. But what is more important for present purposes is the fact that these roles are ranked. Related roles are higher or lower relative to one another. The mores prescribe how one should act with his peers, with those above, and with those below. This is the dramatic aspects of social structure and is what has been called "ceremonial." Myths authenticate these ways of behavior by giving to them what is supposedly a rational origin but which on examination turns out to be a product of group mythopoeic imagination.

Although such a myth–rites complex has been found in all "primitive" cultures to which the ethnologist has given his attention, there is a general feeling among the more advanced cultures that they are relatively free of any such mental legerdemain. Contemporary Western culture, in which science and technology have been elaborated, are looked upon as "secular" – meaning that they are free from such cherished myth and ritual. In fact, among students of the social sciences there is a general tendency to look upon Western cultures as having been distilled from some kind of teleological secularization process, whereby cultures pass by stages from the sacred to the secular.

However, this is a deceptive bit of conceit. No culture recognizes, readily and unaided, its own myth for what in fact it is. Were it not for the uninitiated foreigner who, owing to his lack of initiation, is at an advantage in differentiating cultural fancy from fact, it would be almost impossible to identify those elements of a culture which are mythopoeic from those which are history. Since Western culture believes itself to be uniquely secular, and since members of a culture are at a disadvantage in recognizing such fancies in their own culture anyway, the idea that Western culture is free of myth, or at least free of anything serious along this line, is readily believed. But that which is myth may be imbedded in a matrix of what is highly regarded as the distillations of matter-of-fact science.[2]

In Western culture, economics, compared to the other social sciences, is often looked upon as having reached a high degree of scientific preciseness and abstraction. In fact, some of the other practitioners of social science seem to be envious at times of the scientific heights reached by the economist. The Euclidean diagrams and systems of simultaneous equations present to the uninitiated an appearance of scientific rigor that the more evolutionary social sciences seem to lack. Certainly there is considerable reason for this view. The economist has applied mathematical techniques and definitions – in what is called "equilibrium theory" – to an extent which no other social science can pretend to have reached. By working from the basis of two general forces – demand and supply – the economist has worked out a formidable paraphernalia, the elaboration of which seems to be infinite. The mathematical exploration of an infinite number of demand-and-supply conditions would seem to be limited only by the finite human imagination – and the economist seems never to reach the end of those possibilities of imagination. This scientific appearance has removed economics from any taint of social myth or legend.

But on examination of that which underlies the mathematical façade, the case is not quite so clear. Beneath the geometry and the calculus there lies "dramatic myth." When all the mathematical abstractions are swept away, what is called "demand and supply" can be seen as consumers and entrepreneurs. Consumers have the role presumably represented by the demand curve. Entrepreneurs and others in productive roles lie back of the supply curve, chiefly the entrepreneurs, as economic theory makes clear. In the total demand-and-supply situation, the character of the consumer is rather vague; that of the entrepreneur is much more clearly drawn.

On this level of generalization, economics takes on the characteristics of a drama. Consumers desire certain products. They make their wants known through bids in the market place. Entrepreneurs, ever alert in pursuing the main chance, respond to the wants by producing goods in just the quantity and quality that consumers desire them. The entrepreneur takes on the qualities of a cultural hero who performs miracles of production. He is a creative genius and a master of ceremonies. Although never on the panegyric level of the popular discourse, still the entrepreneur has, in the passages of staid economic treatises, a certain color and flair not granted to any of the other characters in the economic drama. He has a creative role denied to any of the others, including labor.

These entrepreneurs are gifted with the powers of "foresight," "initiative," and "enterprise." By virtue of these extra powers they are able to foresee the economic future, the sweep and advance of technology, in a fashion denied to the populace at large. The economic significance of population growth and shifts, of new lands, and of changes in sentiment is all revealed to these captains of industry. The heroic proportions of the entrepreneur are outlined in the following passage by Joseph Schumpeter:

> We have seen that the function of entrepreneurs is to reform or revolutionize the pattern of production by exploiting an invention or, more generally, an untried technological possibility for producing a new commodity or producing an old one in a new way, by opening up a new source of supply of materials or a new outlet for products, by reorganizing an industry and so on. Railroad construction in its earlier stages, electrical power production before the First World War, steam and steel, the motorcar, colonial ventures afford spectacular instances of a large genius which comprises innumerable humbler ones – down to such things as making a success of a particular kind of sausage or toothbrush. This kind of activity is primarily responsible for the recurrent "prosperities" that revolutionize the economic organism and the recurrent "recessions" that are due to the disequilibrating impact of the new products or methods. To undertake such new things is difficult and constitutes a distinct economic function, first, because they lie outside of the routine tasks which everybody understands and, secondly, because the environment resists in many ways that vary, according to social conditions, from simple refusal either to finance or to buy a new thing, to physical attack on the man who tries to produce it. To act with confidence beyond the range of familiar beacons and to overcome that resistance requires aptitudes that are present in only a small fraction of the population and that define the entrepreneurial type as well as the entrepreneurial function. This function does not essentially consist in either inventing anything or otherwise creating the conditions which the enterprise exploits. It consists in getting things done.[3]

These are rather broad claims, but not nearly so broad as those when the entrepreneur or captain of industry was combined with the role of capitalist. Since the rise of the modern corporation the entrepreneur has become addicted to working his feats of entrepreneurship with "other people's money." But as late as the second half of the nineteenth century, the capitalist-entrepreneur was extolled for his capital accumulation as well as his business acumen. It was because he stinted his own consumption that he was able to save the capital funds which by some mystic transformation became "capital," meaning tools and machines. Although in the large corporation the management has become separated from ownership, the entrepreneur is still a man of large means and a large view. He is familiar with the manipulation of sizable amounts of capital funds – albeit they are those which he has collected from the modern-day version of the capitalist who has lost suzerainty over their usage. However, there are still those who do combine both roles. One need only mention the DuPont, Mellon, and Rockefeller dynasties as cases in point in which fund accumulation and entrepreneurship are still combined, as well as a multitude of small firms, particularly of the proprietorship and partnership type.

Economic history reinforces economic theory concerning the heroic scale of entrepreneurial efforts. According to the usual recounting of the rise of capitalism, there developed in Western man of late feudal times a kind of rational faculty which led to pursuit of the pecuniary main chance. Men suddenly awoke to a new "spirit of capitalism."[4] The actual details and the time of this awakening are conflicting and vague. Some, such as Weber and Tawney, place much emphasis on the Protestant Reformation. Still others, such as Henri Pirenne, date the awakening much earlier than this, claiming that it first came among those sturdy vagabonds unloosed from the soil by a rising population in the tenth century.[5] Others have speculated along other lines, such as the chance accumulation of a large mass of money capital.[6]

There is, however, general agreement that the product of this new-found pecuniary faculty was the source from which came all economic progress. These early captains of commerce and industry are the prototypes of the latter-day entrepreneur. As a result of their foresight and new-found zest for profits, there was a steady technological advance. In fact, the usual method of historical treatment is to precede the Industrial Revolution by what is called the Commercial Revolution, clearly implying that the development of a penchant to buy cheap and sell dear was a necessary prior condition to the development of technology. But what is of primary importance to the present paper is the fact that this technological advance is looked upon in origin as the product of these early captains of industry. The present-day entrepreneur is merely carrying on in the footsteps of these legendary heroes. In seeking his own self-interest, he works "to promote an end which was no part of his intention" as though "led by an invisible hand."

Even to imply that all this economic theory and economic history incorporates a certain amount of myth and legend may seem irresponsible in an age that prides itself on its secularism. Certainly standard economic theory, particularly equilibrium theory, has all the outward appearance of being the product of scientific endeavor. It is equally certain that the economic history accounting for the origin of capitalism is the product of prodigious scholarly effort. Yet there are disturbing facts concerning both the entrepreneurial theory and history that more than hint that there is here an origin legend and a myth which have as their aim to present the entrepreneur in heroic proportions – to rationalize what is essentially a ceremonial role.

It is becoming increasingly apparent that the development of technology is a product of invention and discovery and that both of these are dependent on the prior state of the industrial arts. In a sense, this is circular, for the fact of the matter is that the advance of science and technology does depend upon the prior state of development of science and technology: invention is a process of combining previously existing technical traits in a new way. The automobile was a combination of the internal combustion engine and the buggy; Watt's steam engine, of a separate condensing chamber and the Newcomen engine; and printing was a combination of the wine press, separately cast metal types, oil-based inks, and rag paper. Thus the process of invention has been from the beginning of time. Heroes may come and go, but new technology does not arrive until the state of the industrial arts is such that innovation is possible. And this state is a cultural product, not one of heroes. All the pecuniary incentive and rational pecuniary calculation imaginable could not have achieved the automobile at the time of Leonardo. In fact, it is generally realized that the Industrial Revolution did not suddenly begin in 1760, but that the quickening of invention which is frequently called the Industrial Revolution had been continuous with the whole stream of technological development at least from Paleolithic times.[7]

However, the entrepreneur does play a social role, and it is this role which seemingly obscures the simple origin of technology in that previously existing. Entrepreneurs are those who turn good things to account; they are pursuers of the main chance. But in a pecuniary society the fruit of the industrial arts can be engrossed by ownership and thereby turned to private or corporate gain. Although the sum total of technology is the product of the sum total of human invention and thus is a social heritage, it has always been possible to engross some part of it and utilize it for personal aggrandizement. This has been true of all cultures.[8]

The entrepreneur sits astride a strategic pass along the stream of technological development from which position he allows or disallows the further development and application of already-available new technological possibilities. Since he is a controller of money funds, he acts as master of ceremonies at investitures and divestitures of ownership. He creates ownership equities, such as stocks and bonds, which overlie all the material embodiments in which the advance of science and technology makes itself manifest. In fact, much more than this may be overlaid by ownership claims when these are extended to such intangibles as trade names, patents, etc. Veblen long ago made all this clear:

> The inventors, engineers, experts, or whatever name be applied to the comprehensive class that does the intellectual work involved in the modern machine industry, must prepare the way for the man of pecuniary affairs by making possible and putting in evidence the economic and other advantages that will follow from a prospective consolidation.... His [the entrepreneur's] furtherance of industry is at the second remove, and is chiefly of a negative character. In his capacity as business man he does not go creatively into the work of perfecting mechanical process and turning the means at hand to new or larger uses. That is the work of the men who have in hand the devising and oversight of mechanical processes. The men in industry must first create the mechanical possibility of such new and more efficient methods and correlations, before the business man sees the chance, makes the necessary business arrangements, and gives general directions that the contemplated industrial advances shall go into effect.[9]

It is conceivable that at one time the entrepreneur had also the ability to apply the industrial arts. Take the famous case of James Watt and the Soho works, for example. But as modern technology advanced and became more complex, carrying business along on to a larger scale, the two attributes of the earlier entrepreneurial role – business and industry – were separated; thus the entrepreneur came to concern himself almost exclusively with pecuniary matters. Since invention and technological development by an individual is dependent on intimate familiarity with that part of the industrial arts in which the advance is to take place, the latter-day entrepreneur has been barred from any abilities along these lines because of technological inadequacy. Therefore he not only does not develop the industrial arts but is devoid of any ability to do so.

Nevertheless, the myth lingers on. To the present day the entrepreneur is looked upon as a "captain of industry." This goes as well for the corporate manager in the large corporation in which there has been a clear separation of ownership from control. Thus, during the Second World War, the feats of industrial output, by conglomerations of technology and instrumental organizations, were often attributed to the personal perspicacity of the corporate head – usually head of the business legerdemain only. In a society in which pecuniary transactions, the conglomeration of money capital, the creation of stocks and bonds, and the determination of ownership, with all of the concomitant rights pertaining thereto, must precede any large technological undertaking, it is easy to attribute a causal role to the pecuniary manipulation and to the manipulator of that pecuniary activity – the entrepreneur. Thus, to his activity is attributed all economic progress. Nevertheless, the facts are obdurate. Technological advance is the product of the continuous stream of technological development. Ownership and coercive control are the products of pecuniary activity. As Veblen so frequently pointed out, the latter endeavor may even be at the expense of the former if a profit can be enhanced by suppressing the advance of technology.

In other words, the entrepreneur or present-day corporate manager is a permissive, but not a creative, agent. Exercising pecuniary control, he simulates, by his concomitant pecuniary activity, technological endeavor, the *sine qua non* of effective production. In one sense he is analogous to the magician of the Trobriand society, through whose ceremonial performance ownership is invested and success is assured.[10]

At least since the revelations of Veblen, all these facts concerning the ceremonial role of the entrepreneur have been apparent. Yet the myth persists without too much question. One has but to examine the popular versions of this belief as expounded in the public press to perceive its widespread acceptance. In fact, this popular version gives a clue toward understanding the role that the academic version plays. Despite its formidable-looking mathematical notations and seemingly abstract matter-of-fact presentation, the part of economic theory concerning the entrepreneur appears to be a scholarly or sacred version of a popular folk myth. All societies at all times have had their rites and their myths which explain these rites. Pecuniary rites concern the present-day acquisition and removal of status. The entrepreneurial myth purports to explain why it is so and how it all came to be.

Capitalism is differentiated from other modes of economic organization as a system of status and distribution by status. It is a system of social organization in which the manipulators of capital play the primary role. The whole process of production is explained in dramatic terms, with social-status groups, land, labor, and capital being treated as productive factors. But the first of these is capital, the directive and coercive agent in the actual system of production. It is also the agent that has claim to the first fruits through a scheme of distribution over which it also has primary control. The sentiment and belief of the community reinforces this whole social structure.

In a sense, every market transaction is a rite. The seller is divested of ownership of goods and is invested with ownership of money. The buyer is divested of ownership of money and invested with the ownership of goods. In each case, certain duties, the rights of the other party, are complied with. The transaction is hedged in and rigidly prescribed by a complex of mores. Any violation of these or failure to comply with them may be cause for declaring courts of law determining whether one party to a transaction has been damaged by the failure of the party of the second part to comply with the prescribed ritual. In this process of trading, traders or entrepreneurs are able to enhance their holdings of money and property. By taking full advantage of some new technological concatenation, they are able to secure a differential advantage and a differential gain. Any new advance in the technology of the culture will work itself out in the market place by giving an advantage to the group that is able to acquire ownership and control over that new technology.

Both the theory of the present-day role of the entrepreneur and the conjectural history of the entrepreneur are firmly held to by a community that is by sentiment committed to such belief. This is the myth by which the mores-status complex of capitalist society is justified. To challenge the belief, to ask questions about it, to probe, is, if not dangerous heresy, at least a serious impertinence. As George C. Homans stated:

> That the distribution of wealth is never described as it really is, but only as it is conceived to be according to a traditional mythology is as much true of our own times as it was of the Middle Ages, though most of us, very properly, will be irritated if we are asked to admit this fact. The only myths are the myths of other people.[11]

In Western capitalism, the entrepreneur is a cultural hero; in paying deference to him we are presumably doing nothing more than recognizing that he is the prototype of the fabulous capitalist ancestors who first began to calculate rationally (pecuniarily) and thereby set us on the road of modern science and technology. Under the circumstances it is felt to be only right and good that we contribute a large portion of the usufruct of this technological heritage to their present-day counterparts. Supposedly from their efforts alone comes all progress. Likewise, these latter-day captains of industry should put in public view the fruits of their extraordinary cunning so that all may then enjoy them, if not directly, at least vicariously.[12]

The myth of the entrepreneur assures us that buying and selling is of great social significance. By virtue of pecuniary accumulation, not only are fortunes acquired, but society is advanced. Since fortunes are made by taking advantage of some differential gain made possible by some new advance in the industrial arts, it is simple enough to attribute to fortune-making the cause of the techno-logical advance. That is, since all new embodiments of scientific and technologi-cal advance must be owned, rites investing ownership are performed prior to use and production. Thus it is logically an easy step to assume that the rite, the pecu-niary transaction itself, is the cause of the advance. The entrepreneur, being the master of pecuniary ceremonies, is held to be the catalytic agent. In this way a society in which all economic linkage is symbolized by pecuniary obligations is provided with a rationale and a cultural hero.

Notes

1 For a fuller discussion of this question see Lord Raglan, *The Hero: A Study in Tradi-tion, Myth and Drama* (New York, Vintage Books ed., 1956).
2 E. A. Burtt, *The Metaphysical Foundations of Modern Physical Science* (New York, Doubleday Anchor Books, 1954).
3 J. A. Schumpeter, *Capitalism, Socialism and Democracy* (London, George Allen & Unwin, 1943), p. 132.
4 Max Weber, *The Protestant Ethic and the Spirit of Capitalism* (New York, Charles Scribner's Sons, 1950); R. H. Tawney, *Religion and the Rise of Capitalism* (New York, New American Library ed., 1953).
5 Henri Pirenne, *Medieval Cities* (New York, Doubleday, 1956), pp. 80f. See especially the account of St. Godric of Finchale. See also Pirenne's *Economic and Social History of Medieval Europe* (New York, Harcourt, Brace, n.d.).
6 J. A. Hobson, *The Evolution of Modern Capitalism* (New York, Charles Scribner's Sons, 1908); Maurice Dobb, *Studies in the Development of Capitalism* (New York, International Publishers, 1947).
7 For discussions of the thesis mentioned in this paragraph, see William F. Ogburn, *Social Change* (New York, The Viking Press, 1952); S. C. Gilfillen, *Inventing the Ship* (Chicago, Follett Publishing, 1935); V. Gordon Childe, *Man Makes Himself* (New York, New American Library, 1951), and Childe's *What Happened in History* (New York, Penguin Books, 1946); Lewis Mumford, *Technics and Civilization* (New York, Harcourt, Brace, 1934). For discussion of technological innovation immediately preceding the Industrial Revolution, see John U. Nef, *The Rise of the British Coal Industry* (London, George Routland & Sons, 1932), and S. Lilley, *Men, Machines, and History* (London, Cobbett Press, 1948).
8 For an example of property and ownership among Neolithic people, see Raymond Firth, *Primitive Polynesian Economy* (London, George Routland & Sons, 1939), chap. VII.
9 Thorstein Veblen, *The Theory of Business Enterprise* (New York, Charles Scribner's Sons, 1904), chap. III, pp. 36f.
10 Bronislaw Malinowski, *Argonauts of the Western Pacific* (London, Routledge & Kegan Paul, 1922), chap. V.
11 *English Villagers of the Thirteenth Century* (Cambridge, Mass., Harvard University Press, 1941), p. 340.
12 Thorstein Veblen, *The Theory of the Leisure Class* (New York, New American Library ed., 1953), chap. I.

7   Why is institutional economics not institutional?

American Journal of Economics and Sociology, vol. 21 (4) (July 1962), pp. 309–17

COMMENTARY BY WILLIAM WALLER

This article returns to Hamilton's methodological reflections. He notes that the mainstream of economics misperceives institutional economics for two reasons: the misperception that the term "institution" is synonymous with social structure and the fact that institutional economics in the 1930s became associated with description and atheoretical empiricism. Hamilton acknowledges that the choice by Walton Hamilton in 1919 of the admittedly vague term "institutional" certainly contributed to the problem.

Hamilton goes on to note that Veblen's first two books contain the word "theory." He points out that institutional economics has a well-developed theory of value and a theory of economic progress. He argues that the instrumental value theory of institutionalism, where items are valuable because of the consequences their use has on the provisioning process, will not explain price. But he notes that the explanation of price in neoclassical theory is not so much an explanation as it is an imputation of price along with the assertion that it is equal to value. He also contrasts instrumental valuation with the labor theory of value of the classical and Marxist economists.

Value theory in institutional economics is a tentative assessment of usefulness for the proposed task at hand. It will not tell you why a cup of coffee cost ten cents when this article was written; nor will it prove that capitalism exploits labor because labor is not compensated with the full product of its efforts. But it does connect valuation to the development of technology and knowledge. Since this is the core of the institutional economists' theory of progress, the two elements of institutional economic theory fit together. It is here that the concept of institution becomes relevant because these habits of thought and action are what inhibit the efficacious adoption and use of technology, knowledge, and tools in solving the ongoing problems of provisioning when such use would disrupt the existing system of power and status relations of society.

So Hamilton's question is answered at the literal, methodological, and theoretical levels, showing that institutional economics is not institutional.

WHY IS INSTITUTIONAL ECONOMICS NOT INSTITUTIONAL?

Among orthodox economists there exists a conception of institutional economics which is wholly at variance with modern institutionalism as conceived by institutional economists. A short paper such as this may hardly be the most effective means to rectify what seems to be a total failure of understanding. But any attempt to achieve greater understanding is worth the effort, even when the task seems overwhelming for such slender means.

The task does seem overwhelming, for a formal concept of institutionalism has become imbedded both in the literature dealing with the development of economic thought and in that which is devoted to discussions of methodology. Once such a conception becomes imbedded in the formal literature, it becomes extremely difficult to alter and almost impossible to eradicate. Unfortunately, much of our study of the history of economic thought comes from secondary rather than primary sources. The casual judgments one receives in formal courses in the history of economic thought, both from instructor and text material, seem to have a finality about them which precludes further inquiry. The judgments on institutionalism are most uniformly bad.

That such judgments are made of institutionalism should not cause consternation. The usual conception of institutional economics is not a very flattering one – especially to one interested in institutional economics. To the standard theorist the institutionalist seems to have abandoned theory. The institutionalist has focused economic inquiry on some vague thing called institutions. These are sometimes held to be habits and customs and sometimes to be social organizations such as the banking system. In one manual on the history of economic thought the author characterizes institutionalism in this conventional fashion:

> They [institutionalists] seek the determining forces of most economic activities in economic institutions. These institutions are largely psychological and comprise habits, customs, and existing economic arrangements. As described by Davenport, "Institutions are a working consensus of human thought or habits, a generally established attitude of mind and a generally adopted custom of action – as, for example, private property, inheritance, government, taxation, competition, and credit."[1]

Somewhat the same conception comes through in *A Survey of Contemporary Economics*, edited by Bernard Haley, which, since it bore the imprimatur of the American Economic Association, may be looked upon as an official statement of the orthodox opinion. In that volume, in a chapter entitled "Methodological Developments," Richard Ruggles stated:

The term institutional today is usually reserved for those analysts who are working in applied fields and who use in their work and research the large available body of empirical material on the institutions in these areas. Theory is not usually discarded, but the focus of interest is often shifted to the analysis of the specific institutional factors which are found in a given situation.[2]

This conception of institutionalism seems to penetrate deeply into the current economic literature. One encounters it in some out-of-the-way places. Alvin Hansen in his *Guide to Keynes*, in reviewing the pre-Keynesian state of business cycle theory, stated, "The prevailing theory was neatly logical, but it was often incapable of coming to grips with reality. Many economists, accordingly, turned to descriptive and institutional studies."[3] In this statement Hansen seems to equate institutionalism with description.

This conception of institutionalism seems to imply a fatal disjunction between theory and the study of the actualities of a particular economic system. The dispute between institutional economics and standard economics is reduced to one over description vs. theory. Those standard economists who are more charitably inclined feel that the conflict can be resolved by an inexpensive shotgun wedding of theory and description. If this formulation of the conflict is an accurate one, this would seem to be a logical resolution. The time and energy now wasted in useless conflict could be put to work in the major endeavor of the economist – the analysis of those patterns of economic behavior which in their totality compose an economic system. But to many institutionalists this does not seem to be a satisfactory statement of the issues which divide the parties to the dispute.

The dispute seems to rage over the meaning of the word "institutional." For the confusion on this point both the standard economists and the institutionalists must bear some responsibility. Despite the pride in the rigor with which the standard economist defines his terms, his conception of institution has been unusually vague and lacking in rigor. It may be unfair to accuse the standard economist of any absence of rigor in the use of "institution," because the loose use of this term seems to be a general condition, in all of the social sciences. The economist, seeking a tighter definition, might seek such a definition in the literature of sociology. But unfortunately he is most likely to find just as unsatisfactory a condition in sociology. From the time of Sumner, who seems to contend in his *Folkways* that institutions derive in some vague fashion from mores, the sociologist has tended to equate institutions and all complex patterns of behavior. Hence the term is so comprehensive as a designation that it seems to designate everything and fails thereby to differentiate anything.

Since the adjective "institutional" in the name "institutional economics" seems to point to the institutions as the focus of study, the orthodox economist is easily led to the belief that institutional economists have established the study of economic institutions as the primary task of economics. Economic institutions are then vaguely conceived as private property, contract, free enterprise, and the corporation. In one study manual, even technology is categorized as an institution, which seems to compound the confusion in an already confused situation.[4]

Since the term "institutional" seems to lead to a conception of institutional economics as the study of some vague and ill-defined phenomena called economic institutions, the popular conception of institutional economics is understandable. The interpretation of institutional economics as a descriptive exercise is also understandable. The institutional economist might under these circumstances plead that a failure to understand his position derives from a failure to get beyond a name and a few superficial aspects. Unfortunately, the institutionalist cannot plead in this manner, for the accused does not come into court with clean hands.

Many institutionalists are themselves responsible for the generally unsatisfactory state of affairs. The designation "institutional economics" owes its origin to Walton Hamilton, who used it in a famous paper entitled "The Institutional Approach to Economic Theory." This paper was read before a section of the American Economic Association at its annual meeting in 1918 and was reproduced in the Papers and Proceedings for that meeting. In that paper Hamilton specifically stated, "The thesis here set forth is that 'institutional economics' is 'economic theory.'" He was aware of the danger involved in the use of the designation "institutional," for he went on to say, "This involves putting a particular meaning upon a word which has meant many things." Although Hamilton obviously considered institutional economics as theoretical, even he did not avoid the pitfalls which lie in wait for he who becomes enmeshed in the nebulous conception of institutions. In the development of his thesis he presented "five tests which any body of doctrine which aspires to the name of economic must be able to meet." The third among these was: "The proper subject matter of economic theory is institutions." Those who have read this paper have obviously put great store by this third characteristic. To most economists the study of institutions does not mean a theoretical one, but does mean a descriptive one.

Subsequent to Hamilton's paper, some very prominent institutionalists seemed to encourage such a conception of institutional economics. The influence of Wesley Mitchell was pervasive on institutional economics in the late 1920s and early 1930s. This influence was exercised through Mitchell's presidential address before the American Economic Association in 1924 in which he emphasized the value of "quantitative analysis in economic theory." Even greater influence was had by Mitchell's *Business Cycles: The Problem and Its Setting*, which was published in 1927. Whether Mitchell intended to do so or not is problematical, but the effect of his work was to lead many economists to believe that the primary task of economics in the immediate future was to gather facts. Theorizing could await the amassing of all the facts, whatever "all the facts" in this context could mean. In *Business Cycles*, after a review of past and existent business cycle theories, Mitchell included a long Chapter II which consisted of a description of the "money economy." This chapter has frequently been cited as an institutional approach to the economy. One writer has claimed that it comes nearest to being a "Principles of Institutional Economics" of all institutional writing.[5] In Chapter III, Mitchell made a plea for an empirical approach to the business cycle in which statistical methods would play a primary role. Although in the introduction he made it clear that theoretical and empirical approaches are complementary rather than antithetical, he did seem to make a fatal disjunction between theoretician and empiricist. He suggested that in some manner these two approaches would be brought together, but since he seemed to imply that they would be prosecuted by different practitioners, he left open the question of the meaningfulness of theory done independently of empirical research and of empirical research without benefit of theory.

However this may be, the effect of Mitchell's two chapters was to encourage the identification of institutionalism with description, on one hand, and with a kind of aimless empiricism on the other. This influence was strongest in the early part of the 1930s. It was apparent in the now famous 1930 American Economic Association Round Table Conference entitled "Economic Theory – Institutionalism: What It Is and What It Hopes to Become." It was also apparent in *Economic Behavior: An Institutional Approach*, which was edited by Willard E. Atkins of New York University. The conception of institutionalism as a fact-gathering and descriptive exercise stems largely from this episode in the development of institutional economics.

But if these series of circumstances are sufficient to explain the widespread notion that institutional economics is the study of institutions, it is nevertheless true that institutional economics does not fit this conception. Nowhere in Thorstein Veblen, who is admittedly the intellectual godfather of institutionalism, is there to be found such a conception of economics. As Veblen is alleged to have pointed out to critics who accused him of neglecting theory, the titles of both of his first two major works began with the word "theory." Commenting upon both this misconception of institutionalism and the character of Veblen's work, Eric Roll stated:

> Even if one were to accept the interpretation that Veblen's chief legacy is an emphasis upon statistical studies, one could yet point out that Veblen's own writings were almost wholly theoretical in the same sense as the works of the classics are theoretical.[6]

In commenting upon the character of present-day institutional economics, John Gambs stated unequivocally, "It is not statistical economics; it is not welfare economics; it is not social criticism. Finally, it is not institutional. The currently-used word of identification bears roughly the same sort of relationship to a social institution as the word 'romanticism' bears to a Roman."[7]

If institutional economics is not institutional – that is, if institutional economics does not direct us to study this rather nebulous stuff called institutions – just what is it? Put in another way, we may ask the question, "Why is institutional economics not institutional?"

First, it can be said that it is not institutional because it does possess a rather well-developed body of theory, a body of theory which includes a theory of value and a theory of economic progress, which may be contrasted with the two major systems of economic thought which seem to be contending for allegiance today – that of classical political economy and that of Marxism. In this sense, institutionalism is an alternative way of interpreting those affairs we term economic.

Almost all conflicts in economics have raged over the question of the locus of value. The major distinction between classical and neo-classical economics seems to be made on the question of value. The theory is looked upon as a major break with the older labor theory of value. The Austrian school stands as a kind of dividing line within the orthodox stream between ancient and modern-day theories of economy. Even to the present time, the disputes between Marxian and neo-classical economics are apt to rage over the labor theory of value. The neo-classicist will usually insist that Marxian economics, retaining the labor theory of value, is incapable of explaining market price. The Marxian will usually reply that Marx was not concerned with explaining market price but was occupied with explaining historic social change. His theory of value is a key part of his explanation of the downfall of capitalism.

What is often overlooked by the casual student of institutionalism is the existence of a theory of value within institutional economics. This oversight may be attributable to the obsession of the orthodox economist with the question of price. Certainly the institutionalist, like the Marxist in this case, is not concerned with explaining why a cup of coffee costs ten cents. Nor is the student who seeks in institutionalism for an alternative theory of price likely to be satisfied with what he finds there. Nevertheless, ever since the work of Veblen, institutionalism has possessed a theory of value.

In *The Theory of the Leisure Class*, Veblen was concerned with the use of goods as symbols of status. Conspicuous consumption, conspicuous leisure, and pecuniary standards of taste, all terms which derive from that volume, connote the status side of consumption. Veblen did such an excellent job of drawing in the institutional aspect of consumption patterns that he seems to imply, to the hurried reader at least, the notion that our valuations of goods are a matter of custom and habit and that this is all there is to the matter. There is no disputing tastes.

But implicit in the *Theory of the Leisure Class* is another criterion of value. Valuations are not entirely a question of ascertaining the social authenticity of economic goods. Behind all of the Veblenian irony there is an implicit assumption that goods are also instruments and that as instruments their merits can be evaluated. What is implicit sometimes becomes explicit. In a discussion of waste, Veblen makes his criterion of value quite clear.[8] There he points out that all goods must possess at least some pretense of being instrumentally useful. The ultimate test of usefulness, as he puts it, is whether the item in question "furthers the life process taken impersonally." We use goods simultaneously as symbols of status and as instruments to achieve some end in view. As Veblen puts it:

> It would be hazardous to assert that a useful purpose is ever absent from the utility of any article or of any service, however obviously its prime purpose

and chief element is conspicuous waste; and it would be only less hazardous to assert of any primarily useful product that the element of waste is in no way concerned in its value, immediately or remotely.

In his analysis of waste, Veblen reveals a theory of valuation in terms of demonstrable consequences. In this position he is not as explicit as some latter-day institutionalists,[9] but he is sufficiently clear to indicate wherein he places the locus of value.

Certainly this theory of value does differ from both the labor theory of value of the Marxist and the utility theory of the neo-classicist. To the Marxist, intent on demonstrating that capitalism is a system of exploitation and that the failure of labor to receive the full product of its efforts is the root of capitalism's eventual downfall, the instrumental theory of value of the institutionalist may seem hardly a theory of value at all. Certainly it does not point in the direction of economic change by virtue of class warfare.

To the neo-classicist, who locates value in varying intensities of subjective feelings which are allegedly measurable in infinitesimal increments, the instrumental theory of value of the institutionalist may seem to lack rigor. Certainly it is not a theory of value by virtue of which one may ascertain the conditions essential to a state of maximum satisfaction. Nor is it a theory which will aid in the eternal quest to ascertain the reason for the price of tea.

Goods have value as instruments to achieve some end in view. The very word used to denote the objects of economic endeavor seems to beg the question "Good for what?" And the question "Good for what?" seems to imply some kind of ongoing economic activity in which the good fills a void. It is a means to achieve some end in view, and as a means, its goodness or instrumental efficacy may be judged. The institutionalist argues that the life process is one series of adjustments to new situations. Goods serve as instruments in making these adjustments. As such, their worth may be ascertained on the basis of the outcome from the employment of the good in a problem situation. The employment of the good implies the existence of a hypothesis concerning the efficacy of the good as an instrument. If this good is employed in this fashion, the result will be such and such. Verification of the hypothesis awaits employment of the good under the prescribed conditions. Its value or worth depends on the outcome of its employment.

There is no certainty in this type of endeavor. The results cannot be judged with the kind of finality and preciseness that a value theory which relates price and value seems to give. But to the institutionalist the preciseness that follows from the relation of price and value seems to be a spurious one. All valuations are tentative at best and subject through further activity to constant rejudgment and reassessment. This being the position of institutionalism, the institutional economist is not concerned with this seeming failure to develop a new mode of identification of price and value.

The value theory of the institutionalist derives from his concept of technology. To the institutionalist the tool-using and -developing capability of man is very significant. It is significant because it is not only the locus of verifiable valuations, but also the locus of economic progress. When the institutionalist contends that valuations are based on the use of economic goods as instruments, he is arguing that in his capacity as a tool-using animal, man makes valuations on the basis of the consequences of the employment of tools. But tools and instruments, both material and conceptual, are by their very nature capable of employment in new ways and new combinations. Their worth in such new employments also rests upon the consequences of such employments.

It is by virtue of the employment of tools that man secures a living. The life process is the process of tool employment and tool development. Human well-being is uniquely a function of the industrial arts taken in the broadest sense. An expansion of well-being hinges upon the expansion in the tools and skills associated therewith which man has at his command. An integral part of the tool-developmental process is the process of judgment. Thus, the institutionalist, by identifying economic welfare with tool development, integrates his theory of value with his theory of economic progress.

Institutions, from which the term "institutional" is derived, are of significance only to the extent that they impede the tool process and hence economic progress. The institutionalist admits that his analysis of tool behavior is not exhaustive. There is, as Veblen so aptly pointed out, another aspect of human behavior within which tools are used as symbols of rank and status. Much of human behavior is directed to the honoring of the supposed differential qualities of man. By exploiting these alleged differential qualities, men are able to secure an unearned increment such as is alleged of the landlord in classical economic theory. In the modern world much of human behavior is directed to the procurement of such differential gains. Veblen's distinction between business and industry is a genuine one. He was pointing to these two streams of human behavior, the use of tools as instruments and the simultaneous honoring of status, characteristic of all cultures at all times. But unlike the classicist, Veblen found the locus of progress and of genuine value in the tool function. Looked at in this fashion, it would probably be more correct to state that it is the classicist who is the institutionalist. For it is the classicist who locates the key to economic progress in a system of capitalism in which the institutions are bent to the greater glorification of capital.

It is possible to dispute the contention of the institutional economist that his theory is adequate to the analysis of the contemporary economy. The truth of the institutional analysis will ultimately be determined on the basis of its efficacy as an analytical tool. If the institutionalist is guilty of any major crime, it has been his failure thus far to apply his theory in many areas of economic analysis. But he is not guilty of deserting theory, nor is he wanting in analytical tools.

Notes

1 Frank A. Neff, *Economic Doctrines* (New York: McGraw-Hill, 1950), p. 432.
2 *A Survey of Contemporary Economics*, vol. II (Homewood, Ill.).

3 Alvin Hansen, *A Guide to Keynes* (New York: McGraw-Hill, 1953), p. 4.
4 Russell A. Dixon, *Economic Institutions and Cultural Change* (New York: McGraw-Hill, 1941).
5 John Gambs, *Beyond Supply and Demand* (New York: Columbia University Press, 1946), p. 98.
6 Eric Roll, *A History of Economic Thought* (New York: Prentice-Hall, 1946), p. 500.
7 Gambs, op. cit., p. 9.
8 Thorstein Veblen, *The Theory of the Leisure Class* (New York: Modern Library, 1934), pp. 97–101.
9 C. E. Ayres, *The Theory of Economic Progress* (Chapel Hill: University of North Carolina Press, 1944).

8 Drawing the poverty line at a cultural subsistence level

Southwestern Social Science Quarterly, vol. 42 (March 1962), pp. 337–45

COMMENTARY BY WILLIAM WALLER

Two years before the beginning of "The War on Poverty," David Hamilton entered the debate regarding the meaning of poverty. He explores the classical meaning of the term derived from early economic writers from Adam Smith to Karl Marx who argued that competition for jobs in capitalism tended to push wages to a subsistence level. He notes that typically this referred to a standard of living sufficient for the laborers to subsist and perpetuate themselves as a race. Marx added to this level of sufficiency the ability to "live in a normal state as a laboring individual" and argued that the level needed to do so was affected by the climate and "the degree of civilization of a country." Anything below this level was considered poverty.

Hamilton discusses B. S. Rountree's attempt to classify poverty by looking at actual consumption of goods and services sufficient to maintain physical efficiency. This was an early attempt to define an absolute standard of poverty. Hamilton discusses further efforts in this direction in the United States by employing so-called emergency budgets. But he notes that all efforts to establish a minimum level of subsistence below which absolute poverty lies seem arbitrary, as do all measures of relative poverty. Measures of relative poverty designate some percentage of the income distribution, say the bottom 10 percent, and people living below this level are considered to be living in poverty. This is arbitrary, because no matter how high the standard of living of the bottom group, they are by definition living in poverty.

Hamilton notes that neither absolute nor relative definitions of poverty are adequate. He notes that relative definitions are arbitrary and that earlier attempts at absolute definitions have failed to define a level based upon physical and biological requirements. He notes that the latter attempts fail because they are based on the mythical notion of an individual living in a state of nature. Human beings always live in social cultural groups. Consequently, their ability to survive, subsist, or thrive is dependent on their ability to function in that culture.

Therefore, subsistence is defined as being able to continue to function within a particular culture; survival means continuing to stay alive within a particular culture; and thriving means living well within a particular culture. All of these levels of living are conceptually and materially dependent on the state of the productive arts of that particular culture. Hamilton illustrates this by noting that in American culture, prior to World War II automobiles were playthings of the rich, but afterwards they were a necessity for getting a living. Similarly, radio and television were luxury items, but they eventually became essential for obtaining news and information. Thus Hamilton concludes that poverty must necessarily be defined by the cultural context in which it is occurring.

DRAWING THE POVERTY LINE AT A CULTURAL SUBSISTENCE LEVEL

Economists and sociologists concerned with the study of living standards have labored long over the construction of a measure for poverty. Everyone seems agreed that there is such a thing as poverty, but no two people seem agreed on its definition or on its extent.

The difficulty in defining poverty and in determining its extent is over the definition of the "poverty line": that minimum plane of living below which lies poverty. Once the poverty line has been drawn, the extent of poverty can be determined by pricing the poverty line level of living and then ascertaining from income distribution data how many family units lie below this level. This final operation is itself sufficiently complicated by the necessary allowances which must be made for varying family size, age, and other factors.

But drawing the poverty line is even more fraught with complexities than is determination of the extent of poverty once the line is drawn. It is necessary to distinguish between relative and absolute poverty. Failure to distinguish between these categories of poverty has confused the issue on many occasions. Everyone in any society is in poverty relative to those on a higher plane of living. In the absence of total income equality, relative poverty would exist in any society no matter what the state of general abundance. Poverty would most certainty be identified with some lower fraction of the income receivers, who would be defined as in poverty relative to the general pattern of income distribution. Thus, it might be perfectly legitimate to define relative poverty as the level of living attained by anyone in the lowest tenth of the income receivers.

But in measuring absolute poverty this definition would be unsatisfactory. It might be argued that in a society to which the state of the industrial arts afforded a high level of living, relative to that provided in other societies, even the poor might not suffer from anything more pernicious than relative poverty. The idea that absolute poverty might, with the advance of science and technology, vanish from the earth seems to be a corollary to the concept of relative poverty. This would seem to be the preconception of those who argue the affluent society doctrine.[1] The advocates of this notion seem to have concluded, at least subconsciously, that absolute poverty has disappeared and that even the poor have a minimum above what could be called the absolute poverty line. Only relative poverty remains in the industrial economy.

Even though these definitional problems of poverty seem to complicate the matter of measurement, the early economists were untroubled in defining the poverty line. From the time of Malthus, the classical economists contended that labor, as a social category, was paid a wage which tended toward the subsistence level. Not all of them defined subsistence in the same manner, but Ricardo's definition can be taken as typical. He contended that the "natural price of labour is that price which is necessary to enable the labourers, one with another, to subsist and to perpetuate their race, without either increase or diminution."[2] Real poverty and wretchedness occurred when the general rate of wages fell below this so-called natural subsistence rate.

Marx, who learned well his economic lessons from Ricardo, also contended that wages were determined by subsistence. To Marx, subsistence consisted of an amount sufficient to allow the labor power used up in the act of production to be replenished. According to Marx, the laborer's "means of subsistence must ... be sufficient to maintain him in his normal state as a labouring individual."[3] But the normal state was something which was affected both by the physical and climatic conditions of the country in which the laborer lived and by the degree of civilization of a country."[4] The last determinant would seem to indicate that Marx believed that subsistence was something which increased with the advance of the material arts. Poverty and wretchedness would exist, then, when the remuneration of the laborer either failed to advance with this subsistence minimum or when it was driven below it, as he contended it would be, in a capitalist society by employers intent on maintaining surplus value.

Both the classical economists and Marx drew the poverty line at a plane of living which was related to some vague concept of subsistence, whether defined in physiological terms, as Ricardo seems to have done, or in physiological and "historical" terms, as seems to be the case with Marx. Utter degrading poverty would then exist among those parts of the population who were, for some reason or another, driven below this subsistence level.

Serious attempts to measure the extent of poverty were not made until the latter half of the nineteenth century.[5] A vague concept of subsistence as a dividing line between poverty and some higher level of living was found to be inadequate. People such as Charles Booth and B. S. Rowntree in England attempted to establish a more definite standard which could be used as the poverty line. Booth in his justly famous study of London poverty drew the poverty line in terms of crowding.[6] He found a negative correlation between housing density and income. He argued that those people who were living three or more to a room, of a size typical of the poor districts of London, constituted what he called the "very poor." Booth estimated that 18s to 21s per week was essential to provide a minimum standard of living at which no one could be considered destitute. However, those living at this level did possess only the minimum necessities. Below this level were the "very poor." He found that those who were below this level of income corresponded with those who were living three or more to a room.

B. Seebohm Rowntree, in his classic study of York,[7] classified poverty as primary and secondary. Poverty existed when the level of living fell below the minimum essential to maintain "physical efficiency." Primary poverty consisted of those families whose money incomes were insufficient to procure even this minimum standard of living. Secondary poverty consisted of those families whose money incomes were sufficient to procure the minimum standard, but who failed to reach this level because of an allocation of expenditure which would not maintain mere physical efficiency. Rowntree's minimum standard of living to provide for mere physical efficiency was drawn on the basis of some physical subsistence minimum. Since the minimum standard did include a complete budget for food, housing, and household sundries, which he broke down into clothing, light, fuel, and all other expenditures, his subsistence line was drawn in more concrete terms than had been characteristic of subsistence concepts heretofore. But the basis of the standard was a rather vague concept of "physical subsistence." Some thirty years later, in a sequel to this early study, Rowntree commented that "It was a standard of bare subsistence."[8] He went on to call attention to the stringency of the standard on which the poverty line was drawn. The concept of the poverty line as defined by Rowntree was a distinct improvement on earlier attempts to define poverty. Rowntree did attempt to establish subsistence minimums for each category of consumption. Earlier allusions to subsistence had left the term general and rather vague.

Other students of poverty subsequent to Rowntree have followed his lead and have defined poverty as any level of living which falls below some predetermined standard which is alleged to provide the minimum essentials. Early in this [twentieth] century in the United States, budgets which provided a minimum of health and well-being were constructed for purposes of administering assistance. These budgets were based on the minimum necessary to maintain a family on public assistance. The budgets were referred to "assistance" or "subsistence" ones. Subsequent to this early period, budgets were drawn which provided for a standard of living above the subsistence level. These budgets were frequently referred to as providing a comfort standard or one of health and decency. Since these budgets provided for something more than what was looked upon as a subsistence level of living, they were not used as devices for drawing the poverty line – at least, not a line which demarcated absolute poverty.

During the depression of the 1930s, budgets which were based on a subsistence concept once again made their appearance in the United States. These budgets became necessary when a large number of people were seeking depression assistance. Since assistance funds at the command of those administering relief were limited and the number seeking assistance seemingly undifferentiated, it was necessary to make the funds cover as many cases as possible. The relief payments were based on the standard of living budgets. For the WPA [Works Progress Administration, later the Works Project Administration] two budgets were constructed. One would provide what was called a "maintenance" standard of living. This was supposedly above the subsistence level, but below what the WPA considered to be a satisfactory American standard of living. For setting WPA payments, however, an "emergency" budget was used. This was derived by cutting some of the items from the "maintenance" standard. The emergency budget was one which was closer to subsistence and may have been even below such a level. It was called "emergency" because it was supposed to provide a level of living sufficient to maintain life, but if prolonged over more than two to three years could seriously impair health and well-being.[9]

But all of these efforts to establish some minimum level of subsistence have been unconvincing as lines which demarcate absolute poverty. The established minimums, below which supposedly lies absolute poverty, have seemed to be arbitrary. The very terms used to designate the level provided by the poverty budget seem to have a cultural significance. For example, the term minimum of "health and decency" raised a question concerning the relativeness of these two terms. What is held to be minimum health in one culture may be considerably above that which prevails in one with less advanced medical arts. And certainly "decency" varies widely among various cultures. To many students of the standard of living, these budgets, if used to measure poverty, seem to measure only relative poverty. They appear to be relative to a culture and hence do not measure some bare minimum; thus they do not reveal absolute poverty. Poverty is relative to some arbitrarily chosen bench-mark which reveals the predilections of the one establishing the standard. Thus, in a culture possessing highly developed industrial arts, the minimum standard below which poverty is said to exist would reveal only relative poverty – what in that culture has been considered to be a poverty level of living.

All of these difficulties indicate that the meaning of subsistence needs to be examined. The word "subsistence" conveys the notion of some physical minimum below which the individual may not fall without suffering irreparable physical damage.

This connotation of subsistence has intellectual antecedents in the eighteenth century. Smith and other writers of that era were wont to refer to man in the "original state of nature." This was an imaginary state in which man lacked a cultural dimension. He possessed only those attributes of sense perception with which nature had thoughtfully endowed him. He lived on the usufruct of a bountiful nature just sufficient to meet his minimum physical needs. With the advancement afforded by the invention of tools he was able to rise above this subsistence level. The perpetuation of the species at a subsistence level even with the advance of tools and skills was a product of the rate of growth of population.

The notion that there was such an "original state of nature" has been exploded by the subsequent work of the archaeologist and anthropologist. Everywhere that there is evidence of the prior existence of man there is evidence of culture. As a matter of fact, in some very early archaeological finds, the only evidence for the existence of man is a cultural one. Thus, the level of living even in very "simple" societies is one which is conditioned by the state of the industrial arts – even if these are of a very elementary sort.

Effective participation even in the simplest culture demands a mastery of certain tool skills and hence some minimum standard of living which will provide sufficient nutritional, educational, and other needs to the successful prosecution of these tool skills. This point may be amplified by referring to the condition of so-called simpler societies which exist adjacent to cultures much more advanced technologically. The Aborigines of Australia exist in such a condition. They are on the edge of an industrial culture, although their own culture is still largely a Paleolithic one. A person acculturated in the Aboriginal culture has Paleolithic skills and abilities which unsuit him for any kind of participation within the industrial culture of Australia. Certainly the Aborigines do possess a subsistence level of living within their own culture, but it is a subsistence almost totally lacking in those elements essential to successful participation in the industrial culture which surrounds them.

The plight of these so-called simpler societies which are in repeated contact with a much more advanced culture is one over which social scientists are concerned today.[10] The rapid expansion of the industrial cultures poses problems concerning the ability of the members of the simpler societies to make any kind of adjustment which is compatible with survival. All of these societies do possess a minimum standard of subsistence. Their survival thus far is evidence of this fact. But the subsistence is such that it does not provide the minimum essential to effective participation in the culture by which they are about to be overwhelmed. Since man cannot live without society, his standard of living must be sufficient to enable him to participate in some capacity within the society of which he is a member, by birth, by choice or by circumstance.

In the study of living standards this point has been missed by overemphasis on the ceremonial determinant of these standards. The word "decency" used to describe minimal standards of living is one which focuses undue attention on ceremonially derived minimum standards. Decency seems to have a ceremonial authenticity only. What is decent in one culture may be indecent in another, and vice versa. Since this is the usual interpretation, any minimum standard of decency seems to demarcate only relative poverty. Those below this standard lack the finer attributes of living which demarcate cultural gentility. That is all that can be said about the matter.

But such is not the case. As the state of the industrial arts advances, so does the minimum or subsistence standard of living essential to successful participation within any culture. New items which are a product of the advance of the industrial arts are diffused through the culture. They become part of the standards of living. But in being adopted as a part of the standard of living they alter the way of life of the whole society and eventually become essential. In other words, items which were looked upon as luxuries initially force such changes in the way of life of a people that they eventually become necessities.

The automobile is an excellent example of this effect. In American culture the automobile, shortly after its initial introduction, was viewed as a plaything for sons of the rich. But as the diffusion of the automobile proceeded, it worked a change in the American way of life so that eventually what was a luxury became a technological necessity.[11] This fact was recognized clearly during World War II when allowances of gasoline were made to owners of automobiles in order that they might get to work. The automobile had made it possible to live long distances from the usual place of work, but in allowing such residence it became a necessity to this way of life. In the western American cities which have grown and developed largely since the automobile era, the very structure of the city presumes the existence of the automobile as a means of transportation.

We might argue similarly for systems of wireless communication. The dissemination of news and information is essential to the continued existence of any society, and participation by any individual within that society presumes receipt of such news and information. In western culture the radio and television each were first introduced as novelties. But as their possibilities for the dissemination of information and news were realized, they became common media for this purpose. And as they became common media, the society came to depend upon them. In no case is this point made more forcefully than in the plans for civil defense, in which the radio and television are key instruments. The assumption is made that these instruments are generally available to the members of western society. They are now necessities. Certainly they are still luxuries and even possibly playthings in the remoter regions of the Papuan culture. But this is not true within the industrial economy.

What these automobile, radio, and television examples seem to indicate is that as the state of the industrial arts advances, so does the minimum standard of subsistence below which lies absolute poverty. The poverty line rises with the improvement in the state of the industrial arts. Certainly the poverty line is a culturally determined one, but it is not whimsically determined, a matter of the mores, "decency," and "all that." It is a function of technology. The criterion, therefore, for a minimum standard of living is not one of physical survival in the usual meaning of this concept, but one of cultural survival – the survival of an individual within a culture in any kind of meaningful sense. This also means that even in so-called affluent societies such as that of America it is possible to have absolute poverty.

In order to participate effectively in American culture, certain minimum health and educational standards are essential. But these are standards which rise with technological advance. For example, chronic malaria is not compatible with effective participation in western culture. It is incompatible with participation in the industrial process. The lack of access to preventive and curative medical attention for malaria in western culture would be taken as evidence for the existence of absolute poverty. Yet among the peoples of Papua prior to World War II malaria was practically endemic. Its presence could not serve as the basis for concluding that a member of Papuan society was in absolute poverty. Having chronic malaria did not unfit one for participation in Papuan society.

Medical advancement brings with it a rise in the general level of health and physical well-being. As this comes about, the activities of the culture presumes the possession of this minimum level of well-being. To lack access to such a level means that a person may not possess the physical well-being to participate in the various activities of the culture which presuppose its possession.

Similar conclusions can be drawn concerning educational minimal standards. The minimum education essential to an effective cultural participation rises with the advance of the industrial arts. In our own culture today, those with only a grammar school education are at a serious disadvantage in finding employment.[12] Those with only a few grades of schooling are almost unemployable, given the skills and level of knowledge demanded by industrial types of employment. As the state of the industrial arts has advanced, the employment opportunities for those with a limited education have diminished. Without gainful employment and hence a source of regular pecuniary income, a member of western society is hardly a participating member. He may become a charity case and live on the perimeter of society. The test for receipt of such charity is the absence of the ability to participate effectively in the affairs of society.

All of these considerations would seem to indicate that the poverty line, that level of living which demarcates absolute poverty, is a moving one. With the advance of the industrial arts the minimum level of living essential to effective participation in a culture rises. Thus, even within a society which is generally in the affluent class, it is possible to have absolute poverty.

Notes

1 See, for example, J. K. Galbraith, *The Affluent Society* (Boston: Houghton Mifflin, 1958); J. W. Krutch, *Human Nature and the Human Condition* (New York: Random House, 1959); Frederick Lewis Allen, *The Big Change* (New York: Harper, 1921.

2 David Ricardo, *Principles of Political Economy and Taxation* (London: J. M. Dent Everyman's Edition, 1937), p. 52.

3 Karl Marx, *Capital* (New York: Modern Library edition, n.d.), p. 190.

4 Ibid.

5 One cannot ignore Friedrich Engels' *The Condition of the Working Class in England* (New York: John W. Lovell, 1887, originally published in 1844); but this work does not attempt a rigorous assessment of the proportion of the working class who were living in absolute poverty.

6 Charles Booth, *Life and Labour of the People in London* (London: Macmillan, 1903), vol. 5, chaps. 1 and 2.

7 B. Seebohm Rowntree, *Poverty: A Study of Town Life* (London: Macmillan, 1910), chap. 4.

8 B. Seebohm Rowntree, *Poverty and Progress: A Second Social Survey of York* (New York: Longmans, Green, 1941), p. 102.

9 For discussion of these budgets see United States Department of Labor, *How American Buying Habits Change* (Washington: U.S. Government Printing Office, n.d.), chap. 10; and for a discussion of these budgets during the depression of the 1930s see C. R. Daugherty, *Labor Problems in American Industry* (Boston, Houghton Mifflin, 1958), pp. 135ff. See also Dorothy S. Brady, "Family Budgets: A Historical Survey," *Monthly Labor Review*, vol. 66 (February, 1948), p. 171.

10 Margaret Mead (ed.), *Cultural Patterns and Technological Change* (New York: New American Library, 1955). This was originally published as a UNESCO document.

11 For an excellent account of this effect, see Lloyd Morris, *Not So Long Ago* (New York: Random House, 1949).

12 See Robert J. Lampman, "The Low Income Population and Economic Growth" in Study Paper No. 12, Joint Economic Committee (Washington: U.S. Government Printing Office, 1939).

9   The great wheel of wealth

A reflection of social reciprocity

American Journal of Economics and Sociology, vol. 24 (July 1965), pp. 241–8

COMMENTARY BY WILLIAM WALLER

Hamilton rejects Karl Polanyi's assertion that modern industrial capitalism differs from all preceding forms of economies by being organized on the market principle rather than reciprocity. Hamilton defines reciprocity, drawing from the work of cultural anthropologists, most notably Bronislaw Malinowski, as meaning that "everything done by one person to favor another must be reciprocated by the latter."

Hamilton notes that the anthropologists are drawn to the more spectacular manifestations of this form of economic organization, such as the Kula exchange of arm shells and necklaces described by Malinowski. But Hamilton also discusses the trade in other, mundane goods that goes on simultaneously with the primary exchange of symbolically important goods. From this Hamilton notes that the symbolically important goods are part of a ceremonial exchange that reinforces social solidarity. The trade and barter in mundane goods is a manifestation of the technological interdependence among the people engaged in reciprocal exchange, based on division of labor and specialization of different groups in the employment of specific tool skills to produce useful items.

Hamilton observes that the ceremonial aspect of reciprocal exchange is reduced, but not eliminated, in modern industrial culture. The technological exchange of goods and services that represent division of labor and specialization in our culture is accompanied by a reflected set of ceremonial financial exchanges employing money – a formal mechanism for authenticating exchange in our culture. The technological movement is shown by the flow of goods and labor between households and firms. The ceremonial movement is represented by the flow of money in the opposite direction; said pecuniary flow inscribes ownership, power and status relations in our society. All these flows take place in a great wheel of wealth, now usually depicted in the economics manuals as a circular flow diagram.

Again Hamilton uses anthropology to illustrate the importance of culture in understanding economic systems.

THE GREAT WHEEL OF WEALTH: A REFLECTION OF
SOCIAL RECIPROCITY

Karl Polanyi in his *Great Transformation* argues that the contemporary economy differs from all preceding forms of economy by being organized on the market principle.[1] He contended that all preceding economies had been organized on the basis of reciprocity, but this principle had been replaced in the Western economies sometime in the early decades of the nineteenth century by that of the market.

Reciprocity is a principle of social and economic process for the explanation of which we are indebted to the anthropologist Bronislaw Malinowski. Malinowski best stated the principle in his *Crime and Custom in Savage Society*.[2] Despite the title, this little volume is devoted to an exposition of primitive economics as much as it is to "crime and punishment." Perhaps credit may also be given to Marcel Mauss for contributing some understanding of this basic process, although his claim is partially clouded by virtue of the fact he had the benefit of some of Malinowski's work.[3] But no matter to whomever we should pass the bouquets for first formulation of the concept, their largely independent work would seem to reciprocally authenticate one another and hence the principle of reciprocity.

Polanyi used the concept of reciprocity as formally stated by Malinowski rather than the slightly more complicated form in which Mauss stated it. According to Malinowski, all primitive economic exchange proceeds on the basis of reciprocity. In fact, this principle is a general one which applies to all social interaction. As he contended, everything done by one person to the favor of another must be reciprocated by the latter. A favor done requires a return favor which is socially sanctioned and readily recognized as equivalent to the initial favor. This complex is perhaps most clearly and simply illustrated to the reader unfamiliar with anthropological literature by reference to the gift exchange in our own culture which is very apparent during the Christmas season. We all have various categories of Christmas-time friends with whom we exchange gifts. This gift exchange is, however, not a random phenomenon. Despite the saying that it is the spirit of giving rather than the thing given which is significant, a moment's reflection will indicate that this is only partially the truth. The gifts we exchange with one another are always what we call "appropriate," and appropriate means something which is approximately equivalent to what we anticipate receiving. Although it might intrude a jarring note into what is looked upon as a manifestation of pure generosity, we all have our $2, $5, and $10 friends.

Malinowski enlarged the principle to explain social order itself. But we are largely concerned with its more narrow economic implications. In every society examined by the anthropologist the principle of economic reciprocity has manifested itself in a system of circulation, the most notorious being the Kula circuit among the island dwellers off the northeast coast of New Guinea. In this complex, red shell necklaces pass clockwise through the islands while white shell bracelets pass counterclockwise. Inter-island trading partners are linked to one another through these objects. The islanders of the Trobriand Archipelago are linked to those of Dobu through this exchange. The Trobrianders call upon the Dobuans and they receive from their respective trading partners necklaces. The Dobuans counter this by calling upon their Trobriand partners in anticipation of receiving arm shells, which are looked upon as of equal social worth. In other words, the Trobriander who has received a necklace from his Dobuan trading partner must reciprocate to him by the gift of an arm shell held to be of equal social worth to the necklace he has received earlier. This complex circuit is a closed one, for it extends through the islands in a complete circle.[4]

Such circular systems have been found by the student of primitive society elsewhere. A similar phenomenon has been found in northern Australia in what is called Arnhem Land. There the objects exchanged are referred to as gerri.[5] In East Africa even the matter of marriage is tied into the economy through the circuit flow of brides and cattle – brides going in one direction and cattle in the other. In fact, the cattle–brides complex can be diagrammed in very much the same fashion appropriate to the Kula traffic in the Trobriands.[6] Although not worked out to precisely the same high degree, reciprocity has been demonstrated to set up a circuit flow of objects among the Maori,[7] the Tikopia,[8] and the Ontong Javanese.[9] Not all systems of reciprocity which establish a circuit of exchange have the beautiful symmetry of that of the Kula, but all can be diagrammed circularly in which one set of items is indicated as passing in one direction while another set of items passes in reverse direction.

Students of reciprocity have, however, emphasized its more lurid details and in doing so have seemingly missed its technological basis. As usually expounded, the principle of reciprocity seems to rest on emotional feelings of social solidarity which are refired and rekindled by the exchange. If this were the sole basis for the phenomenon, one could, as did Polanyi, see its disappearance with the rise of market economy. The relationships which prevail within the market between trading partners do seem to have lost some of the personality which did prevail in earlier societies.[10] However, reciprocity is in another sense the manifestation of a technological interdependence which is one essential dimension of the tool process. We are and always have been technologically interrelated. The division of labor perhaps could be said to have begun when Eve was split off from Adam's rib and immediately thereafter picked up a blunt instrument. All tool activity is complementary and hence reciprocal. The city garbage collector complements the work of the physician, who reciprocates by maintaining the health of the city garbage collector. And both of these activities complement all of the other tool functions being performed in a complex industrial culture.

These interrelationships could be mapped and their reciprocal or complementary nature clearly demonstrated. It would be possible to begin perhaps with coal and iron mining and show how these tool operations were complemented by the manufacture of iron, which was similarly complemented by the production of steel and further finished products. From here it could be shown how this activity was complemented by the manufacture of automobiles, watches, and mining machinery, all of which enabled the coal and iron miners to get from their homes to the mines on time in order to mine more coal and iron to keep the circuit going.

All of this perhaps seems so obvious that we miss its significance in understanding reciprocity. It is a similar, but less complex, technological interdependence, for the tool skills are less advanced, which underlies reciprocity among all of those peoples the anthropologist has studied. The Kula traffic proper is such a large and obvious bit of the institutional complex of Trobriand society that its technological base is obscured. But Malinowski does call attention to the fact that much more than the ceremonial exchange of arm shells and necklaces is involved. As he put it,

> The ceremonial exchange of the two articles is the main, the fundamental aspect of the Kula. But associated with it, and done under its cover, we find a great number of secondary activities and features. Thus, side by side with the ritual exchange of arm shells and necklaces, the natives carry on ordinary trade, bartering from one island to another a great number of utilities, often unprocurable in the district to which they are imported, and indispensable there.[11]

The circulation of gerri among the Arnhem Land people is also clearly based on a technological specialization. Although these are a people with an essentially Paleolithic tool complex, having neither domesticated plants or animals nor pottery, they do have specialized tool skills. As Thomson put it, "In many of these [tool] processes the possession of special skill is recognized by the use of a distinctive name, and in their technology there is evidence of the beginning of craft specialization."[12] Even among such people as the pygmies of the Ituri Forest, who have perhaps an even simpler technology than that of Arnhem Land, evidence exists to indicate complementary interrelationships based on tool skills.[13]

Technological reciprocity is a fact. This, it seems to me, is the meaning of Durkheim's concept of organic solidarity of which he made so much in his *Division of Labor*.[14] There he argued that as the division of labor proceeded, the individual members of society became increasingly interdependent. The type of mechanical solidarity which had characterized earlier forms of society was displaced by an organic solidarity enforced by increasing specialization.

Thus far we have implied that social reciprocity has in fact two aspects, one which is technologically based and the other which is ceremonial in nature. As we noted above, it is this latter aspect which heretofore has been emphasized by the ethnologist. He has not done so wholly, but neither has he made a clear distinction between the two. The technological aspect proceeds on a matter-of-fact basis in which each tool skill in some way possesses a complementary relationship with every other tool skill. Admittedly some of these relationships are quite remote and not immediately apparent until, by some concatenation of events, our attention is focused upon them.

But the ceremonial aspect of reciprocity is of such a nature as to attract our immediate attention. It is based on the concept of authorship and the honoring of this authorship. Man has never been satisfied to accept the matter-of-fact relationships characteristic of his technology. The outcome of technological activity is at best uncertain. But man desires certainty.[15] To secure this certainty he has repeatedly resorted to the occult. This is what is responsible ultimately for his successes, or at least so it seems. And among men it is those master workmen, the kings, priests, and warriors, individuals in most frequent and repeated touch with the occult, and hence of greatest repute, who are ultimately responsible for all good things. Thus the ceremonial aspect of reciprocity is one in which man honors this attribution of mystic potency. We pay our respects through great feats of gift giving and ceremonial exchange in such notorious events as the potlatch of the northwest Indians[16] and the formal Kula trading of the Trobriand circuit.

The ceremonial reciprocity in other words simulates what is going on technologically. But ultimate authorship is attributed to the mystic potencies which are at the basis of an elaborate system of status. The upshot of it all is, however, to establish a system of circulation in any tribe, ancient or modern, part of which is ceremonial in nature but which simulates a genuine technologically based interdependence.

If this is a correct interpretation of social processes, then Polanyi made a wrong turn when he contended that market economy was to be distinguished from all of those economies which preceded it because of the absence of the principle of reciprocity in the market economy. This wrong turn may have been made because reciprocity as an economic process has usually been explained as a ceremonial phenomenon. And certainly the market is a bit more impersonal and less sensational than is the potlatch – although Veblen, familiar with the market as well as the potlatch, saw clearly the similarities in these two complexes. And anyone who reads Malinowski's account of the precautions taken by a Trobriand Kula trader to achieve great success in his dealings with his Kula partner can find more than just an analogous similarity to the pecuniary machinations of the captains of industry in the heyday of classic capitalism.

But if we focus our attention on technological reciprocity we would be forced to argue, as it seems to me did Durkheim, that reciprocity, or rather complementary tool relationships, are more extensive in the industrial economy than in the simpler agrarian and hunting economies which preceded it. In other words, the technological basis of economic reciprocity is more extensive today than it has ever been heretofore, and will undoubtedly become even more so in the future if man survives the immediately precarious situation with which he is faced.

All of this may be easily conceded. All that it seems to recognize is a fact – the fact that we live in a complex industrial economy. But it also seems to indicate that the market economy is also nothing but a reflection of social reciprocity – both technological and ceremonial.

It is startling that this was not apparent to Polanyi. The "great wheel of wealth," which the economist finds useful in sketching the grosser aspects of our economy, would seem to be nothing but a reflection of social reciprocity. This familiar diagram purports to show that goods pass in one direction while money, in some way socially recognized as exactly equal to the goods, passes in the reverse direction. In fact, it is perhaps a diagram of a Kula ring on a colossal scale which an ethnologist from the Trobriand culture would readily recognize for what it is. In the great wheel of wealth the goods flow is a recognition of technological reciprocity while the money flow is a reflection of ceremonial reciprocity and the honoring of status.

Just as the Kula ring is a manifestation of social reciprocity, so is the great wheel of wealth. Every transaction in the industrial economy presumably represents the passage of a good or service from one individual to another who reciprocates by the passage of money which is defined socially to be exactly equivalent. Nothing so impresses the buyer as to the honesty and fair dealing of the seller as does a claim that the commodity is being sold for no more than it cost. This seems to assure that no gouging is taking place, that the transaction is one governed by the rule of equivalence.

Some students seem to feel that reciprocity as a social process disappeared as money replaced direct transactions of goods for goods, services for services. But this seems to ignore the nature of all pecuniary transactions. Money is a formal object which satisfies the demands of reciprocity. Justice in the pecuniary economy requires that the money passing in one direction is socially exactly equivalent to the goods passing in the reverse direction.

Much of economic theory has been concerned with demonstrating just how this equivalence has been achieved. It purports to demonstrate that in the market economy the utility or satisfaction achieved by the consumer from the consumption of a good is exactly equal to the blood, sweat, and tears that went into its production and that this equivalence is measured by price. In other words, the money being passed by the consumer to his trading partner is precisely equal to the necklace or arm shell received.

The dispute between Marx and the mainstream of classical political economy seems to be over this point. The standard theory argues that all of the rules of reciprocity are satisfied in market economy or capitalism. Marx argues that this is not the case. The rules of reciprocity are not being met as long as there is surplus value. But all of this hardly seems to indicate the demise of reciprocity, although the market may have introduced a degree of impersonality which is not present in non-monetary transactions.

The reciprocal obligations by virtue of which a family unit is bound together still seem to contain an emotional element absent in the same degree from market transactions. But even in this case we often allude to the decay of the extended family in which such obligations are much more extensively recognized. They now do not seem to extend far beyond the bounds of the nuclear family. But what has happened to reciprocity in the family seems to be characteristic of what has happened to reciprocity in the market economy. The expansion of technology has bound together larger and larger groups of individuals while simultaneously reducing the extent of personal relationships. It is this depersonalization of reciprocal obligations for which the industrial revolution is responsible – not the substitution of market economy for reciprocity. By extending and enlarging our technological interdependence the industrialization of Western economy has enlarged the area over which reciprocity prevails.

The great wheel of wealth is merely testimony to the fact that reciprocity is still an aspect of market economy. And we cannot rid ourselves of it, at least of that aspect which recognizes a technological reality. Our problem has been one of eliminating that aspect of reciprocity which is ceremonial and which impedes the full utilization of our technology. The abrasive aspects of market economy which Polanyi deplores are generated by the ceremonial aspect of reciprocity. Much of our trouble in managing our economic affairs is a product of this. Technologically, reciprocity means increasing abundance. Ceremonially, reciprocity means conspicuous consumption and poverty.

The whole phenomenon of reciprocity in our economy was encompassed in Veblen's dichotomy between workmanship and exploit, industry and business. This is precisely what is reflected in the great wheel of wealth, in which all of the fruits of workmanship (goods) are supposedly equal to all of the fruits of business (money).

The upshot of all this would seem to indicate that the economist has much to gain by borrowing from the cultural anthropologist. Thus far the borrowing has been almost totally in the other direction. The ethnologist has attempted to use the concepts familiar to modern economics in his study of simpler economies. The results have not been fruitful.[17]

This is not surprising. It denies type continuity, which is so evident in what Max Otto referred to as the "human enterprise." It makes a false disjunction between so-called primitive economies and more modern-day ones. The consequence of this is to send the economist off hunting for the unique historic events which represent a great watershed between the present economy and all simpler ones. It constructs a distinction between modern and primitive economies on a false base. A genuine distinction can be made, of course, on technology, but this does not deny historic continuity, as do such theses as that of Max Weber concerning the development of a spirit of capitalism out of the Protestant Reformation.[18] The economist would seem to be able to benefit from the study of primitive economics in the same way that the sociologist has benefited by the encroachment of the anthropologist onto once hallowed sociological ground.[19]

Notes

1 Karl Polanyi, *The Great Transformation* (Boston: Beacon Press ed., 1957). See also Polanyi, Conrad M. Arensberg, and Harry W. Pearson (ed.), *Trade and Market in the Early Empires* (Glencoe, Ill.: The Free Press, 1957).
2 Bronislaw Malinowski, *Crime and Custom in Savage Society* (Paterson, N.J.: Littlefield, Adams, 1959, originally published in 1926).
3 Marcel Mauss, *The Gift: Forms and Functions of Exchange in Archaic Societies* (Glencoe, Ill.: The Free Press, 1954 ed.).
4 Bronislaw Malinowski, *Argonauts of the Western Pacific* (London: Routledge & Kegan Paul, 1922), chap. III.

5 Donald F. Thomson, *Economic Structure and the Ceremonial Exchange Cycle* (Melbourne: Macmillan, 1949).
6 See for example E. Jensen Krige and J. D. Krige, *The Realm of a Rain Queen* (London: Oxford University Press, 1943), p. 145.
7 Raymond Firth, *Primitive Economics of the New Zealand Maori* (New York: E. P. Dutton, 1929).
8 Raymond Firth, *Primitive Polynesian Economy* (London: G. Routledge, 1939). See also his *We the Tikopia* (New York, American Book, 1936).
9 H. Ian Hogbin, *Law and Order in Polynesia* (New York: Harcourt Brace, 1934).
10 This impersonality of exchange has perhaps reached its apex in the vending machine. In this situation the buyer is related only remotely to his trading partner, whose agent is a wholly impersonal machine. Money in this case becomes hardly more than an actuator of a mechanical process.
11 Malinowski, *Argonauts of the Western Pacific*, op. cit., p. 83.
12 Thomson, op. cit., p. 9.
13 Colin Turnbull, *The Forest People* (New York: Anchor Books, 1962).
14 Emile Durkheim, *On the Division of Labor in Society* (New York: Macmillan, 1933).
15 John Dewey, *The Quest for Certainty* (New York: Capricorn Books ed., 1960).
16 Irving Goldman, *The Kwakiutl of Vancouver Island*, in Margaret Mead (ed.), *Cooperation and Competition among Primitive Peoples* (Boston: Beacon Press ed., 1961).
17 Daniel B. Fusfeld, "Economic Theory Misplaced: Livelihood in Primitive Society," in Karl Polanyi, Conrad M. Arensberg, and Harry W. Pearson, op. cit., pp. 342–56.
18 Max Weber, *The Protestant Ethic and the Spirit of Capitalism* (New York: Charles Scribner's Sons, 1958 ed.).
19 See for example the work of James West, *Plainville, U.S.A.* (New York: Columbia University Press, 1945); and W. Lloyd Warner, *Social Class in America* (New York: Harper Torchbooks ed., 1960).

Part II

Structural policy and economic theory

Part II contains sixteen articles, each with an introduction. All but one of the sixteen are from the *Journal of Economic Issues* (JEI), so a word about that one article first. David Hamilton's "The U.S. Economy: The Disadvantage of Having Taken the Lead" was published in 1982 in the *Review of Institutional Thought*, a short-lived but intensely institutionalist journal published by the Association for Institutional Thought (AFIT). AFIT stopped publishing the *Review* but went on to become a lively association of institutionalists, holding its annual meetings at various cities in the western United States. A number of David Hamilton's works were first presented as papers at these meetings and were frequently the occasion for lively discussion.

The fifteen articles from the *Journal of Economic Issues* were published over the twenty-five-year period 1967–1991. Since its beginning, the JEI has been the leading journal in institutional economics. The articles are grouped into four sections: Section 1 contains articles on Poverty Theory and Poverty Policy; Section 2 contains Consumption Theory; Section 3 contains Hamilton's Critique of Neo-classicism; and Section 4 contains articles on the Elements of Institutionalism. Each section warrants a few comments.

The way I understand it, David Hamilton's approach to poverty in Section 1 is actually quite simple. Because he understands that poverty is a social problem with its roots nourished by a hierarchical structure of status, Hamilton is a reconstructionist as opposed to a redistributionist. Reconstructionists propose reconstructing the social institutions that support the hierarchical structure of status. The idea is to take away the social support for poverty and inequality, thereby making permanent progress against them possible. If the social support is left in place, the redistributing of income to those on the bottom of the social pyramid will be half-hearted, unpopular, and temporary. This was the fundamental short-coming of the War on Poverty waged in the 1960s. It was mainly redistribution-ist. Only a few aspects of the War on Poverty, those aimed at empowering the poor, were reconstructionist. To be successful, Hamilton emphasizes, the institutional support for an inegalitarian society must be reconstructed into institutional support for an egalitarian one. The War on Poverty failed to bring about such a reconstruction. And that failure is a great shame, because Hamilton explains that there is no technological reason for poverty. The current state of the industrial arts is sufficiently advanced to lift us all out of its grip. The cause of poverty lies elsewhere.

Hamilton explains that one meaning of reform is bogus – is a form of ceremonialism. The bogus, ceremonial meaning of reform takes reform to be a return to some mythical golden age of harmony. Reaganomics, Hamilton shows, provides us with an informative example of ceremonial reform. The Reagan administration claimed to be reforming the economy by returning to the truths of the allegedly golden age of the lazy fairy (Hamilton's phrase for laissez-faire).

In Section 2, Hamilton explains that consumption is socially learned behavior, not behavior dictated by divine inspiration or by individual utility. So to explain consumption, Hamilton insisted, you must go back to the institutionalist Thorstein Veblen. Rejecting hedonism and divine inspiration, Veblen became the first professor of marketing science by explaining consumption behavior in terms of socially learned human behavior. Such behavior is both symbolic (status oriented) and instrumental. On one hand, the symbolic behavior of consumers is ceremonial. It is intended to signify the consumer's superior performance of the ancient rites of conspicuous consumption and invidious distinction – showing off the ability to pay, to be blunt. On the other hand, the instrumental behavior of consumers is practical. It is intended to achieve some practical end in view: buying new tires to replace the worn set on the car, getting hot coffee on a cold morning, trying new bifocals for reading.

In Section 3, Hamilton explains that much of what the standard textbooks teach us about the economy is little more than myth. It is ideological rather than instrumental. It elaborates on the myth of the lazy fairy. It is a species of old-time religion that, instead of being the cure for many economic problems, is their cause. My favorite quotation from the articles in this section sums it all up: "There is no invisible hand." And, of course, there is no lazy fairy, either.

If David Hamilton the institutionalist, the evolutionary economist, does not believe in the invisible hand and the lazy fairy, then what does he believe in? What are the basic elements of his approach to the economy? In the three articles grouped into Section 4, Hamilton focuses his attention on the question, how should we study the economy? Hamilton has taken great care in selecting and applying his approach. His approach is institutionalist. He is a follower of Thorstein Veblen. However, like most of the intellectual mavericks in institutionalism, he is his own man. His institutionalism is his own unique institutionalist approach. Although he certainly runs with the other institutionalists, his is not new institutionalism, not Marxist institutionalism, not radical institutionalism, not Karl Polanyi institutionalism, but David Hamilton institutionalism. He discusses one or more of the basic elements of his institutionalist approach in virtually all of his articles. Those elements are seven in number.

Element 1: evolution

Hamilton's institutionalist approach is evolutionary. He explains change in a particular way. It is non-teleological, the result of a continual sequence of cause and effect, not the result of divine direction or intervention. Evolution results in structural change, not just mechanical movement around an equilibrium or central tendency. Using contemporary modeling jargon, you could say that evolutionary change is endogenous rather than exogenous and that it involves changes in the behavioral relations as well as in the parameters. Furthermore, evolutionary change results in real movement that involves alterations and/or complete replacements in the social structures that human beings use and modify in their daily activities. Such changes are not swings back and forth around the equilibrium tendency of a pendulum, but permanent changes in a continuing process. Each change becomes the starting point for the next change, in a continuing cumulative sequence.

Element 2: technology

Hamilton argues that the dynamic factor in social evolution is technological change, not capital accumulation. Capital is one of the so-called factors of production, terms invented by classical economists to signify the alleged contribution made to the community's production of goods and services by those with a vested interest in receiving income. Certain powerful members of the modern (industrial) community have acquired a vested interest in the receipt of profit and interest, and so classical economists make-believe that these powerful members of the community actually contribute to the community's production of a flow of goods and services. Such community members are called capitalists and the manna they contribute is something called capital. This capital (manna) is alleged to accumulate through the painful saving of capitalists, and its accumulation drives the economic growth of the community.

Hamilton rejects this fairy tale and argues that the modern (industrial) community is able to produce a certain flow of goods and services because of the state of the industrial arts used by the community. Furthermore, Hamilton approaches changes in the state of the industrial arts as products of the community as a whole, not as the heroic acts of a Schumpeterian inventor. If Thomas Edison had not invented the light bulb, somebody else would have. The state of the industrial arts had reached such a point that the light bulb was just waiting to turn on in the head of anybody who was familiar enough with what the community already knew.

Element 3: learned, instrumental behavior

Human behavior is not utilitarian. It is not simply the sum of responses to expected pleasure and pain. It is far more rational and cumulative than that. It is rational in the sense of being instrumental, being aimed at achieving certain ends in view by manipulating the relevant part of the environment, where the relevant environment is composed of malleable causes and effects. That is, the immediate vicinity of the actor is treated as a series of potential tools and expected results, and they are used in order to achieve certain objectives. Humans do things. We do not just experience pleasure and pain. We are active, not just passive.

Human behavior is also cumulative because we learn from our own experience and, most importantly, we learn from others as well. Our community teaches us, both through formally organized activities and through informal ones. As we learn in this communal context, we change ourselves and our communities. Our behavior is not fixed. It evolves, always in a learned, communal context. That context is our culture. Hamilton's approach to human behavior is instrumental and culturally contextual.

Element 4: poverty is unnecessary

Hamilton insists that absolute poverty can be avoided in the modern economy. Absolute poverty, meaning insufficient real income to support effective participation in the activities and values of one's culture, is not necessary in a modern industrial economy.

The state of the industrial arts is sufficiently advanced to produce enough goods and services to allow everyone effective participation. And yet we still have absolute poverty, even in the technologically advanced economies. We can measure it and discuss its incidence. A sufficiently advanced state of the industrial arts is necessary, but not sufficient. Institutional reconstruction that undermines the support for social stratification is also required. Hamilton's approach to poverty goes beyond simple redistribution and emphasizes the state of the industrial arts and the need for institutional reconstruction.

Element 5: collective action

Hamilton's approach to the economy considers state collective action and other forms of collective action to be important and potentially beneficial. The welfare state can take action to improve the position of the poor. Markets can be regulated by state agencies in the public interest. Public education can spread enlightenment. Public health programs can spread good health. Private activities are not the sole source of value. Public activities can stimulate as well as direct. In Hamilton's approach, the lazy fairy and the invisible hand are both myths. Humans can direct the course of events through collective action.

Element 6: instrumental economics

Hamilton eschews ideology in his approach. He is not oriented toward either the preservation or the destruction of the status quo. He does not support "the system." Nevertheless, he does not support its overthrow, either. What he does support is problem solving. Poverty is a problem, so we should try to solve it, even when our efforts require us to confront the myths and sacred cows of our own culture. The problem is the main issue, to Hamilton the pragmatist.

Element 7: rich context

Although Hamilton is not an economic historian, and although he is a master of the short article, his approach is still rich in context. He uses many stories from history and anthropology to provide a rich context for his work. Context is important for full understanding. Hamilton's wide reading in anthropology, economics, sociology, history, literature, science, politics, and art provides the context for his institutional economics.

William M. Dugger
University of Tulsa

10 Reciprocity, productivity, and poverty

Journal of Economic Issues, vol. 4 (March 1970), pp. 35–42

COMMENTARY BY WILLIAM M. DUGGER

Hamilton begins this article with a central tenet of institutionalism: there is no technological reason for poverty in a modern industrial economy. And yet, Hamilton continues, even though the United States declared war on poverty in 1964, it persists. The war concentrated on raising the individual productivity of the poor because the warriors assumed that the poverty of the poor was due to their individual lack of productivity. Hamilton explains that this assumption is a widespread cultural belief and is the major block to the elimination of poverty.

Relying on Veblen rather than Polanyi, Hamilton explains that the anthropological notion of reciprocity lies behind this cultural belief. The people in our culture believe that a person's income from society is equal to some prior contribution he or she made to society: No current income, no prior contribution. This belief in reciprocity leads people also to believe that any major redistribution of income to the poor violates an important social norm. The poor would not be so poor if they had contributed more. Likewise, the rich would not be so rich if they had contributed less. Therefore, redistributing from the deserving rich to the undeserving poor violates the notion of reciprocity and is resisted. Therein, Hamilton emphasizes, lies the problem.

RECIPROCITY, PRODUCTIVITY, AND POVERTY

No technological reason exists for poverty in the modern industrial economy. This fact has long been recognized in the United States by economists, who have written about an "economy of abundance" since the 1930s when Stuart Chase, apparently, coined the phrase. This is recognized today in the frequent references made to George's enigma of poverty midst progress.

Certainly the state of the industrial arts is still the primary cause of poverty in the non-industrial countries. But those which now have the most advanced industrial arts have the capability of eliminating utter degrading poverty. The Scandinavian countries may well have done so.

In recognition of this fact, the United States has been engaged in a "war on poverty" since 1964, which some people would characterize more as a skirmish than a war. But no question can be raised concerning our capability of eliminating poverty. The gross national product should reach a trillion dollars in current dollar value by 1970.

A strong argument can be made that we had the capability of eliminating utter degrading poverty as early as the 1920s. At least, the almost forgotten Brookings studies entitled Distribution of Wealth and Income in Relation to Economic Progress seemed to indicate this to be the case. They demonstrated that as early as 1929 it was possible to provide every family in the United States with a minimum income of $2000. This was equal to $3941 in 1965 prices and $4637 in September 1969 prices.

But if we do not lack for productive capacity to eliminate poverty, we cannot blame its continued existence on the lack of distributive instruments either. At the present time we seem to have an abundance of suggestions, from Friedman's miniscule negative income tax to the much more powerful guaranteed income proposal of Theobald. In fact, no reason exists for not casting existing income maintenance minima at some level conceded to demarcate the minimum good life from poverty. One of the great mysteries is why we don't simply culturally borrow the Swedish system of social security. We had no hesitance about borrowing European science and technology on a wholesale scale throughout the nineteenth century and are still at it, as developments in atomic science testify. In any event, there is no dearth of proposed new distributive instruments and evidence elsewhere that at least some of these can do the job. One of the greatest mysteries is the mystery that has been made of poverty eradication by some of the new OEO types attracted by the task.

Small progress against poverty

Despite the rather large claims made for the success of our most recent efforts, they are not as startling as we are led to believe. What inroads have been made are probably attributable more to an accelerated operation of the economy than to the Herculean efforts of the poverty warriors. In fact, the relatively small inroads made on poverty by virtue of an accelerated operation of the economy may be in danger from the policies induced by those economic advisers who consider an approach to full employment as something wicked called an "overheated economy."

A rather startling revelation was made in 1968 that we still have hunger and malnutrition not dissimilar from that found in underdeveloped countries where general poverty prevails because of the absence of essential industrial arts. Students of the poverty problem in this decade usually qualified their descriptions of American poverty with the caution that we did have want, but no one suffered the kind of poverty one could find in the underdeveloped economies. In *Hunger,*

U.S.A. a typical quotation to this effect is given from Michael Harrington's *Other America*: "... to be sure, the other America is not impoverished in the same sense as those poor nations where millions cling to hunger as a defense against starvation. This country has escaped such extremes."[1]

Economists may attempt salvation by pointing out that Harrington is not a member of the guild. But a little effort would turn up some similar statements by guildsmen in good standing. Nevertheless, by 1968 cases of kwashiorkor and marasmus were being reported on the Navajo reservation as well as in other, less remote areas. Even in northeastern United States, a supposedly affluent area, people have been found who suffer from nutritional anemia. The Citizen's Board of Inquiry into Hunger and Malnutrition stated on the basis of extensive investigations that "Participation in government food programs has dropped 1.4 million in the last six years. Malnutrition among the poor has risen sharply over the past decade."[2] In this instance the drop in participation was not a consequence of diminished need. As a matter of fact, just the opposite was true, as increasing evidence of malnutrition indicates.

According to government accounts, 38.9 million lived in poverty in 1959. This was reduced to twenty-two million by 1968. The percentage of the population in poverty dropped from 21.9 to 10.9.[3] Some of this seeming great achievement in one decade follows from the fact that in 1959 the unemployment rate was around 6 per cent for much of the year while in 1968 it was about 3.6 per cent for most of the year.

But to whatever cause we owe the improvement in the statistics, reason would seem to caution against any great optimism. The measure of poverty hinges on the validity of poverty lines which may be criticized as inadequate. Because of the large allowance for income in kind, the rural poverty lines probably fail to honestly pick up substantial amounts of rural poverty.[4] More seriously, the poverty lines have been raised only in recognition of a price increase over the decade. But poverty lines need to have a "productivity" adjustment as well.[5] When adjusted only for price increases, and especially over a ten-year period, they begin to lose their relevance as true measures of poverty. For much the same reason, the consumer price index needs an overhaul periodically for more than just price level changes. In other words, it would be rather absurd to use today a budget, adjusted only for price changes, which demarcated poverty in 1900. Yet that is what we have been doing, and part of our seeming success in eliminating poverty is attributable to faulty measures. In any event, we have not eliminated the poverty way of life, and general agreement seems to have been reached that we will not do so by 1976, the original target date for total eradication of poverty. We are apt now to hear more about hard-core poverty which fails to yield to our best efforts.[6] Disillusionment seems to have replaced the great optimism with which the poverty warriors went about their work only four and five years ago. Even those who hail the readings from the statistical indicators seem pessimistic about making further reductions in poverty.

But the new disillusionment may be a product of an incorrect or weak analysis of the problem of poverty at the start of the war. Certainly the Economic

Opportunity Act, which may be interpreted as the best exemplar of the philo-sophic outlook of the poverty war, was the product of the orthodox interpretation of poverty. People are poor even though we have the industrial arts to eliminate the poverty condition because they do not themselves have the technical capac-ity to extricate themselves from poverty. They lack sufficient productivity by virtue of which they could earn a sufficient living. Programs to elevate individ-ual productivity were predominant in the poverty war. This was no accident.

From at least the time of the Biblical stricture that man should eat his bread in the sweat of his brow, poverty has been looked upon as a product of individual ineptness or inattentiveness to duty. This outlook rejects a universal cultural phe-nomenon which constitutes the major block to the elimination of poverty.

Anthropology and poverty

Economists have largely ignored the efforts of anthropologists, with some note-worthy exceptions. But the anthropologist does have contributions to make to an understanding of modern economic phenomena. And perhaps the reason for our failures to do what technologically can be done lies outside the normal scope of economics.

Veblen[7] in all of his work stressed the inhibitory effects of ancient and honor-able institutions. In one passage he stated that

> [t]he higher theoretical knowledge, that body of tenets which rises to the dignity of a philosophical or scientific system, in the early culture, is a complex of habits of thought which reflect the habits of life embodied in the institutional structure of society.

In this essay in *The Place of Science* he was making the usual distinction between the institutional and the technological way of life but emphasizing the role of habit both in its mental and in its behavioral manifestation. Habits of life are rationalized and justified by equally long habits of thought.

No part of our present economy is more the creature of long habits of practice and thought than is distribution. Veblen noted that matter-of-fact predominated in routine acts of production. Matter-of-fact thought is subject to transformation by experience in practice. Production technology is subject to modification and transformation. But not so the general system of distribution, which rests on claims of individual authorship and prowess. The distributive system supposedly simulates and parallels that of production. But this is largely by virtue of institu-tional imputation rather than any matter-of-fact demonstration.[8]

One notion the anthropologist has to offer that may be helpful in disentan-gling the mystery of poverty in the midst of plenty is that of reciprocity. Karl Polanyi and his followers have made some use of it in economic analysis, but even they have ignored its significance in the industrial economy.[9] The concept of reciprocity is, however, at the base of our whole market system. The market reflects "social reciprocity."[10]

The concept is one which was apparently independently discovered by Bronislaw Malinowski and Marcel Mauss.[11] Briefly, the concept recognizes that in institutional processes everything done by one individual or group to the favor of another individual or group requires a reciprocal socially defined equal return. The receiver of the initial act must in return do something to the giver of equal social worth. This has its counterpart on the negative side in that everything done of social detriment must be reciprocated by something of equal social detriment. The equalities have nothing more substantial behind them than social custom and habit. No outside individual could possibly objectively measure the straw mats that exchange for the fish or taros and see any kind of equality unless he too had been conditioned in the ancient and honorable institutions that sanctified the equality.

In any event, reciprocity does set up a system of distribution. The Kula traffic of Melanesia is the most widely known. But similar circular flows are to be found wherever the anthropologist has looked into systems of distribution. But what is critical is that behind the whole system lies the notion that income received is equal socially to some prior contribution to income given.

This phenomenon is no less true of modern systems of distribution than it is of those in so-called primitive societies. Certainly this notion is what lay behind Locke's tortured justification of private property. And certainly it is what lies behind our more modern-day notions of income justification by the mystic stuff called productivity.

Again we may refer to Veblen. In *The Theory of the Leisure Class* he argued that wealth may be acquired by matter-of-fact application of technologically certified methods as well as by stealth. But by whatever method acquired it must be placed in evidence as testimony to the productive capability of the owner. In other words, authorship and therefore rightful claim was honored by institutional public display.

In the industrial economy, reciprocity assumes the form of productivity. A person establishes a right to income in some employment if the product of that work is looked upon as socially equivalent to income in the other direction. Or he may acquire the right to income by ownership of property which in some way is imputed to contribute to the final product an amount socially equivalent to that received by its owner. In actuality, claims may be rather ethereal when we consider intangible property such as trade names and trade marks, but no more so than in some primitive cultures, as the West Coast potlatch easily demonstrated.

Individuals not so employed or so owning property must establish a relationship to someone who does receive such a socially sanctioned income. Kinship involves a set of obligations and reciprocal benefits which, particularly in earlier agrarian society, established these necessary economic connections. This still holds, but in the industrial economy does not extend much beyond the nuclear family.

We do extend income to individuals who have neither of these justifications. But this is referred to as charity and simply recognizes that we do not feel that anyone should die by virtue of absence of any legitimate income claim. But even in these cases reciprocity has some bearing. We have maintained the Elizabethan "means" test, and the notion that such welfare income should be only for the "deserving poor" is still to be found. Efforts to rehabilitate the poor, which means to put them in a position to receive income by virtue of productive employment, are always lauded. A recent passage is illustrative:

> However varied the approaches to breaking the multifaceted cycle of poverty, they all must have one ultimate goal: the encouragement or enrichment of the incentive for self help on the part of the poor. Only by attacking the impoverishment of motivation among the poor is the final goal of the elimination of poverty feasible. Antipoverty efforts should be distinguished from traditional and merely ameliorative welfare benefits by being directed to stimulating motivation and hope.[12]

Welfare economics, which pretends to a scientific neutrality equaled by none, participates in the same concept. The premise that social welfare can be enhanced only in a condition in which no one loses income, no matter how outrageously in actuality it may have been acquired, has lurking behind it the hidden preconception of reciprocity. The premise would be untenable in its absence.

As a matter of fact, much of economic theory is dedicated to demonstrating the equality of productive effort and receipt and enjoyment of income. Certainly the ultimate state of equilibrium would be one in which all factors of production receive income exactly equivalent to their contributions to the ultimate product and all consumers receive satisfactions exactly equal to that which has been forgone. And all is measured by price. But since the receipt of income is presumably from a productive source, the satisfactions received are equal to the efforts expended. Reciprocity reigns supreme.

Reciprocity is what gives to income distribution its socially derived rigidity. A decade or so ago we heard much about the new equalitarian society. This was worked by the progressive income tax and by regressive welfare expenditures. In actuality this was, of course, not the case. Income distribution has not undergone any massive change from the time we have reliable data to the present. Kolko has fairly well demonstrated this to be the case in the United States.[13] Barbara Wootton demonstrated this to be the case for Great Britain in the periods following World War II and Titmuss has done so for a more extended period.[14]

Incomes are distributed on some basis of social ethics which seems to equate certain social occupations and roles with productive efficacy. The income can be justified if some socially convincing demonstration can be made that the productive output is precisely equal to the income output. Not only is this true, but incomes are compared with one another and invidiously compared as to productive efficacy. This means that if a rise in the income of one occupation can be socially justified, all others must be adjusted so that the relative income position of each may be maintained.

This holds even with those who have left the work force by virtue of retirement. In retirement each receives in accordance with his previous contribution and thus each receives at a relatively lower scale but in the same proportion to others as he received when in the work force. Benefits are tied to preceding earnings.

Nothing short of a massive institutional change can eliminate poverty in the industrial economy. But this means that ancient and honorable habits of thought which reinforce and justify ancient and honorable institutions must give way. Picking away at poverty by such devices as "black capitalism" and miniscule income substitutes such as the negative income tax as proposed will not do the job.

The whole notion of income justification by productivity or reciprocity stands in the way of complete elimination of poverty. And such corollary ideas that something meritorious surrounds productive effort while there is something wicked about consumption is incompatible with a full employment of the industrial economy. Industrial abundance is compatible only with abundant consumption. But the ideas that the production of cigarettes is productive while the consumption of education is, if not wicked, a privilege are incompatible with the elimination of poverty.

Notes

1 Quoted in Citizens' Board of Inquiry into Hunger and Malnutrition in the United States, *Hunger, U.S.A.* (Boston, Beacon Press, 1969), p. 9.
2 Ibid., p. 10.
3 National Advisory Council on Economic Opportunity, *Continuity and Change in Antipoverty Programs* (Washington, D.C., U.S. Government Printing Office, 1969), p. 1.
4 National Advisory Commission on Rural Poverty, *The People Left Behind*, (Washington, D.C., U.S. Government Printing Office, 1967), pp. 7–8.
5 David Hamilton, "Drawing the Poverty Line at a Cultural Subsistence Level," *Southwestern Social Science Quarterly*, March 1962.
6 Ben Seligman, *Permanent Poverty* (Chicago, Quadrangle Books, 1968); Sar Levitan, *The Great Society's Poor Law: A New Approach to Poverty* (Baltimore, Johns Hopkins Press, 1969); Daniel P. Moynihan, *Maximum Feasible Misunderstanding* (New York, The Free Press, 1969).
7 Thorstein Veblen, *The Place of Science in Modern Civilization* (New York, Viking Press, 1942), p. 4.
8 C. E. Ayres, *The Problem of Economic Order* (New York, Farrar & Rinehart, 1938), chap. III.
9 Karl Polanyi, *The Great Transformation* (Boston, Beacon Press, 1957). See also K. Polyani, Conrad M. Arensberg, and Harry M. Pearson (eds.) *Trade and Market in Early Africa* (Glencoe, Ill., The Free Press, 1957) and Paul Bohannon and George Dalton, *Markets in Africa* (New York, Doubleday, 1965).
10 David Hamilton, "The Great Wheel of Wealth: A Reflection of Social Reciprocity," *American Journal of Economics and Sociology*, 24, no. 4 (July 1965), pp. 241–8.
11 Bronislaw Malinowski, *Crime and Custom in Savage Society* (Paterson, N.J., Littlefield, Adams, 1959); Marcel Mauss, *The Gift: Forms and Functions of Exchange in Archaic Societies* (Glencoe, Ill., The Free Press, 1954).
12 *Continuity and Change in Antipoverty Programs*, op. cit, p. 12.
13 Gabriel Kolko, *Wealth and Power in America* (New York, Frederick A. Praeger, 1962).
14 Barbara Wootton, *The Social Foundation of Wage Policy* (London, Unwin University Books, 1962); Richard Titmuss, *Income Distribution and Social Change* (London, George Allen & Unwin, 1962).

11 The political economy of poverty

Institutional and technological dimensions

Journal of Economic Issues, vol. 1 (December 1967), pp. 309–20

COMMENTARY BY WILLIAM M. DUGGER

In this article, Hamilton asks two fundamental questions: First, what determines the average level of living in a society; and second, what determines who will live in relative poverty and who in relative plenty? He finds the answers given by orthodox economists to be wrong. Institutionalists, he claims, give the right answers, and he explains them. As usual, Hamilton gives a rich contextual background to his explanations. Such attention to context is a characteristic of institutional analysis.

Hamilton points out that neoclassical economists and even Marxists attribute the average level of living in a society to the capital accumulated by its members. Veblen provided the appropriate correction to this shared misconception when he explained that a society's average level of living was a result of the state of the industrial arts in the community. The correct answer to this first question is the level of technology, not the quantity of capital.

Neoclassical economists answer the second question – who enjoys plenty and who suffers poverty? – primarily with the marginal productivity theory of income distribution. However, Hamilton points out that their answer is circular. A person is paid little or much because their productivity is small or large, but their productivity is measured by their pay. The correct answer is that relative income is determined by relative status ranking. High status is paid high income. Low status is paid low income. The income distribution is a product of the institutional structure of status.

THE POLITICAL ECONOMY OF POVERTY: INSTITUTIONAL AND TECHNOLOGICAL DIMENSIONS

The latecomer to the poverty problem is apt to conclude that poverty is a phenomenon of recent occurrence and discovery. Not over a decade ago we were being told that we were in a new era. Danger came not from too little but from superfluity, as one critic asserted.[1] The industrial economy had made goods so plentiful that we lived in a period of mass culture. The time was rapidly approaching when we would all be on one plane of living. Individual differences, tastes, and standards would be reduced to one mass level. Already one could not tell the difference between the executive in his Brooks Brothers suit and the working man in his mass-produced imitation. The Cadillac in which the executive arrived at the office could hardly be differentiated from the Chevrolet in which the worker arrived at the plant.[2]

Although Professor Galbraith's *The Affluent Society* challenged this point of view, the book, because of its unfortunate title, was interpreted by those who run while reading as giving an economic authentication to the superfluity argument. In a sense, it did. In order to effectively contrast the shabbiness of the post office with the glitter of the night club, Galbraith did give many readers the impression that private expenditure was now for superfluities. This was undoubtedly an unanticipated effect of *The Affluent Society*. Other readers, perhaps slower but more perceptive, got from the book a different message. Thus, in a most peculiar sense Galbraith's *Affluent Society* may be looked upon as the last shot fired in the superfluity argument and at the same time the opening shot in the war on poverty.

The economic complacency of the 1950s has given way before a flood of articles and books pointing to some or all aspects of poverty in the American economy. It is doubtful that we have had such an outpouring of literature on the matter of poverty in the midst of plenty since the era of the "muckrakers."[3] The economic neophyte, whose counterpart a decade ago perhaps concluded that everyone was living in superabundance, now may easily conclude that poverty is a newly discovered problem.

Despite its seeming newness, the question of poverty, of course, is as old and as large as the study of economics itself. In fact, Adam Smith defined economics or political economy as the study of poverty. At least, that would seem to be one warranted interpretation of the meaning of *An Inquiry into the Nature and Causes of the Wealth of Nations*. The very first two paragraphs of *The Wealth of Nations* indicate clearly that it is a study of both wealth and the absence thereof. Ricardo is often viewed as having redirected economic inquiry from the wealth of nations to the division of the spoils among the so-called factors of production. But inasmuch as these factors had meaning only because they represented social categories of income receivers, and since there was a differential receipt of income, the question of relative poverty still remained.

The great nineteenth-century schism in classical political economy resulted in two major branches, neo-classicism and Marxism, which are still largely divided over the issue of poverty. The neo-classicists argued that relative poverty was essential to capital formation. The lot of the poor might be a difficult one, but it could be remedied in the long run by capital accumulation. Since this accumulation could occur only if we had the rich, the savings of the rich became a virtue. In fact, the richer the rich and the poorer the poor, the faster would be capital accumulation. And the faster capital accumulation took place, the shorter the duration of the poor in economic purgatory.

The chief adversaries to this optimistic view, the Marxists, did not disagree in essence. They too, as good classicists, identified progress with the mystery of capital accumulation. However, the process, according to the Marxist interpretation, was one of exploitation of the poor by the rich, who appropriated, by means of private property, the wealth created by the poor. Although this was an essential stage in the evolution of economic society, it was a temporary one. Because of the alleged inherent contradictions, and given the inverted Hegelian dialectic, the system would eventually collapse and be superseded by the economic millennium. Whatever their differences, Marxists and neo-classicists were agreed that poverty was an essential element of a capitalist economy. But in both views, it was a passing phase with a promise of something better in the future. Neither theory held much promise for the present.

Alfred Marshall had a few suggestions concerning poverty which he passed on for what they were worth. They were given more in the form of casual, off-hand suggestions than as hopeful ways out.[4] He suggested that education would improve the skills of the poor and hence their productivity. He also sanctioned certain public health and housing standards. And he argued that a small increase in the income of the poor yielded more than commensurate satisfaction. This was, of course, because the marginal satisfaction of an additional mouthful of bread to the poor exceeded by far that of an additional mouthful to the rich. But Marshall was unenthusiastic about a minimum wage and argued its disemployment effect. And he did feel that any major redistribution of income was dangerous to the initiative and high spirits of the entrepreneurial class.

But the Marxists were probably even less hopeful in the short run. The ameliorative suggestions of the neo-classicist were looked upon as "bourgeois reform." By reducing the misery of the proletariat in the short run, they would delay that time when the proletariat would overthrow the system. However, given the inevitable fall of surplus value, the eventual overthrow of the system could not be avoided. Reform had nothing to contribute save perpetuation of a system of exploitation for longer than it would otherwise have survived.

Some part of the confusion concerning the sources of progress and poverty is attributable to the failure to note the two-pronged nature of the problem itself. Although Smith and Ricardo both seemed to be discussing poverty – or wealth, if you prefer – they were each writing on two different problems. Edwin Cannan, several decades ago, pointed clearly to this whole issue in his very useful definition of the "fundamental questions of economics." He did so in the preface of the first edition of *Wealth*, which it is appropriate to quote at this point:

> The really fundamental questions of economics are why all of us, taken together, are as well off – or as ill off, if that way of putting it be preferred – as we are and why some of us are much better off and others much worse off than the average.[5]

This definition of the "fundamental questions of economics" seems to point directly to the structure and organization of society itself. And in doing so it seems also to open the way to an effective analysis of poverty.

All cultures and hence all economies may be characterized by the major tools and concomitant skills by virtue of which they secure a livelihood. In fact, the anthropologist has, from almost the beginning of anthropology, classified societies on the basis of the tools which seem to predominate. The distinction between Paleolithic and Neolithic cultures is based on tools. Advanced agrarian and handicraft cultures are distinguished from industrial cultures by the tools they use. It is possible thus to speak of salmon cultures, buffalo cultures, tuber cultures, and hunting and gathering cultures. And in doing so it is clearly intended to make a distinction on the basis of the predominant tools which are used to secure the salmon, the buffalo, the tuber, and roots and berries. For example, the Plains Indians were primarily hunters of roots and berries and possessed a crude, digging-stick agriculture until such time as they secured the horse, apparently by accident, from the Spanish conquistadores.[6] Having secured this new instrument, they found it possible to make the buffalo a major object of their food quest. Thus the economy itself is said to have been transformed by virtue of the horse.

As Veblen would have put it, the answer to Cannan's question of "why all of us, taken together, are as well off" as we happen to be is to be found in the state of the industrial arts. As we advance our industrial arts, all of us, taken together, live on a more elegant level than was previously the case. Not all benefit equally from such an advance, but, as Clarence Ayres has remarked, even the slaves in a slaveholding culture benefit from a general advance in the industrial arts.

The significance of the industrial arts, or of the entire technological process, has been overlooked by the mainstream of economics. All economists have conceded that there is some connection between levels of living and the state of the industrial arts, but most have failed to see its full significance because they have viewed technology purely as things. Hence they have sought elsewhere than in the tool process itself for the accumulation of tools. The perennial quest has been for the source of the capital, with capital accumulation seen as a by-product of some other activity – fund accumulation.

The implication has been given, even if not intended, that fund accumulation is identical to or simultaneous with tool creation, although the tool-creation process itself has been neglected by economists. Unfortunately, the economist has been led off on a chase to locate the source of the funds. The economic historian, for example, has become almost obsessed with the question of the locus of the funds which set off "the industrial revolution." The role of funds has been obscured along with the tool process. If the term "fund accumulation" had been used rather than "capital accumulation," the confusion might have been reduced; certainly it more clearly points to the true role of funds in any culture. Fund accumulation enables the accumulation of ownership and the appropriation of artifacts or the rights to their exclusive use. This is the case, for instance, with the exclusive right to the use of a certain fish weir within a fish culture or with a patent right to the exclusive use of a glass-bottle machine within an industrial culture. Before ownership or exclusive use can be conferred, there must be something already technologically feasible on which ownership can be conferred.

The recognition of the primacy of technology has been long in coming, but there are signs of an increasing awareness among some economists. Veblen attempted to redirect our attention to the tool process itself. In recent decades, and particularly since Keynes' *General Theory*, we have begun to realize that anything which is technologically feasible can be funded.[7] In fact, a thing's technological feasibility is prior to its funding. The latter is merely an act which gives the technological process institutional sanction; it has much the same function as a Papal blessing prior to undertaking a medieval crusade.

But technology is a social process and as such it is autochthonous. It advances by virtue of tool combination or invention. Within a particular culture, in contrast to the sum total of human cultures, technology may also be advanced by diffusion or borrowing. Its advancement is made by men who put things together in new combinations. And as technology advances, so does the sum total of human skills. As V. Gordon Childe pointed out, man makes himself: "Human history reveals man creating new industries and new economies that have furthered the increase of his species and thereby vindicated its enhanced fitness."[8]

Modern technology or tool behavior is continuous with that which preceded it. The modern advances in nuclear physics and in space flight are continuous from the *coup de poing* [hand-ax] and the spear-thrower or atlatl of Paleolithic technology. The difference between the level of living of the Arunta near Alice Springs in Australia and the level of living of the participants in American culture today is one explainable in terms of the possession of and access to tool skills. That Edwin Cannan was well aware of this fact is evident in his very perceptive essay "Capital and the Heritage of Improvement," in which he notes:

> A characteristic of man which seems to divide him from the other animals is a certain flair for improvement. The other animals alter their habits and alter the materials used in the construction and furnishing of their homes – which we call their "nests" – to suit changes in environment; but they do not seem to have any capacity for adopting, as time goes on, better methods and securing greater quantity or better quality things which they require to satisfy their needs. Man alone seems, for the most part at any rate, to possess the power and the will to improve and make his surroundings more suitable for his purposes from age to age.[9]

Just why man grows two grains of wheat where but one grew before is probably an unanswerable question. And it probably does not need an answer. All we know is that the tool process, by virtue of which we have advanced our level of living, has been characteristic of the human enterprise since the beginning of time. It is one of the major dimensions of being man. In fact, the fossilized remains of early man are indistinguishable from his simian ancestors. We take the existence of tools as evidence for the existence of man.[10]

Thus, the differences in levels of living are differences in tool skills. And the differences in tool skills are themselves traceable to natural causes, to the vagaries of geographic isolation, and to institutionally induced social isolation so that diffusion was either physically restricted or institutionally prohibited. The lagged state of tool development among the Aborigines of Australia is usually ascribed to geographic isolation, at least until recent centuries, when social isolation probably became a more significant element. The case of the Amish peoples in southeastern Pennsylvania is one of social isolation.

Some nations now struggling consciously to develop an industrial economy are running up against the limitations to a full utilization of modern technology which are imposed by sovereignty, an institutionally derived vestigial remain. The industrial economy does not recognize such institutional barriers. And as Wendell Gordon has pointed out, some national boundaries inhibit and make impossible the taking of full advantage of modern industrial arts.[11] Some national boundaries are too constricting for a full employment of the most advanced industrial arts. But whatever the explanation for these differences among nations, it is the differential possession of the heritage of improvement which explains the varying levels of living which prevail among the world's peoples.

Economists today, especially those working in the underdeveloped economies, are becoming increasingly aware of these facts. Of course, there are still those who define the problem of economic development in terms of fund accumulation and asceticism in the true classical tradition. This is despite the fact that those about whom they write already possess the requisites for development in the classic manner – a few rich capital accumulators on one hand and a mass of consumers at and below the poverty line on the other. But other economists more frequently define the problem of development in terms of the struggle between the introduction of new technology and the resistance caused by ancient and honorable institutions.

It was noted earlier that the problem of poverty is two-pronged. Our discussion thus far has been devoted to only one facet of the question: the differential levels of living which prevail among the people of the world. Our explanation of this phenomenon in terms of access to and possession of tool skills does little to explain the differential levels of living which prevail within various cultures. In other words, we have not addressed ourselves to Cannan's second fundamental question of "why some of us are much better off and others much worse off than the average."

Standard theory has devoted much time to this question. It is possible to argue that those who have worked in the tradition of Adam Smith have been largely concerned with the first of Cannan's two fundamental questions while those working in the Ricardian tradition have been concerned largely with the second. We know that in every culture, including the most unsophisticated technologically, some individuals seem to fare better than others. There is relative poverty in all.

The classicist, following Malthus and Ricardo, attempted to explain this type of poverty in terms of the pressure of population. The iron law of wages seemed to indicate that poverty was a function of the tendency of the masses to breed up to the maximum allowed by subsistence. This was looked upon as a natural law. Some of the current specialists in development economics have dusted this explanation off and are reapplying it to the existence of relative poverty in so-called underdeveloped countries. But for this reincarnation, this explanatory law would be of only historic interest. However, this argument always exempted the rich from any such breeding potentialities, and, in doing so, it failed to answer why certain occupations were perennially cursed with the stigma of poverty. For instance, why are the bhangis [low-caste Indians who clean latrines or handle dead bodies] of India, since their function is essential to health and well-being and the very existence of the group at large, confined to such an inferior level of living? Why are they, rather than the maharajahs, maintained on such a poverty level? Or to ask the same question in our own culture, why are garbage collectors maintained on such a low level of living in contrast to medical doctors? In a more general way, why must certain occupations bear the burden of poverty while others live in superfluity? The population doctrine will not give a satisfactory answer.

Neo-classicism attempted to satisfy this question by the marginal-productivity argument, much of which, in a qualified form, is still in use today. But this argument probably raises as many questions as it seemingly answers. For one thing, as usually given, it is circular. The wage is taken as the measure of marginal productivity, about which nothing is known except as it manifests itself in the wage or income.[12] The theory, although circular, is greatly attractive: it seems to indicate that each person receives exactly as he contributes. Thus, the rich are such because of their great contribution to the whole product and the poor are such because of their inferior contribution. It is, as such, an ethical doctrine since it seems to indicate that we receive in the same proportion as we give. It satisfies all the requirements of social reciprocity. It indicates that the present society is indeed a just one. Perhaps this unconscious appeal to justice, rather than any inherent logic, perpetuates this doctrine in economic theory. But assuming that the doctrine is correct, it begs the question of why each should receive in accordance with what he produces. Since we consume in family units, by and large, why should the incompetence of the fathers be visited upon the sons, yea, unto the seventh generation?

Since it is the community through the market mechanism which evaluates the productivity of these contributions, recourse to the theory of marginal productivity leads merely to more difficult questions. Since garbage must be collected and carrots must be dug, the theory does not explain why the community places such a low valuation on garbage collection and carrot-digging. In other words, why should ditch-digging, technologically essential in an industrial economy, stigmatize the ditch-digger and hence socially justify his poverty? None of the economic reasoning thus far has been of any help in settling these questions. Yet they are ones which must be answered if we are to eliminate utter, degrading poverty, as we have indicated we intend to do by the current war on poverty.

The answers seem to be locatable. Modern social theory indicates that every known society has been characterized by some system of ranking. And these ranking schemes seem to have, in all cases, an economic dimension. The ceremonial roles assigned to each individual in some way predetermine his level of income and hence his level of consumption. Throughout history, mankind has devoted much effort to keeping the poor in their place. And this place is circumscribed by an inferior receipt of income.

As long ago as *The Theory of the Leisure Class*, Veblen tied together both a theory of consumption and one of production. He indicated that occupations differ in the degree of meritoriousness with which they are viewed by the populace at large. Certain tasks are looked upon as highly honorific while others are stigmatized as unworthy. Some tasks are viewed as exploit and others as drudgery. The activities which are seen as exploit are those in which the active agent is alleged to move mysterious forces which can only be so moved by an individual who himself possesses a superior mysterious force. Thus, the hunt, warfare, and religion carry great prestige for those most successful in these activities, thereby demonstrating that they possess vast amounts of spiritual force, or *mana* as the Polynesians and certain of the Melanesian peoples designate this alleged attribute. Those who tend to the matter-of-fact everyday affairs of the group, the practitioners of well-recognized tool skills, are looked down upon as possessing little in the way of spiritual force. Their activities are explainable in matter-of-fact terms and are easily demonstrated.

This distinction and gradation among occupations serves also as the basis for a differential flow of income. In view of the great mysterious force he exercises over the growth of taros, it is only right and good that the largest share of the taro crop should flow to the chief of Ornarakana.[13] Similarly, the king should live in Versailles and the maharajah own a Taj Mahal. The differential flow of income must be put in evidence, as Veblen indicated. But what many readers of *The Theory of the Leisure Class* have missed is the fact that the inferior consumption of the lower grades must be in evidence no less than is the superior consumption of the highest grades. The conspicuous consumption of the rich would have little meaning if the inferior consumption of the poor were not also conspicuous.

We are apt to read about status aspects of culture, the caste system of India and the marked distinction of rank among some of the Polynesian peoples, for example, and ignore this aspect of our own culture. After all, we are a sophisticated culture presumably beyond such elementary beliefs, the obvious condition of the Negro notwithstanding. But C. E. Ayres has very effectively pointed out that such is not the case:

> This sort of thing may seem at first to be utterly remote from modern life, but students of the social sciences are agreed that it is not. Modern society has inherited these ways of thinking and acting from ancient society, and they comprise a very large part of ordinary behavior. The evidence of this is by no means limited to ceremonial expressions such as that of the public official who prefaces his declarations with the words, "By virtue of the

authority vested in me." The whole system of status rests on the assumption that the different orders of society possess different degrees of mystic potency. It would be quite intolerable otherwise. A belief on the part of both whites and Negroes in some sort of ineffable difference is essential to the maintenance of the color line and unquestionably will continue so long as the line exists. The difference is one of mystic potency to which the investigations of geneticists, ethnologists, sociologists, and others, are quite irrelevant; and the same is true of the rich and the poor."[14]

All of this scheme of ranking implies a set of culturally defined roles.[15] The alleged *mana* of an individual in whatever role is not primary in ascertaining the status position of that role. The king, no matter who occupies the throne, is always at the top of the status pyramid. And this is no less true of the corporate president and his academic counterpart. We do not alter the ranking of the roles in accordance with the alleged *mana* of those occupying them. If a high-status role is momentarily occupied by a time-server, we do not place that role below those to which it has by tradition been assumed to be superior. It is the role which carries the mystic potency and this is conveyed to the new occupant by virtue of the rite which sanctions his occupancy.

In some cultures the scheme of roles may be quite unelaborate while in others it may be very extensive and ever present. A small village culture, because of its very size, will possess a less extensive system of roles than that which exists in a large culture coterminous with a national state. For example, the role system in the United States is more elaborate than that of Tikopia. But a role system exists in each culture.

It should also be made clear that this does not imply that every role in as elaborate a culture as the United States can be ranked from the highest to the lowest. But within one segment of the social order the roles may be ranked with some degree of confidence.[16] Given such a scheme of status relationships, it should not be surprising that income distribution patterns are not subject to startling change over fairly long periods of time. Despite the often-made statement that through the progressive income tax the rich in the United States have been reduced to the level to which the poor have been elevated because of welfare payments, the income distribution figures do not indicate vast changes.[17] The same has been found for England by Richard M. Titmuss.[18]

Barbara Wootton in her investigation of wage determination in England found that, in the period she studied, everyone's income had gone up; but at the end of the period all incomes, relative to one another, were in essentially the same places they had been at the beginning. In this study she devoted her attention to the wage-determination process in various occupations. By studying wage determination in practice, she found that it was tied to the social ordering of various roles. Between two occupations a certain wage differential was acceptable, but if it became larger, efforts were made to reduce it, and if it became smaller, efforts were made to enlarge it. All occupations were linked in the manner of the chain links in a coat of mail. The result was a remarkably stable pattern of income distribution.[19]

The system of status thus sanctions certain roles which are looked down upon as demeaning, and even loathsome and untouchable, as are the bhangis of India. A group feels it only right and good that they should receive income and hence consume on a level commensurate with their status. Sumptuary laws were used in feudal times to maintain each in that station in life befitting his calling.[20] Although we no longer have sumptuary laws and do not punish the pauper in the Cadillac, income distribution does a fairly effective job of keeping each at his appropriate consumption level.

And it is this whole structure plus its reinforcing sentiment, myth, and legend which maintains poverty in the midst of plenty. One can hear and read almost every day the legends which testify to the shiftlessness and lack of moral fiber characteristic of the welfare client. The success of the war on poverty hinges upon whether we can cut around this vestigial remain from the feudal status system just sufficiently to get people over the poverty line, at whatever figure it happens to be drawn. It is all well and good to raise the skills of the populace; but even if all have master's degrees there are still carrots to be dug and garbage to be removed.[21] The stumbling block status and proper differentials remain. Since goods are used as symbols of status, the acquisition of goods indicative of a higher status than that actually occupied threatens the worthiness of those occupying the status emulated. In other words, those in the higher-status category for which the goods are traditionally sanctioned may feel that those emulating them are not properly keeping their place. We like the poor as long as they maintain their place, and staying in their place means perpetuating those levels of living which signify their station in life. As John Ise once stated facetiously in a public address, "We must not debauch the poor!"

The answer to the problem of poverty will be well on the way to solution when we answer the question: Why must the garbage collector be paid so little? Why must the bhangis of India still be among the untouchables of the world? More generally, why must there be occupations which denote untouchability?

These are questions that are pertinent to both categories of poverty to that among societies as well as that within an affluent society. Gunnar Myrdal has argued that the rich nations are getting relatively richer and the poor, relatively poorer. But even the solution of this problem is blocked by the institutional structure or status arrangements. Any solution would involve introducing new industrial arts. And new industrial arts threaten an established system of status as sanctioned by ownership and symbolized by consumption. Charles Wagley, in his study of a small Amazon town and its development, made the point very well when he summed up the situation of poverty and absence of growth in the Amazon:

Never in its history has the best of Western Technology been available to the people of the Valley. Never has Amazon man had the use of knowledge and skills available in more advanced regions for exploitation and control of the physical world. The lack of technical equipment, the emphasis upon an extractive economy, a rigid class system and other social and cultural factors have combined to keep the Amazon a backward area. These factors have always been greater barriers to change than the Amazon climate or soil, or the so-called tropical diseases. There are man-made barriers, and not immutable barriers which would make the development of the Amazon Valley impossible.[22]

Economic science has thus far been singularly unimpressed by these man-made barriers. The economist has concentrated on physical laws of production and consumption, to the almost total exclusion of social forces in their institutional and technological manifestations. But the problem of poverty will not yield an answer until translated into its institutional and technological dimensions.

Notes

1 Joseph Wood Crutch, *Human Nature and the Human Condition*, New York, 1959.
2 For expositions of this point of view, see Frederick Lewis Allen, *The Big Change*, New York, 1952; and David Riesman, Nathan Glazer, and Reuel Denney, *The Lonely Crowd*, New Haven, 1950.
3 See, for example, James N. Morgan, Martin H. David, Wilbur J. Cohen, and Harvey E. Brazer, *Income and Welfare in the United States*, New York, 1962; Gabriel Kolko, *Wealth and Power in America*, New York, 1962; Michael Harrington, *The Other America*, New York, 1963; Harry M. Caudill, *Night Comes to the Cumberlands*, Boston, 1963; Ben H. Bagdikian, *In the Midst of Plenty*, New York, 1964; Herman P. Miller, *Rich Man, Poor Man*, New York, 1964; Nathan Glazer and Daniel Patrick Moynihan, *Beyond the Melting Pot*, Cambridge, Mass., 1963; Leon H. Keyserling, *Progress or Poverty*, Washington, D.C., 1964; Edgar May, *The Wasted Americans*, New York, 1965; *Economic Report of the President, 1964 and 1965*, Washington, D.C., 1964 and 1965.
4 Alfred Marshall, *Principles of Economics*, 8th ed., London, 1920, pp. 712–20.
5 *Wealth: A Brief Explanation of the Causes of Economic Welfare*, 3rd ed., London, 1946, p. v.
6 Robert Lowie, *Indians of the Plains*, 1963 ed., Garden City, N.Y., 1963, pp. 42–6.
7 David Bazelon in *The Paper Economy* (New York, 1963) did valiant service in emphasizing this point. Stuart Chase in *Money to Grow On* (New York, 1964) repeatedly makes the point that if something is technologically feasible it can be financed.
8 *Man Makes Himself*, Thinkers' Library Edition, London, 1948, p. 15.
9 *Economica*, November 1934, pp. 381–2. In this essay, Cannan independently comes to much the same conclusion concerning the meaning of capital as did Veblen in his two essays, "On the Nature of Capital," reprinted in *The Place of Science in Modern Civilization*, New York, 1919.
10 L. S. B. Leakey, *Adam's Ancestors*, New York, 1960.
11 *International Trade*, New York, 1958, pp. 558–62.
12 J. A. Hobson, *Free Thought in the Social Sciences*, New York, 1926, part II, chap. III; C. E. Ayres, *The Problem of Economic Order*, New York, 1938, pp. 50–4.
13 Bronislaw Malinowski, *Coral Gardens and Their Magic*, New York, 1935, vol. 1.
14 *The Theory of Economic Progress*, New York, 1962, p. 166.
15 For a clear discussion of this concept, see Walter Goldschmidt, *Man's Way*, New York, 1959, pp. 81–90.
16 See, for example, Hortense Powdermaker, *Hollywood, the Dream Factory*, Boston, 1950. In this study an anthropologist examines the status hierarchy of Hollywood.

17 Kolko in *Wealth and Power in America*. Miller in *Rich Man, Poor Man* took issue with some of Kolko's assertions, but his own data also indicate that we are far from the "income revolution."

18 *Income Distribution and Social Change*, London, 1962.

19 Barbara Wootton, *The Social Foundations of Wage Policy*, London, 1955.

20 Frances Elizabeth Baldwin, *Sumptuary Legislation and Personal Regulation in England*, Baltimore, 1926.

21 Recently the *New York Times* carried an account of a successful educational program in New York City which enabled some kitchen helpers to qualify as cooks and chefs. Some who had previously been vegetable scrapers were now cooks in prominent restaurants. The point of the article was how, through training, the unskilled were raised to skilled occupations. But assuming that the vegetables are still being scraped by someone who has taken the place of the previous scrapers and that vegetable scraping is still just as unremunerative as before, the poverty level remains. The real question is why vegetable scrapers must be rewarded at a poverty level. Why must the minimum wage be pitched at $3,300 a year? *New York Times*, "Program Offers Future for Cooks," Sunday, April 18, 1965.

22 *Amazon Town: A Study of Man in the Tropics*, New York, 1964, p. 289 (italics in the original).

12 The U.S. economy

The disadvantages of having taken the lead

Review of Institutional Thought, vol. 2 (December 1982), pp. 1–13

COMMENTARY BY WILLIAM M. DUGGER

This is institutionalist storytelling that puts social theories and events in their historical context and leads to broader insights into the human condition. Hamilton describes the origin, nature, and result of the social malaise that drove the United States off course in the 1980s. He explains that the loss of the two wars that the United States had started in the 1960s left the majority of Americans with an abiding cynicism toward government.

President Lyndon Johnson had declared war on poverty and set a goal of ending the poverty level of living by 1976. With enough resources and with the right changes, the goal could have been met, but the resources were not provided and the changes were not made. The war on poverty was lost. The war in Vietnam was lost as well. The War on Poverty should have taught us that poverty was deeply embedded in the social structure and to eliminate it, we would have to change the social structure that supported it.

Instead of learning practical lessons from the war on poverty or from the war in Vietnam, most Americans came to believe that government was largely ineffective. This has led to a return to laissez-faire economics. Now Americans blame all problems on a government that has grown too large and powerful, and place all their faith in a return to the market. Hamilton warned in 1982 that they were wrong. He was right.

THE U.S. ECONOMY: THE DISADVANTAGES OF HAVING TAKEN THE LEAD

Much of the decade of the 1960s and all of that of the 1970s were very frustrating for the American people. It has been fifteen years of bad news without much good news to offset the stress created by the bad. Some of the causes of the frustration have been real; some of them have been imagined. But paranoia and depression can be brought on by either real or imagined causes. To the victim, both have an equal validity.

Undoubtedly the marketing of news is a factor in the general feeling of frustration. The competition for an audience, especially on television, leads purveyors of news, if not to manufacture the product, to put a crisis emphasis even on events and circumstances which represent problems on the way to solution or disappearance. Routine affairs, both domestic and foreign, are treated with an amount of solemnity and gravity that the occasions hardly warrant. This daily and weekly bearing of sad tidings is conducive to perpetual social paranoia. People otherwise not disposed to more than average worry conclude that things must truly be bad, just as the news media indicate.

But even without the efforts of the news-people to secure an audience, sufficient events have occurred to discourage some of the most hearty. We began two wars in the 1960s, neither one of which could be said to have been won. One of these, Viet Nam, was the traditional war taking a heavy toll in human life. The other, the War on Poverty, was a non-traditional one to prevent the heavy human toll from social and economic deprivation.

In their own ways, each of these wars contributed to the present cynicism toward government action to solve any kind of problem. The government during several administrations, and despite substantial opposition, persisted in Viet Nam in a hopeless undertaking. It was possible to succeed only by destroying that which was presumably being saved. The solution was far worse than losing the war. Long after this became apparent to the mass of the people, the government persisted single-mindedly in prosecuting a losing war. Rather than condemn the administrations specifically responsible for this persistence, it seemed much easier mentally to conclude that government per se was at fault. The war was not the product of certain bungling and bunglers; the problem was government. Ironically, on this ground, the liberals, who largely opposed the Viet Nam war, joined cheek to jowl with the conservative vested interests, who have always been against government, especially when its actions have been beneficial to the general welfare, an effort that liberals traditionally uphold.

The war on poverty began with high hopes. Sargent Shriver, the first director of the war on poverty, declared at its inception the admirable purpose to eliminate the poverty level of living by 1976. That the war on poverty would not eliminate the poverty level of living was almost foregone at its inception. What the poor need is money. The war on poverty was so designed as to give them everything but money. They were to be trained for jobs, largely nonexistent as it turned out, and certainly not relevant to a large part of the poverty population, the senior citizens and the children and youth and their guardians, largely female. Certainly there is nothing wrong with providing people with skills and opportunities to use them. Unfortunately, the skills provided the poor were not matched with the opportunities to use them.

A real war on poverty would transform income in such a fashion as to eliminate the poverty level of living. Doing so would also stimulate the economy so that the increased demand would provide the opportunities for employment.

During World War II, when we operated the economy at the highest level we ever achieved before or after, the problem of poverty was minimal. The war on poverty failed, by virtue of misdiagnosis of the disease at its onset. That is not to say that the great middle class would have been receptive to transferring any more income than it was to the limited war on poverty. Nevertheless, something that set out with very high hopes achieved only limited success. In 1976, as today, we still have the poverty level of living. Those with little staying power declared the objectives unattainable, a conclusion joined enthusiastically by those who always find the poor themselves offensive. That the high goals of the war on poverty were not met lends credence to the cliché that problems cannot be solved by "throwing money at them." Government is twice discredited; automobile bumpers disport stickers such as "Make Organized Crime Not Pay: Turn It Over To The Federal Government."

The disenchantment with federal government has its counterpart at the local level. New York City is the prime example, and, being our largest city and supposedly our capitol for many things other than government, attracts a nationwide attention and becomes symbolic for the alleged "collapse of our cities." Clever phrases, such as "New York is ungovernable," are given a credence that leads to serious discussion as to whether it is or is not. The real plight of New York and other cities similarly situated is wholly ignored in a mood of unwarranted cynicism. Actually, New York's problems are largely financial ones that relate to the fact that the governmental and taxing unit is not coterminous with the Metropolitan area. The real problem is how to ungovern, if it may be put that way, the municipal, county, and state satrapies that cut and divide one area calling for one government. Until this problem of local sovereignty is recognized as an institutional barrier to effective metropolitan government, New York's problems will not be on their way to solution.

We have other metropolitan areas suffering from a similar situation, including Boston, Pittsburgh, and Cleveland. All of them have central city areas, losing population to the escape hatches in the suburbs, and all suffering from urban neglect. Ironically, a long-standing sentiment against "large" government precludes a solution to the problem, which is a nagging contributor to a more general despair of government. In short, the sentiment is self-fulfilling. Local government cannot govern simply because it is local.

The environment is despoiled. That the environment has been despoiled in the sense it has been altered has been true since man the tool-maker arrived on the scene. Having been born and partially reared in the Pittsburgh region, I can well remember when I took it for granted that air had a sulfurous odor. Since those times we have come to recognize new sources of air and water pollution brought about by the very new industries that were allegedly to be our salvation. The promise of a new life, free from the filth and pollution of what Lewis Mumford referred to as the Paleotechnic period of technical development, does not seem to have materialized. New environmental problems exist today that provoke nostalgia for an idealized past when no such problems existed. And there is truth to the nostalgia, to the extent that our contemporary experimental problems did not exist; but environmental problems did. Nevertheless, the new concern over the environment, which in truth is a hopeful sign, contributes to the general state of despondency.

According to much of the thinking of the last century, the United States and the North American continent in general represented a boundless resource cornucopia. The contrived oil shortages of the 1970s rather starkly called attention to our dependency upon known resources in general and emphasized that non-renewable resources had a life expectancy that would not sustain the boundless cornucopia view. The observation that we were not "energy self-sufficient" had an effect on our morale somewhat analogous to that which occurred in England in the decade of the 1790s when that nation became generally cognizant of the fact that it was no longer "food self-sufficient." This latter recognition is partially what led to the Malthusian population doctrine and gave impetus and meaning to the corn law controversy, a controversy that today seems tedious and dull. That resources are defined by the state of the industrial arts is much more difficult to comprehend than that some particular substance, for the moment a critical resource, is limited in amount. Projectionists – and who does not enjoy applying linear regressions to phenomena to demonstrate the year of the Apocalypse? – in the masquerade of science have a field day. Actually, our new awareness of resource conservation, like our new awareness of environmental pollution, is a hopeful sign. But, unfortunately, it too has contributed to the general malaise.

Our dependence upon importing resources, which we always had, but not to the same degree as Holland, Belgium, England, Sweden, Norway, Denmark, and Japan, all of which have somehow managed to survive, has given us a problem in our balance of payments. The payments problem is evidence of the fact that the international trade sector of our national income and product accounts is relatively more important than it once was. We have come of age. We just may have lasting nagging problems of payment on somewhat the same relative scale as those nations mentioned above. But to people in Peoria or Kankakee or Muleshoe, who never knew there was such a thing as a balance of international payments, here is a new, frightening problem.

To some, the problem of international payments is a function of a loss of productivity. The productivity of the American worker was a legend. The perspicacity and enterprise by virtue of which the legendary captains of industry managed and organized that productivity made America the workshop of the world in the twentieth century as England was alleged to have been in the nineteenth. During World War II we were the "arsenal of democracy." To the conventional mind, something is wrong with today's American working man. You just cannot get any good and faithful servants any more! They just do not work as hard as they used to! Trade unions are most frequently pointed to as the cause of reduced productivity. And it is contended that American working men have become too content, too well off. They expect too much. We all need to put on the hair shirt and get down to work. To all of us who have been told about the new life of leisure that modern technology promised, the outlook is grim indeed.

With our new dependence on the rest of the world and our loss of productivity is a belief that we no longer lead the world. Henry Luce's "American Century" has turned to ashes. We have lost the world. The fact that it was never ours to lose does nothing to deter those who wish to despair over the loss. After all, the fact that China was never ours did not deter those who insisted that it had been lost through duplicity and treason. Their enthusiasm in searching out the responsible agents for the loss was not diminished one whit by the fact that nothing had been lost, any more than the enthusiasm of the hunters of the Loch Ness monster was ever diminished by its non-existence. Non-existence cannot be proven, which, to those of great faith, means that the existence of that in which they have faith, is real.

Last in this tale of woe, we are beset by both inflation and unemployment, a condition which the vaunted Phillips curve testifies cannot be. Like the Loch Ness monster, there are those who say the Phillips curve is still there, but lurking somewhere over to the right. "Tradeoff" is a word that just does not seem to be around any more.

All of these real as well as alleged events have brought on a new despair and even cynicism concerning the decade ahead. It is all a kind of failure of nerve.

Gilbert Murray, a renowned classic scholar early in this century [the twentieth century], wrote of a failure of nerve in Greek society. This was a period that followed the great classic period of Aristotle and Sophocles and was most marked in the early Christian writers prominent in the first two centuries A.D. He wrote of the difference that characterized these later writers and teachers as

> ... a rise of asceticism, of mysticism, in a sense of pessimism; a loss of self-confidence, of hope in this life and of faith in normal human effort; a despair of patient inquiry, a cry for infallible revelation; an indifference to the welfare of the state, a conversion of the soul to God. It is an atmosphere in which the aim of the good man is not so much to live justly, to help this society to which he belongs and enjoy the esteem of his fellow creatures; but rather, by means of a burning faith, by contempt for the world and its standards, by ecstasy, suffering, and martyrdom, to be granted pardon for his unspeakable unworthiness, his immeasurable sins. There is an intensifying of certain spiritual emotions; an increase of sensitiveness, a failure of nerve.[1]

In the last century [the nineteenth] something like this was experienced by the Indian people of the Great Basin and the Plains. Buffeted on all sides by the invasion of the whites, by the extension of the railroads, and by the disappearance of control over those factors by means of which they secured a livelihood, such as the buffalo, despair took hold. In this atmosphere the Ghost Dance phenomenon spread among them in the 1870s and down into the 1890s. It represented an attempt by performance of the Ghost Dance ritual to return to the ways of the ancestors. It was a promise that the whites would disappear and life would once again assume the idealized form it allegedly had once possessed.

A somewhat similar phenomenon occurred among the peoples of the north coast of New Guinea and in the Admiralty Islands following World War II. These peoples had their lives disrupted by the Japanese invasion and occupation and then further disturbed by the subsequent invasion and occupation of the Allies. A kind of despair took hold and what was known as the Cargo Cult promised a way out by a return to an idealized past that probably never existed. The promise was to the effect that if they would return to the ritual purity of the past a great fleet would appear on the horizon bringing all kinds of wondrous things.

The climate of opinion in the United States has changed in somewhat the same fashion over the past two decades. The decade of the 1960s began with new hope and determination to overcome what economic and social problems beset us. It was the time of the New Frontier and a new faith in human intelligence and in human action. We were masters of our own destinies. We could solve the problems that confronted us. And all without dogma and revelation.

To some people today that viewpoint seems to be arrogance. A general despair seems to characterize our thoughts about the human condition. Catch phrases such as "New York is ungovernable" get an unwarranted ready acceptance. Inflation and employment are considered to be problems for which there is no intelligent solution. Government in general is looked upon as hopeless; government employees are viewed with contempt. There is an urge to turn to an idealized past and to scuttle much that has been constructed in the twentieth century.

Cults flourish. They run the gamut from innocent little health cults to the bizarre cult that took a terrible toll in Guyana. Things of the intellect are discounted; emotions and feelings are extolled. Human intellect is denied; gut reactions are prized. Discredited ideas of the last century are dusted off, such as supply-side economics, and presented much in the same manner as the many faces of Richard Nixon. Science and technology are denigrated; revelation is viewed as the way to warranted belief.

This despair is partially understandable in view of the total experience of the American people between 1960 and now. But most of it is not understandable in terms of any real deterioration in life styles, because such a real deterioration just has not taken place. For example, although not the last word, disposable per capita personal income nearly doubled over that period and, at least through 1979, had continued to inch upwards. This is in real terms, meaning that, despite inflation, life in general was not deteriorating insofar as it is measured by disposable personal income.

The attitude now prevalent, among liberals as well as conservatives, is much like the cynicism that prevailed in the Weimar Republic in Germany in the 1920s and early 1930s. Having a government they felt had been foisted upon them by the Treaty of Versailles, a government blamed for the runaway inflation of 1923, a government seemingly incapable of coping with the great depression of the early 1930s, the Germans, especially the lower middle class, turned to the nostrums peddled by the Nazis. They sought scapegoats for their problems, the Communists, Socialists, and Jews; they sought panaceas that would solve all problems for eternity. They took to a government that promised to get things done and a philosophy that appealed to an alleged greatness that existed in the past. Those days would return if they but adhered to the rather simple nostrums and ceremonies offered by the Nazis.

While not ignoring the fascist elements in American society, we are not today about to be taken over by the American Nazi Party or a reasonable facsimile. But in our despair, largely unwarranted, we are being offered nostrums from the nineteenth century that will, we are assured, solve all of our economic and social problems. If we but take certain simple actions, if we forgo the behavior by which we have deviated from the "truths" of the past, life will become a thing of beauty and a joy forever. To get there, as with all such prophecies, we must bear a period of suffering or sacrifice. The virtues of the hair shirt are touted.

In economics we are offered doctrines that stem from the middle of the last century when the Manchester School of economics reigned supreme in England, when the gospel of wealth was being preached in the United States by such as Andrew Carnegie in the business world and William Graham Sumner in the academic, and when Herbert Spencer offered the last word on "the survival of the fittest" and laissez-faire. The simplicity of these doctrines today is sometimes not apparent because of the self-assurance, credentials, and technical virtuosity of today's advocates.

What is being said is that we need to get back to an abiding faith in the market as the governor of our economic affairs. Supply-side economics is merely a set of policy recommendations that follows from the "free" market faith.

Faith in something called the "free market" has been an abiding one for the business community in the United States for decades. In a way, and especially in its popular form, it serves as justification for the primacy of the role of business in American society as well as an origin legend concerning how we came to have the particular form of economic life that now prevails. It emphasizes the supreme role of the business entrepreneur, the heroic accomplishments of entrepreneurial heroes of the past, Carnegie, Morgan, Rockefeller, Vanderbilt, and even Gould, Fiske, and Drew, three buccaneers correctly named "robber barons." Today it rationalizes and romanticizes the activities of the rather impersonal and faceless corporate officials who have assumed the role once occupied by the legendary captains of industry and finance of the past.

In the very opening sentence of his *Theory of Business Enterprise*, Veblen stated: "The material framework of modern civilization is the industrial system, and the directing force which animates this framework is business enterprise."[2] The theme of the book is an explanation of just how "investment for profit" frustrates and thwarts the most effective application of the machine process. As he went on to put it,

> The business man, especially the business man of wide and authoritative discretion, has become a controlling force in industry, because, through the mechanism of investments and markets, he controls the plants and processes, and these set the pace and determine the direction of movement for the rest.[3]

Unlike that of Veblen, the conventional interpretation of the economic development of the United States, as noted above, is essentially that which we find adequate to interpret the earlier "industrial revolution" in England of the eighteenth and early nineteenth century. T. S. Ashton's conventional and now classic account of those events, *The Industrial Revolution: 1760–1830*,[4] is hardly more than a panegyric to the entrepreneur operating under the divine guidance of the principles of investment for a profit. The accounts of both the new and old economic history of the United States are simply all extension of this conventional view of the American scene.

It is unfortunate that Veblen, in his *Absentee Ownership*,[5] did not devote his attention to answering the question concerning American industrial preeminence in the first quarter of the twentieth century that he asked concerning that of Germany. The technological difference between the United States in the first half, and perhaps even three-quarters, of the nineteenth century and Great Britain through the same period was even more marked than was that between Great Britain and Germany. Yet by the opening of World War I, the United States, as had Germany, had surpassed Great Britain technologically. The full implications of this were not commonly recognized until the early years of World War II and the years immediately after that war.

Had Veblen asked the question, there is no doubt the answer would have been much the same as that which he found in the case of Germany. We had all of the advantage of the technological borrower doubled in spades. Unlike Germany, we Americans were uninvited guests on a continent occupied by a people with a Neolithic, and in some cases Paleolithic, industrial art. No vestigial remains of a preceding industrial technology stood in the way of the most advanced application of the latest technology. It is more flattering to our sense of self-importance to attribute the accelerated technological development to some American *geist* or genius, a self-indulgence most peoples seem to allow themselves. But the veritable transmission belt for science and technology provided by the late-nineteenth-century parade of American youth to the centers of learning in England, Germany, and France is testimony to the conscious and deliberate borrowing on which American preeminence was built. Evidence of this dependence was to be found in the American graduate schools even after World War II in the almost rigid requirement that all graduate students acquire ceremonial adequacy in French and German, proficiency in English being presumed. Such proficiency supposedly gave access to the then known world of science and technology.

The United States in the latter half of the nineteenth century sent its youth to the most advanced centers of learning, just as the contemporary underdeveloped countries send their "finest" to the United States. The very structures of our universities bear evidence to this period of borrowing. Our undergraduate colleges, especially those catering to what are referred to as the humanities, operate more on the British system in spirit, if not organization. Our graduate and professional colleges, largely founded in the latter half of the nineteenth century, bear a heavy Germanic hand. An examination of Charles Singer's *A History of Technology*[6] reveals that, up to the opening of the twentieth century, the vaunted American contributions are rather modest ones indeed. While an English and Continental bias could be expected because of the locus of most of those who contributed to the volumes, there is no mistake in the general account. It is quite clear that Europe is where the technological action was located in the nineteenth century.

If we look at the American case in this fashion, our prodigious technological accomplishments of the twentieth century rose clearly on a borrowed base, no less than in the cases of Germany and Japan, both of which were recounted by Veblen. Ironically, we [i.e. Americans] obliged both Germany and Japan in this second half of the twentieth century by eliminating, during World War II, much of the obsolete technological system perpetuated by investment for a profit. Obsolete technology, protected from elimination or even improvement by ownership equities, found no such immunity from aerial bombardment and other means of physical destruction.

Through World War II we had no reason to question our technological dominance and therefore we had no reason to question long-established use and wont. The steel barons were content with their dominance of that industry. The automobile industry, hoisted on the petard of its own propaganda, was convinced that the American people demanded a built-in living room in their automobiles and that the demand, not of the automobile makers' creation, of course, was of genetic origin. The railroad barons moved the freight in World War II and were singularly confident in their capabilities, unimpressed with new ways and new techniques. They deliberately scuttled passenger traffic at a time when the motor-truck was cutting into their staple source of revenue; they refused to accommodate to an adjustment between railroading in its traditional form and the over-the-road truck. Our textile industry, faced with a textile revolution brought about by a chemical revolution, blamed all of their difficulties upon recalcitrant labor unions and moved south to so-called cheap labor. They were bested in that game by Korea, Formosa [Taiwan], and Japan, just as the Italian shoe industry undermined the obsolescent one of New England.

We are now showing the other side of Veblen's coin. We are now technological lenders. The advantages to the technological borrower turn out to the same extent to be eventual disadvantages to the one who initially took the lead. The lender has an extensive technological fabrication, only part of which is representative of the most advanced technological capabilities. Institutional considerations prohibit a full and unrestricted proliferation of technology, this inhibition in the modern industrial economies being worked largely by investment for a profit and the protection of ownership equities. As Veblen put it,

> All of this apparatus of conventions and standard usage, whether it takes the simpler form of use and wont or the settled character of legally competent enactment and common-law rule, necessarily has something of this effect of retardation in any given state of the industrial arts, and so necessarily acts in some degree to lower the net efficiency of the industrial system which it pervades. But this work of retardation is also backed by the like character

attaching to the material equipment by use of which the technological proficiency of the community takes effect. The equipment is also out of the past,
and it too lies under the dead-hand.[7]

The real problems that furnish some substantial basis for our present despondency largely derive from our beginning to lose the technological leadership. Our
problems with local government are largely attributable to an unwillingness to
experiment with new forms of municipal organization. Our problems with the
balance of payments, other than those largely deriving from oil, are substantially
attributable to a loss of technological leadership in a number of basic industries.
Our almost wholly irrational freight transportation system lays a burden on every
industry it touches. Our energy problems in general are aggravated by an unwillingness and inability to adapt quickly to new sources and new techniques. In
almost every case, down underneath, are the institutional barriers of investment
for a profit and the demands of ownership.

Our conventional diagnosis of our present dilemma is almost wholly wrong.
We are being told that business and industry are being strangled by burgeoning
government, especially on the federal level. This premise is almost never questioned even by the economics fraternity. Yet the facts are wholly at variance
with such an interpretation. The burgeoning federal work force has gone down
from 3.6 percent of the civilian work force in 1955 to 2.8 percent in 1978. As a
matter of fact, not only has it gone down relatively, it has gone down absolutely
so that between 1970 and 1978 the federal work force declined by 50,000.
Insofar as regulation is concerned, those economies such as Japan and Germany
which are besting us at the present have far more regulation of industry than we
have. Japanese workers, at least in terms of fringe benefits and most certainly in
job security, are far better off than the so-called "coddled" American worker.
We refuse to even examine the possibility of controlling inflation by price controls, on the implausible pretext that public controls, in contrast to private controls which we now have, "will not work," a premise substantiated by the
irrefutable evidence that when we remove the public controls, or rather when we
do not have public price controls, prices rise.

We have totally lost our confidence in social experiment. We refuse to look at
the facts of existence. We refuse to use the major device we have for resolving
our real, not our imagined, problems. Despite the fact that the most startling and
innovating technological advances of this [twentieth] century have been under
public initiative and some of the most miserable failures have been under private
auspices (the governance of oil, to name but one), we are firmly convinced that
public action is bound to fail.

To the same extent that public employees are demeaned and demoralized,
private entrepreneurs are seen as wearing seven-league boots. The doctrine is
most certainly flattering to the businessman, who has never been known to be
reticent about claiming authorship of all of our technological advances of the
past as well as the present. The consequence is to buttress a status system in
which the business leader sits at the apex, financially secure.

Just like the Plains and Great Basin Indians, the north shore Papuans, the residents of the Admiralty Islands, the Greeks, and, yes, the Germans of pre-Nazi Germany, we are being offered a nostrum in the form of a return to an idealized past. Our Ghost Dance comes in the form of supply-side economics purveyed by old minds in young bodies. Just when we need every public and social device we can muster to get around the institutional encumbrances thrown up in the private sector (traditional sector), we are being told that our problems of the present originated in earlier public action. We need to scuttle public action and have faith in the market. Let competition, in the guise of Exxon, General Motors, General Dynamics, U.S. Steel, Lockheed, Chrysler, take care of things. We have been on the wrong road since the 1930s. Let us return to the old days, under the divine guidance of J. B. Say and the "lazy fairy."

What we are being offered is sophistry, nostalgia, and even worse. And it will not resolve our problems because the solution offered is the problem.

Returning to Veblen for the last word on the subject:

> ... history records more frequent and more spectacular instances of the triumph of imbecile institutions over life and culture than of people who have by force of instinctive insight saved themselves alive out of a desperately precarious institutional situation....[8]

Notes

1 Gilbert Murray, *Five Stages of Greek Religion.* New York: Doubleday, 1955, p. 119.
2 Clifton: Augustus M. Kelley. [1904] 1975, p. 1.
3 Ibid., pp. 2–3.
4 London: Oxford University Press, 1948.
5 New York: B. W. Huebsch, 1923.
6 Charles J. Singer, Editor, *A History of Technology.* Oxford: Clarendon Press, vols. I–V, 1954–8.
7 Thorstein Veblen, *Imperial Germany and the Industrial Revolution.* New York: Viking, 1939, p. 30.
8 Thorstein Veblen, *The Instinct of Workmanship.* New York: B. W. Huebsch, 1914, p. 25.

13 The myth is not the reality

Income maintenance and welfare

Journal of Economic Issues, vol. 18 (March 1984), pp. 143–58

COMMENTARY BY WILLIAM M. DUGGER

In this article, Hamilton adds three planks to the institutionalist platform. First, he explains that poverty is not necessary in a modern industrial economy. Since at least 1929 the United States has had the ability to produce enough goods and services to lift every American out of absolute want. Second, he argues that eliminating poverty through adequate income maintenance programs will help stabilize the economy, not bankrupt the society. Third, the rise of the welfare state (income maintenance programs taken as a whole system) is not due to the misguided efforts of liberal politicians but is a practical response to a real social problem: income insecurity in the industrial economy. Take away the practical response and the insecurity will return. It has returned. Hamilton, and institutionalism, are correct. The myths about the welfare state fostering individual irresponsibility, low productivity, and social decline are not true.

THE MYTH IS NOT THE REALITY: INCOME MAINTENANCE AND WELFARE

Fashions in economics are almost as fickle as those in dress and automobiles. Many of the economic ideas prevalent in the 1960s, which admittedly had positive economic effects, such as those following the 1964 tax cut, are said today to be old hat. Economic and social conditions have in some mysterious manner in the intervening years so changed that what was once a feasible economic strategy is now held to be passé.

No evidence is brought forth to substantiate such a claim. It is based on strong assertion rather than on strong demonstration. The new ideas, just as in fashion, turn out to be those of five or six decades or even of a century and a half ago. J. M. Keynes is dead! Long live Adam Smith, J. B. Say, Jeremy Bentham, Herbert Spencer, and laissez-faire!

So be it with the matter of income maintenance. The fond hopes of eliminating utter degrading poverty, expressed in the mid-1960s, have given way to the meanness that characterizes social welfare administration and what was more properly known as "charity" in the nineteenth century and before. Those notions have been refurbished and put forth as something newly discovered.[1] All of us in the long sweep of history have but a momentary appearance and, hence, of necessity a short memory: with a sense of history learned rather than experienced, we are perfectly set up for the latest in fashion. Our shapers of public opinion at the moment are shaping public fashion, not the long-range public mind. But to deal with real problems we must strip them of the fashionable myths and humbug that hide their stark reality.

The popular myth of the time leads us to believe that income maintenance, a large component of the welfare state, is a function of misplaced sentiment for the welfare of the poor. And, although well-meaning, it is misplaced because it worsens a problem that lies in the flawed characters of the victims. It is the victims who are responsible for bringing on their own downfall, much as it is alleged that rape victims provoke their attackers.[2] For every one of those who take the term "welfare mess" to mean that welfare is poorly administered and mean in spirit, there are two or more who interpret the phrase to mean that the mess is inherent in the concept of welfare itself. The latter critics do not differ in outlook more than a hair's breadth from the Malthusian and Ricardian critics of the poor laws more than a century and a half ago. Both argue in essence that any welfare program, with the possible exception of that provoked by begging, corrupts its beneficiaries. It hurts them worse than it hurts the hesitant giver. Spare the charity and save the child!

Both the past and the present critics have a wholly distorted picture of just how income maintenance systems came to be in an industrial economy – or in any economy for that matter. In one sense all societies are systems of income maintenance, tribal societies with a Paleolithic industrial art no less so than contemporary mass societies with machine, or perhaps computer, industrial art. There are no orphans in the Highlands of New Guinea. Their kinship structure is such that no one is left without some income, whether able to participate actively in the work force or not.

Sometimes in the popular treatment of such matters myth and fancy serve in the place of knowledge. From time to time we are treated to the Eskimo-elder story. We are told that the Eskimos leave an elderly kinsman blocked up in an igloo with two (sometimes three, depending upon the teller) days' supply of blubber. And indeed in some of the recordings of Eskimo culture such events are noted. But the true circumstances are otherwise. The Eskimo peoples followed the caribou and when the caribou went south, to elude the suddenly freezing winters, the Eskimo went south. Sometimes, an elderly and very feeble member of the tribe, feeling unable or unwilling to make one more move, would plead to be left behind. To go, slowing the journey of the others, would have jeopardized the entire family unit.[3] Only under these circumstances did the Eskimos ever leave the elderly, and it was with flagging hearts that they did so. The Eskimo, no less than any other society, was an income maintenance system.

Our distortion of medieval feudalism also leads us astray in interpreting that society. We emphasize the "bound" nature of serfdom, not realizing that everyone in a feudal society was "bound," king no less than serf, albeit if one is "bound" 'tis much better to be so in kingly than in serfly style. George Homans, in his *English Village Life of the Thirteenth Century*, reproduces some written agreements between sons and fathers, both serfs, in which the son agrees to tend to the father's and mother's needs until death do them part on the condition that the father give to the son his rights in the manor.[4] On this condition the son could secure the permission of the lord to marry. Viewed from another perspective, it was a system of social security or income maintenance by kinship and feudal right.

This kinship system of security was built right into rural architecture in the United States. As Clarence Ayres noted long ago in *Science, the False Messiah*, those elegant old homes in rural New England with their seemingly infinite attachments represented an accommodation to an extended family – a family that provided economic security to the lame, halt, and blind, as well as to able-bodied family members.[5] The rambling nineteenth-century adobe structures found in rural New Mexico are similar physical testimony to a family-oriented system of social security that characterized not only New England and New Mexico, but almost all of the rural United States.

Being that people then did not live as long as people do today (so that there were fewer old people), that what old people there were held title much as old people in medieval society held rights, that high infant mortality kept down, to some extent, the number of dependent children, and that the real income on a farm had an elasticity that does not characterize urban cash income, security vested in the family was a feasible way to meet the economic needs of an agrarian-based population.

When we look at longevity figures from New Guinea, from medieval Europe, from rural nineteenth-century New England and New Mexico, in comparison with those of the industrial economy of today, we cannot help but surmise that life today is much more secure than it once was. The industrial economy is more secure in general as evidenced by such measures as infant mortality, longevity, disease, general health, etc., than in previous orderings of society. Machine technology means abundance, not in the sense of limitless goods and services, but in the sense of better health and nutrition, greater literacy, more varied lives. But, nevertheless, it does have some inherent insecurities that were not a part of the older order of life.

For one thing, the extended family has largely disappeared. The nuclear family, an adult or adults with dependent children, has displaced the extended family. Kinship ties, although most certainly still recognized and honored, cannot make the demands in an urban society with two thousand miles separating the related nuclear units that they do in an agrarian economy. The family unit living in a rather small apartment in Manhattan can hardly be called upon to meet the demands of grandfather and grandmother for physical security and income maintenance.

Granted that major changes in the social fabric are the root cause of the development of the welfare state, our argument can be stated more generally. All societies are bound by ties of reciprocity. Social interaction involves two or more individuals, and reciprocity means that anything done by one individual on behalf of another calls for a reciprocal action of equal social worth, by the original beneficiary on behalf of the original giver.[6] The matter of social worth is determined in a rough and ready manner by the society itself. The customs and practices of each tribe define how these interactions shall be settled.

In industrial economies the matter of reciprocity sets up two circular flows, one of goods and one of whatever is defined as money, a standardized unit socially acceptable to settle reciprocal obligations, today ranging from metal coins and paper dollars to simple symbols on a computer printout.[7]

The goods flow represents our technological interdependence.[8] As economists put it, we are all busy doing one another's wash. The money flow represents the ceremonial recognition of that technological interdependence.

In our industrial society, lack of money with which to settle reciprocal obligations mandated by technological interdependence puts a person out of the mainstream; it disallows any access to the technological process by virtue of which the life process is sustained. One of the risks of the industrial society is disruption of the pecuniary flow either socially or to individuals, through all kinds of unforeseen and unplanned circumstances – unemployment, disability, lack of parents through which one can establish a claim, aging and involuntary retirement, injury.

To the two traditional and accepted flows of pecuniary income, that from ownership of property allegedly having some productive efficacy and that from some alleged direct participation in the work force also having some imputed productive efficacy, we have been adding a third stream, independent income. It is independent in the sense that it does not rest on any imputed productive efficacy, although, as we shall argue, it may be very efficacious in supporting the two traditional flows of income.

The industrial economy, as noted, has any number of insecurities built into it by virtue of its major characteristics. We have recognized these insecurities by building, over the last six or seven decades, systems that circumvent stoppages in the usual pecuniary flow. The problem in general in an industrial economy is the termination of cash income for whatever reason.

On the individual level, such termination disrupts or forbids meaningful participation in the life process of the group. On the social level, massive breakdowns in money flows are allowed to so impede the productive process that the very economic and social well-being of the entire group may be threatened. We have the ironic spectacle of want and deprivation in the midst of potential relative abundance. It would be an eloquent person indeed who could explain to an elder of the Mafulu Mountain Folk just why some substantial part of the population had to be without "shoes" because we had produced too many "shoes," or because we were forced to preserve something sacred, the "purchasing power" of the dollar as it was held to be sometime in the past.

One of the first of these terminations that we [in the United States] recognized and accepted as a community, rather than as a family or an individual responsibility, was industrial accidents culminating either in death or in temporary or permanent disability. Workmen's compensation was devised in the second decade of this [twentieth] century to offset the loss of family income from death or injury. This was a feeble beginning in our recognition of a more general problem, but nevertheless a beginning that clearly reveals its origins in the machine process.

In the 1930s we recognized that income could be terminated by involuntary unemployment and recognized this, too, as a cost of industry. And in the horrendous social conditions of that era we finally recognized that the family unit and private charity could not cope with dependent children, the blind, the disabled, and the aged. The Social Security Act of 1935 included provision for all of these economic insecurities. Although provision for health care was originally a part of the Social Security Act, that feature was removed for political reasons. The provisions of the bill were viewed as "revolutionary" enough and any more social change was more than the populace, as represented by their elected spokespersons the politicians, would tolerate. We had to wait another thirty years to get the modest medical care for the elderly that we have today.

That the welfare state is a response to the insecurities of an industrial economy is proven by the fact that every industrial nation has been forced to establish some system – and for the same reasons that we belatedly responded to the same forces – to establish some system of income maintenance and security. It has often been remarked that we in the United States were retarded in our response to those forces, and much is made of the fact that the German system of social security was originally sponsored by Bismarck, and precedes that of the United States by more than fifty years. A better explanation, perhaps, is that the industrial revolution that provoked the social changes to which the welfare state is a response affected Germany before it did the United States, as it most certainly did Great Britain. In any event, leads and lags notwithstanding, every industrial nation has been forced to come to grips with the insecurities peculiarly associated with that form of economic organization.

For most people this analysis of the rise of and necessity for the welfare state is sufficient unto itself. However, to the conventional economist, it was always troublesome. Since the conventional wisdom envisioned an economy in which the market was responsive to human need, these welfare measures seemed to be exogenous intrusions. The market produced goods and services in just the quantity and quality that consumers indicated by their bids that they desired them, and their bids reflected the distribution of income, an income distributed in the same ratio as each had contributed to the final product. It was the best of all possible worlds, almost biblical in that it appeared that people ate bread in proportion to the sweat on their brows.

Since this analysis was held to be a reasonable presentation of actuality, the welfare state and income maintenance programs were taken to be aberrations. Admittedly the system did not always work in such perfect fashion. Some people did, through adversity, fall outside the system. And some had such personalities that they could find no reasonable niche. Hence, for the former, the worthy widows, the orphans, the non-drinking very old, there was private charity, augmented where necessary by some minimal public contribution. For those in the second category, the "sturdy beggars," there was nothing other than a Green River ordinance. [This local ordinance was first passed by the small town of Green River, Wyoming. Its official purpose was to control door-to-door solicitors. Other towns quickly followed Green River and passed their own ordinance. The ordinance was really used by local police to control the large numbers of hobos and vagrants who traveled from town to town begging for food. So, the Green River ordinance became a symbol of the insensitive treatment of the displaced poor. Such local practices were most common during the first Great Depression. They have been largely replaced in the second Great Depression by local ordinances that prohibit people from "camping" on city property or on vacant land. In other words, the Green River ordinance made poverty a police matter.] But anything done even for the worthy poor should be minimal because generosity, even though well intended, always bore the danger of debauching the poor. Neither private nor public charity should become a way of life.

The problems of the welfare state were viewed as outside the economic system – until the great depression of the 1930s. That event was indeed a great eye-opener to those with eyes that could be opened. By its sheer intensity it made manifest to perceptive people the insecurities that were an integral part of the industrial economy. And it provoked an economic theory that could view these economic insecurities as a part of the system, as endogenous rather than exogenous.

Many people totally missed one of the major messages in the back of J. M. Keynes's *General Theory*. In his almost afterthoughts he remarked that two major flaws existed in a capitalist economy: the first was its tremendous instability and the second its very unequal distribution of income. And he argued that mitigating the second flaw, the uneven distribution of income, would go a long way toward remedying the first, the instability.[9]

Income maintenance, from being an exogenous problem, was brought into the main corpus of economic theory. The message was loud and clear for those who cared to hear. In classic theory the extremely uneven distribution of income, particularly apparent in the late nineteenth century, was essential for rapid accumulation of capital. Only by such a distribution of income could the "lower orders" be saved from poverty. Even though the poor might misunderstand, the riches of the rich were in the long run more beneficial to the poor than to the rich. All savings were realized in real investment. The rich, by virtue of their saving, were public benefactors. Any kind of income maintenance, some of which might be essential for purely humanitarian reasons, represented a cost. If funded by transfer from the affluent, it would reduce savings and hence capital accumulation.

The contrary message from Keynes was quite clear. Extremely uneven distribution of income, far from advancing the general level of income, impaired the maintenance of income and employment and real capital accumulation. The very rich, far from being public benefactors, impaired economic progress by attempting to accumulate savings that were never realized. Saving was a result of income, not a cause of income. Income maintenance programs that registered in a Lorenz curve as a move in the direction of more income equality were not a cost that had to be borne. They were essential to real economic stability and growth. Such a message ran counter to long-held economic theory as well as to long-established economic practice. The traditional theory made of practice a convenient social virtue, to borrow a Galbraithian term. A system of income distribution in accordance with a system of social status had the endorsement of the keepers of the higher economic verities.[10] Is it any wonder that the strategies suggested by Keynes did not survive long in the post-World War II world? Viewing the welfare state as an instrument for maintaining economic stability was threatening to the economic theorist as well as to those whose incomes were unconsciously (?) justified by the theorist. In the past two decades, income maintenance has once again come to be viewed as almost solely an economic cost. Somehow, in what is referred to as the neo-classical synthesis, in which the fallacy of composition endemic to micro-economics was glossed over, only the Keynesian mechanics were left. The message in the back of the book was lost.

If we view the welfare state as a monstrous growth, as more or less an economic cancer that has grown on an otherwise well-articulated system, then we most certainty must view it as a cost. But if we view it as a means of resolving the inherent problems of a system flawed by an inability to distribute income in a manner that will sustain income and employment, then we must consider it a strategy to balance an unbalanced system.

In the period immediately after World War II the latter view predominated. William Beveridge, in his *Full Employment in a Free Society*, taking up on Keynes, argued for security from the cradle to the grave as not only a matter of humanity, but a means of economic stability.[11] In this country [the United States], Alvin Hansen, although more or less insisting that our major emphasis should be on government investment to compensate for insufficient private investment, when getting down to naming those public investments named categories clearly consummatory in nature – education, parks and recreation, and public facilities whose major impact would show up in a consumer budget.[12]

Public investments would represent direct contributions to raising the general level of living, but the contribution to the lower income groups would be much greater than they would be to the rich. Late in the 1950s in *The Affluent Society* Galbraith put the argument for public expenditure in just that way. By redressing the balance between public and private expenditure in favor of the former, more would be done to lift the levels of living of the lower income groups than of the rich.[13] However, Keynes's emphasis on economic stability was lost or at least weakened by the manner in which Galbraith stressed the existence of affluence in the private sector. To a great extent he also downgraded the necessity for economic stability, which had been Hansen's major emphasis.

Two other books published after World War II, one by H. Gordon Hayes, *Spending, Saving, and Employment*, and one by C. E. Ayres, *The Divine Right of*

Capital, directly connected public spending as an instrument to redress the balance between public and private spending and at the same time resolve the problem of economic instability.[14] Both authors argued that our system of income distribution, by maintaining a weak propensity to consume, constantly threatened the ability of the economy to operate at full capacity. Both argued for active governmental policy that would alter the pattern of income distribution in favor of the lower income receivers. In so doing, they lent support on this side of the Atlantic to the Beveridge program.

Such a conscious use of welfare measures to maintain economic stability was never implemented. Yet a belief that it had been accomplished underlay the myth of the "affluent society" so prevalent in the 1950s. People firmly believed that there had been a rather large shift in income distribution during the 1930s and 1940s. This shift in income distribution was alleged to be a function of two actions. One was the establishment of welfare state programs in the 1930s. The other was the extension of the income tax during World War II, so that a larger proportion of higher incomes was taken in taxes than had previously been the case. The evidence that this shift in distribution, attributable to the welfare state and the income tax, was a meaningful one in real terms and real well-being was that our productive capacity had greatly enlarged during World War II. The argument made throughout earlier times that redistribution of income was hazardous for all, because such a redistribution would do relatively little for the poor while reducing the well-being of the rich, came to seem irrelevant because of the large increase in real per capita income.

Government leaders of the times did come to the stabilizing effect on the economy of income maintenance programs. During the Eisenhower administration the allegedly stabilizing character of our limited welfare state was acknowledged in the term "built-in stabilizers." It was noted that the budget effect of these programs, partially by virtue of the manner in which they were financed, was to contribute to an unbalanced federal budget during a recession. Outlays to meet claims for social income and welfare increased during a depression while the revenues from social security and unemployment compensation taxes, as well as from the income tax and other conventional taxes, fell. The administration of that era viewed depressions with some equanimity, having recognized this budgetary phenomenon.

It cannot be argued that the United States made a conscious attempt to follow a Keynesian strategy, raising the propensity to consume or using the consumption function as a device to partially offset the savings gap by an emerged stream of consumption expenditure at any level of income, full-employment or partial-employment level. The level of unemployment tolerated as well as the amount of persistent poverty is testimony that such a strategy was not followed at any time after World War II. And certainly no such strategy is being attempted today. Indeed, quite the contrary!

But despite the fact that we have not created a welfare state based upon any consistent economic philosophy or theory, we do have a crazy quilt welfare state with here a patch, there a patch, everywhere a patch. It came into being as we recognized specific problems of income insecurity in an industrial economy. Taken as a whole, the patchwork does provide for a guaranteed income of sorts. To the extent that very few can possibly fall through the welfare net, we have managed to build an income floor corresponding to a guaranteed income in a rough and ready way. However, that floor is so low that a person can take an almost death-dealing fall before finding support. Any review of the average payments under many of our programs quickly disabuses all but the most calloused of the notion that our income maintenance programs provide for the rich life. Table 13.1 shows average payments nationwide under various support programs.

The minimums that we have established under our income maintenance programs almost insure that the recipients will fall below the poverty line. In other words, poverty is written into the system and almost legitimized by virtue of the governmental payment. We do indeed have a welfare state, but it is a welfare state that goes it on the cheap.

Despite the low level of support for welfare, we are told (and it is rather widely believed) that our welfare state has been growing at such a monstrous rate that is it a threat to general well-being. This belief is based on some elementary statistics allegedly showing that we are about to be overwhelmed by the costs of the welfare state.

Welfare costs, according to this legend, have been growing by leaps and hounds, particularly since the mid-1960s when the Great Society doctrine prevailed. On first examination the numbers seem to warrant the alarm. In Table 13.2 we show figures for social welfare expenditures for the period 1960–79, the period during which the Great Society programs are supposed to have taken hold and mushroomed.

These are numbers that those wholly opposed to social expenditure can use to advantage. But they are not nearly so alarming when we examine the total context in which they exist. For one thing, if put in constant dollars, thus adjusting for inflation, the sheer magnitude of the growth is severely diminished. But it is even better for relieving anxiety if we examine more carefully the various categories that make up the total. If we remove social insurance and education, items that

Table 13.1 Average monthly payments on income maintenance programs

	1979	*1980*
Retired worker	$294	$341
Disabled worker	322	371
Widows and widowers	270	308
Unemployment compensation (as % of weekly wage)	388.57 (35.9%)	428.39 (37.5%)
Aid to families with dependent children	123	128
Aid to aged Supplemental Security Income	123	128
Aid to disabled Supplemental Security Income	182	198

Source: *Statistical Abstract of the United States*, 1981, pp. 329, 340, 343.

Table 13.2 Growth in Social Welfare Expenditures, 1960–79 (in billions of current $)

	1960	1970	1979
Social insurance	$19,307	$54,691	$193,588
Public aid	4101	16,488	64,649
Health and medical programs	4464	9907	24,496
Veterans programs	5479	9078	20,523
Education	17,626	50,845	108,279
Housing	177	701	6226
Other social welfare	1139	4145	10,640
Total	52,293	145,856	428,401

Source: *Statistical Abstract of the United States*, 1981, p. 318.

are not exactly welfare or income maintenance, we have a total expenditure in 1979 of $126.466 billion. Public aid, one of the more controversial of our income maintenance programs, constituted 1 percent of the GNP in 1960; in 1979 it was 2.5 percent, which does represent an appreciable relative growth, but certainly nothing alarming. The items accounting for the largest relative growth are food stamps and Medicaid, neither of which was significant in 1960. The conventional "welfare" part of this expenditure was 7 percent of GNP in both 1960 and 1979. We can take another look at the impact of our "welfare state" on both state and federal government in Table 13.3, where we give the total expenditures as a percentage of total government expenditures as well as a percentage of GNP.

We must again interpret these numbers with some caution. The largest contributors to these percentages are social insurance and education, items available and open to all persons regardless of income. More than one-half of all state-level expenditure for social welfare is accounted for by education. Certainly these numbers taken as a whole indicate that social programs, not all income-maintaining by any means, are a larger part of our economy today than they were twenty years ago. But only those who are deliberately alarmist would project on the basis of this twenty-year experience that they were about to overwhelm us. It is possible, of course, to project their growth into the infinite future so that they constitute all of the GNP. That is a statistical possibility; it is not a statistical probability.

Table 13.3 Growth in social welfare expenditures as percentage of GNP and of all government outlays

Year	% of GNP			% of government outlays		
	Total	Federal	State and local	Total	Federal	State and local
1960	10.5	5.0	5.5	38.4	28.1	60.1
1970	15.2	8.1	7.1	48.2	40.1	64.1
1979	18.5	10.1	7.1	56.8	55.0	60.4

Source: *Statistical Abstract of the United States*, 1981, p. 317.

The whole matter of income maintenance and welfare is obscured by the money illusion. When we relate it to the pecuniary measure of gross national product and to governmental expenditure we see only its pecuniary side. We need to view it in real terms. How much of that ongoing flow of real goods and services are we going to allocate to the lame, the halt, and the blind? The questions over money are matters of bookkeeping. Not that bookkeeping does not have its effect on individuals and how much we are going to allot to each. But when we view the problem in real terms it becomes quite apparent that we can afford the "welfare state." In fact when we see it as an answer to income insecurities in an industrial economy we know that we cannot afford to be without it.

Our limitations are institutional, not technological. This fact should be apparent from the Brookings Institution studies of the performance of the U.S. economy in the 1920s.[15] In that now long-forgotten study, the Brookings Institution argued that had we produced the additional 19 percent of industrial output of which we were then capable, and had we distributed this additional 19 percent to those spending units at the bottom of the heap, no American family would have been below $2000 in annual income. In today's (1982) dollars, that would amount to $11,251. This amount is approximately $2000 above the poverty line for a family of four in 1982. While not lavish, this means that our economy as early as 1929 was capable of eliminating utter degrading poverty. It also means that today we are even more capable of sustaining income maintenance programs well above the poverty lines – even more so than in 1929, a year in which our real per capita disposable personal income was considerably less than half of what it is today.

The irony of the present malaise concerning the welfare state is the widespread belief that we somehow cannot afford it even in the face of overwhelming evidence that we can. Unless one assumes that the involuntarily unemployed, the untended dependent children, the elderly, the injured, and disabled can be made somehow to disappear, we would have to maintain some kind of minimum income even if economically strained in doing so. Sometimes we try to wish these problems away by assuming some natural rate of unemployment or by arguing that all involuntary unemployment is in fact voluntary or by arguing that the welfare system itself provokes personal habits that create dependent children. These are all verbal solutions to real problems that will not vanish by wishing them away. Since we obviously can and we obviously will maintain our welfare state, what are the real rather than the imagined problems? First and foremost is our understanding of the welfare state and how it came into being. The belief persists that it was all somehow the creation of "liberals" rather than the product of hard answers to social realities. We need to become fully aware that it is not something that we can do away with any more than we can do away with urban water systems. Both are essential parts of urban and industrial culture. Far from being social luxuries that we can ill afford, we must somehow begin to understand that the multitude of programs identified with the welfare state are essential to both social and individual income levels. The tendency of the pecuniary aspects of the industrial economy to impede the operation of the industrial side through inadequate flows of income must be acknowledged. The notion that the system automatically operates to create just such reciprocal flows of goods and monies (Say's law), that depression cannot occur, is theology, not science, no matter the credentials of those who see fit to purvey it.

Second, which also requires a change in the conventional outlook, we need to see income maintenance not as a cost, but as a necessary part of the economy. Having a healthy, well-educated, and working populace, far from being costly, is a dire necessity. The whole message of Harrell R. Rogers's book is that the real cost of human neglect is one that we cannot afford. Economic stability is encouraged, not hampered, by effective income maintenance programs.

Healthy-mindedness on welfare is essential to solving what administrative problems actually do exist. The funding of social security is one of these. That we can afford it and that it is not going "broke" is readily apparent. The problem, if there is one, is our insistence on funding it with an earmarked tax. We are the only industrial nation that does this. This manner of financing almost ensures that the system will be constantly on the edge of going "broke." It is a system well designed to perpetuate paranoia among those who depend on it for income security.

We have been modifying some of our social security legislation to conform with the new family styles that have come to prevail in the second half of the nineteenth century. The original social security act was designed to aid the then-current conception of a "normal" family. That "normal" family consisted of two married parents, one of whom, the female, remained in the household, and two children, preferably a boy and a girl. Increasingly that is no longer the typical family. As a matter of fact, it could perhaps be said today, with some justification, that there is no typical family. We need to modify our social security legislation to secure for each individual benefits as a right and as a social necessity.

Overall, every one of our income maintenance provisions needs to be constructed so that it has at least a minimum payment no lower than the poverty line. That we could eliminate poverty, as currently defined, in one fell swoop was evident in 1966 when it was estimated that it would have taken approximately $11 billion dollars to have raised everyone below the poverty line to that level; in 1966 the gross national product increased more than five times this amount. But we cannot do so when our income maintenance programs are pitched at the meager levels they are today.

Although it is not within the scope of this article, we need to take seriously the aims of the original Employment Act of 1946. We cannot resolve even the administrative problems of our "welfare" state with vast amounts of unused resources. With these resources fully employed we can easily maintain the" welfare state" at decent levels of funding. So long as inflation is viewed as an intolerable problem of first magnitude while unemployment is viewed as a device for curing inflation, the welfare state, composed of all of our income maintenance plans, does indeed place both a pecuniary and a real strain on the performance of the economy. It does so in several ways. When the economy operates with substantially less than full employment it means that Adam Smith's product of the "annual labor" is smaller. The pile of real goods and services from which must come the contribution to "the lame, the halt, and the blind" is in real terms smaller. Second, on the funding side there are fewer government revenues from which to make income maintenance payments. The government has fiscal problems in managing welfare state payments in chronic depression conditions. From 1949 to 1983, unemployment has been below 4 percent in only seven years. Viewed from the immediate post-World War II outlook, this is chronic unemployment and chronic lingering depression.

If we were to face the problem of unemployment with the same dedication given to national defense, there is no reason we could not achieve the unemployment rates of 2 and 3 percent that we once identified with full employment. At such levels we would generate a much larger real output within which the transfer for income maintenance would take place; simultaneously we would reduce the size of those needed transfers. If achieving this takes wage and price controls, so be it. The opposition to such controls is an emotional one, not a reasoned one. The argument that they require a huge bureaucracy is denied by the experience we have had with their administration in the past. The argument that they "distort the market" presumes that private price making has not already "distorted" that idyllic condition and figment of the mythopoeic imagination. This argument also fails to note that public price controls inject the public interest into what heretofore has been viewed as strictly a private matter by a large segment of the economy, that 70 percent dominated by the Fortune 500. Just as feudal lords were outraged by the intrusions of the king, so we can always anticipate such outrages from the corporate principalities that govern various segments of the U.S. economy. Lastly, the argument that price controls will not work because prices soar when they are removed is a weak argument. All it says is that prices are relatively stable with price controls; in their absence return the very conditions that recommend them in the first place.

In summary, we are capable of eliminating poverty and of providing a decent standard of living for all who have been left out in the industrial economy. That we have not chosen to do so is largely attributable to institutional inhibitions that perpetuate a system of income distribution in accordance with status. Our rising "welfare costs" in recent years, rather than being reason for alarm, are evidence that we had been going in the right direction. The problems that agitate us most are bookkeeping problems. These are most certainly surmountable. But before we can successfully solve even the nit-picking problems, we must transform our conception of income maintenance programs. We need to view them as essential to a healthy and thriving economy.[16] Until there is such a transformation, we can expect only a hard life for those who have been passed over by our economy.

Notes

1 George Gilder, *Wealth and Poverty* (New York: Bantam, 1982).
2 William Ryan, *Blaming the Victim* (New York: Vintage Books, 1971).
3 Peter Freuchen, *Book of the Eskimos* (New York: Fawcett Premier Books, 1961); see especially chap. 8, "The Eskimo Mind." See also Wilhjalmur Stefansson, *My Life with the Eskimo* (New York: Collier Books, 1962).

4 George Homans, *English Villagers of the Thirteenth Century* (Cambridge, Mass.: Harvard University Press, 1941).

5 C. E. Ayres, *Science, the False Messiah* (Indianapolis: Bobbs-Merrill, 1927), pp. 100–2.

6 Marcel Mauss, *The Gift* (Glencoe, Ill.: The Free Press, 1954); and Bronislaw Malinowski, *Crime and Custom in Savage Society* (Paterson, N.J.: Littlefield, Adams, 1959).

7 Emile Durkheim, *The Division of Labor in Society*, book I (New York: The Free Press, 1966 printing); David Hamilton, "Interdependence in Economics," in *Interdependence: An Interdisciplinary Study*, ed. Archie Bahm (Albuquerque: World Books, 1977).

8 Harrell R. Rogers, Jr., *The Cost of Human Neglect: America's Welfare Failure* (Armonk, N.Y.: M. E. Sharpe, 1982); see especially chap. 4.

9 J. M. Keynes, *The General Theory of Employment, Interest, and Money* (London: Macmillan, 1936), pp. 372–81.

10 Barbara Wootton, *The Social Foundations of Wage Policy* (London: George Allen & Unwin, 1955). This book has not received the attention that it warrants. After indicating the weaknesses of conventional wage theory in a very thoughtful way, Ms. Wootton went out to see how wages were in fact determined in Great Britain. The results strongly suggested that wages were determined in accordance with an established system of status.

11 William Beveridge, *Full Employment in a Free Society* (New York: W. W. Norton, 1945), pp. 90–104 and part IV, sections 1 and 2.

12 Alvin Hansen, *Economic Policy and Full Employment* (New York: McGraw-Hill, 1947); see especially chap. 16, "Public Investment." See also his later *The American Economy* (New York: McGraw-Hill, 1957), especially chap. 8, "Standards and Values in a Rich Society."

13 J. K. Galbraith, *The Affluent Society* (Boston: Houghton Mifflin, 1958). Also see the introduction to the third edition, in *The Affluent Society*, 1977.

14 H. Gordon Hayes, *Spending, Saving, and Employment* (New York: Alfred A. Knopf, 1945), especially part II; C. E. Ayres, *The Divine Right of Capital* (Boston: Houghton Mifflin, 1946).

15 The relevant volumes are Edwin G. Nourse, *America's Capacity to Produce* (New York: Review of Reviews, 1934), and Maurice Leven, Harold G. Moulton, and Clark Warburton, *America's Capacity to Consume* (New York: Review of Reviews, 1934).

16 Benjamin L. Page, *Who Gets What from Government* (Berkeley: University of California Press, 1983). This whole book is an assessment of public expenditure fiscal policy, but is especially a critical examination of our notion that we have an effective welfare state.

14   The paper war on poverty

Journal of Economic Issues, vol. 5 (September 1971), pp. 72–9

COMMENTARY BY WILLIAM M. DUGGER

In institutionalism, context is the key. In this short article, more like a review essay, Hamilton sets the literary context of the U.S. war on poverty. He does so first by discussing the books that influenced the declaration of war. Although the war was declared in 1964, Hamilton explains that a number of 1950s books had painted the picture of a society in which poverty was unnecessary or was not a big social problem. In most of these books, social conformity and the lack of authenticity in suburban life were made out to be far more significant. However, John Kenneth Galbraith's *Affluent Society* came out in 1958 and made poverty amid plenty an enigma. Galbraith's book also made poverty in the United States hard to justify. Then, in 1962, came several books on the existence and severity of the poverty problem in America. Still remembered today is Michael Harrington's *The Other America*. Dwight McDonald reviewed Harrington in *The New Yorker*, and put *The Other America* in the limelight. A number of other books were also important, explains Hamilton, among them Gabriel Kolko's *Wealth and Power in America*.

Continuing to set the context of the war, Hamilton next explains how the conduct of the war was affected by cultural context. The cultural setting determined the choice between two strategies: an income maintenance strategy or an individual salvation approach. Income maintenance was out because of the onus placed on "welfare." So, the poverty warriors fought against their foe by trying to save the poor. Trouble was, the poor neither wanted nor needed to be saved.

In evaluating the war, Hamilton introduces the reader to a number of books that explored how the war was going. In these books, the Community Action Program was probably the most controversial part of the war on poverty. It may also have been a more successful part of the war because it did not try to save the poor. Instead, the Community Action Program tried to empower the poor, something entirely different.

Hamilton also suggests that the war may have changed economics, at least for a time. On this point, Hamilton mentions George Rohrlich's book *Social Economics for the 1970s*.

THE PAPER WAR ON POVERTY

Launching the war

An avalanche of literature is probably the one certain accomplishment of the war on poverty. If the poor have not been elevated above the poverty line by virtue of that war, relatively impecunious academic and popular writers certainly have increased the gap between their income and the poverty line. In fact, the course of the war can be charted by the size and character of the literature.

According to the legends which purport to explain the origin of the war, it all began with a few books published in 1962 (although one might date it from the appearance of Galbraith's ill-named *Affluent Society* in 1958). In any event, the literature did have some connection with the whole episode. In 1962 Gabriel Kolko published his *Wealth and Power in America*, James Morgan *et al.* their *Income and Welfare in the United States*, Michael Harrington his *The Other America*, and, last but not least, Dwight McDonald published his review article of Harrington in *The New Yorker*. This was the beginning of the literary war on poverty. A steady barrage has been maintained ever since.

The earlier literature was largely concerned with pointing out the poverty problem. It was an essential antidote to the insipid material appearing in the 1950s as alleging that we had one common, affluent, but demeaning, level of living in the United States. The poor, in their Stein and Robert Hall copies of Brooks Brothers suits, could not be distinguished from the rich in all their authenticity. The danger to all was the common leveler represented by suburbia. Candidates campaigning in West Virginia for the 1960 presidential nomination found that this dangerous level of conformity had apparently not reached to the hills and hollows of that coal-mining state. At least, we are told that John F. Kennedy was greatly affected by the economic want, not the abundance, he found there.

Given the mind-set engendered by the popular and scholarly literature of the 1950s, the early poverty literature of the 1960s was an essential ingredient to get the poverty war under way. The census data of 1960 rather impressively indicated that not everyone had yet reached easy street. In fact, quite clearly, 25 percent of the population had some distance to go before reaching the lower end of easy street.

The affluence concept of the 1950s was inimical to launching a war on poverty only to the extent that it implied poverty-level living did not exist any longer. But to some people, aware of the continued existence of poverty, it appeared enigmatic that amid the affluence, poverty continued to exist. This, at least it seems to me, is what Galbraith was arguing in *The Affluent Society*. The

United States had reached such a level of output that it was difficult to justify a poverty level of living. Traditionally, poverty had been rationalized on two grounds. One was personal failure: People were poor because they lacked innate intellectual or physical ability, or because they lacked something nebulous called moral fiber. There would always be poor. No matter what we did for them, their own ineptness was sufficient assurance that they would soon retrogress to the poverty level. This might be referred to as the contributory negligence argument.

The second, and more serious, argument was that elimination of poverty would entail some redistribution of income. It was stated that redistribution would actually mean very little to the poor, but it would jeopardize capital accumulation. Even a totally equal redistribution would not elevate the poor very far above their present level of living. While little would be done to alleviate the misery of the poor, the ability and incentive of the rich to accumulate capital would be seriously curtailed. A slower rate of capital accumulation would mean the poor, redistribution notwithstanding, would remain at a low level of living for a longer period of time than otherwise would be the case. The key to economic progress for all was rapid capital accumulation. Following this logic, an even more uneven distribution of income would be of greater benefit to the poor; the general level of living of all, poor as well as rich, would be raised faster.

The conventional wisdom relied heavily on both these arguments, the first being most congenial to the popular mind and the latter to the scholastic. Both suggested that poverty would not yield to direct assault. However, with a general recognition in the 1950s of the potential abundance of which the economy was capable, these arguments no longer could serve as strong deterrents to doing something about poverty. To this extent, the affluence and superfluity literature of the 1950s did help launch the war.

Regardless of who or what is responsible, once decided upon, two strategies were available. These, in fact, are as old as economic theory itself. One approach, income maintenance, dates back at least to the Elizabethan poor laws under which some basic minimum income was established. Over two centuries later, in 1795, the magistrates at Speenhamland [in Berkshire, England] were attempting to establish a minimum income that would vary with the cost of living. Even Malthus argued that the expenditure of the landed gentry would afford employment and thus income for the working classes. In fact, those who followed in the Malthusian tradition, down to Beveridge and Keynes, felt that poverty would yield to some kind of income maintenance scheme.

The other strategy might be referred to as the individual salvation trick. Individuals could be raised from poverty by opening for them new opportunities, and by providing them with the skills to take full advantage of these opportunities. Those who push this strategy argue for education, training, elimination of job barriers, and better labor market information. This too is an old approach. Much of the push for public education in the early part of the last century [i.e. the nineteenth century] was justified on the grounds that it would improve the lot of the poor by making it possible for them to better serve themselves.

In economic theory it was implicit in Ricardian economics and explicit in that of Marshall.

Once it was decided to eradicate poverty in the United States, a decision had to be made as to which of these two general strategies to follow. As Clarence Ayres has pointed out several times, we have been developing a new type of income through the general social security devices that have been employed since New Deal days. Traditionally, income was justified if it could be related to employment in the work force, or if it could be demonstrated to derive from property owned and which was employed "productively." (The latter we need not go into when it is remembered that this might include such things as patents not used, trade marks and trade names, and so forth.)

In the twentieth century we have been developing a third type, which Ayres calls independent income. It is independent of both employment and property ownership, and derives largely from tribal membership. All of our varied social security income maintenance schemes, old age and railroad retirement plans, welfare programs, workmen's and unemployment compensation plans, and even farm payments place a floor below which no one can fall, and for eligibility require absence from the work force. Ayres argued that the problem of poverty, as well as economic stability, could be resolved by placing these floors at a sufficiently high level.[1] His argument was an instrumental one. We already were committed in this direction; by consciously structuring the payments, we could eliminate poverty in the midst of plenty. We merely needed to enlarge our commitment.

However, when the war on poverty was being conceived, welfare and everything related to it was in disrepute. An unconscious alliance had developed between those who deplored the whole idea of welfare and those who disliked it because of the degrading practices its administration had developed. Proposals for an enlargement of the entire social security program ran afoul of those who opposed its something-for-nothing aspect and those who opposed its inhumane administration. None of the critics at either extreme were noted for fineness of discrimination, and hence found nothing enigmatic about being bedfellows.

Conceived in this atmosphere, the war had to find new solutions. This almost forced an individual salvation approach. It was argued that welfare was wrong because it was self-perpetuating, and nothing was being done to break the welfare syndrome. We needed programs that would get people out of welfare and make them self-sustaining. The position was argued with almost religious fervor. The problem was one of saving economic souls.

The design of the war on poverty reflected this entire climate of opinion. The very title of the act reflected it. The stress was on economic opportunity, and no provision was made for income maintenance. The authors of the act were proud that in its design they had avoided the pitfalls of the older welfare approach, which paid out money and did nothing to eliminate the need for payments. After six years under the new dispensation, the literature is concerned with assessing the new approach.

Evaluation

One of the first full-scale evaluations was by Sar Levitan (1969). Levitan made a project by project examination of the war on poverty, community action, Head-start, Upward Bound, legal aid, health centers, population planning, Vista, rural loans, migrant labor, Job Corps, and the Indian programs. In each instance he gives the legislative background of the program, the purposes, the funding level, its operation, and an evaluation of its successes and failures.

This book apparently set a pattern for others, perhaps already in the works. In any event, the Brookings Institution traversed much of the same territory in a book written by Joseph Kershaw (1970). Kershaw discusses the dimensions of the poverty problem at the beginning of the volume, then traces the legislative background of the poverty war and its administration. In addition, he examines the various income maintenance, family allowance, negative income tax, and family assistance schemes. Finally, he too evaluates our positive efforts to eradicate poverty under the new dispensation.

Another book in this same vein is by Robert A. Levine (1970). The study is interesting because it is the product of a former poverty warrior; he was assistant director for Research, Plans, Programs, and Evaluation in the Office of Economic Opportunity from 1966 to 1969. He also reviews OEO programs one by one, but from the standpoint of research and evaluation. Mr. Levine argues from the beginning of his study that the OEO was somewhat confused by two different objectives which never were fully clarified. The conflict, waging an anti-poverty war and creating equal opportunity, he sees as rather large, although it seems that creation of equal opportunity, if successful, should clear the way for the elimination of poverty. At least, that supposedly was in the minds of the authors of the program.

One thing emerges from all these studies: The verdict on the war's success is unclear. The campaign began with brave claims that it was new, different from the older welfare and social security approaches. By creating new opportunity for the poor it would be possible to break the permanent cycle of poverty. It was rather strongly argued that the older welfare approach was ameliorative, while the newer approach would eradicate poverty by eliminating its causes. Good scores are given to some programs such as legal aid, family planning, and Head-start. Mixed evaluations are given to others, such as community action, Vista, and Upward Bound. The most severe criticism is reserved for the Job Corps.

The overall effectiveness of the war on poverty is moot. Each of the authors feels that undoubtedly some inroads were made, but none wish to make specific claims. In 1963, 36.4 million people, or 19.5 percent of the population, were below the poverty line. In 1968, 25.4 million fell below, which was 12.8 percent of the population. On the surface, this looks like rather remarkable success, but the issue is confused by the growth rate in the economy during the same period of time. In the early 1960s the growth rate was around 2 percent; in 1965–6 it moved up remarkably to 6.5 percent; between 1965 and 1968 it was 4.6 percent. This had its impact on the unemployment rate. In 1961, unemployment hit a high of 6.7 percent, but fell below 5 percent in 1965, and was down to 3.6 percent in 1968. The inroads made on poverty could be attributed to the upward thrust of the gross national product and the concomitant employment effect. Lending plausibility to the argument that the major inroads on poverty are attributable to a swifter growth rate is the fact that in the period November 1964–June 1969 the average annual expenditure in the poverty war was $1.5 billion. Such a paltry sum could hardly be expected to do much to eliminate poverty. Further evidence that the employment and growth rates were more important than the poverty warriors were willing to admit is the fact that in 1970, when the unemployment rate rose and real gross national product fell, the number of poverty-stricken rose 1.1 million.

In the entire war the most prominent instrument to organize the poor and to implement policies was the Community Action Program; it was also one of the most controversial. The CAP program had two objectives: (1) to provide the poor with services hitherto unavailable, or less available than they were to the middle classes; and (2) to organize the poor to assert themselves and make their wants known to the "establishment" in a manner to which the middle classes were already accustomed. The latter objective, in particular, is the one that shook city halls and the social establishment. To have the poor demanding rather than coming cap in hand was as disconcerting as it must have been to the Girdlers of America when, in the 1930s, the formerly docile labor force confronted them as organized labor. Patrick Moynihan argued in his *Maximum Feasible Misunderstanding* (1969), I think incorrectly, that this aspect of the program was a built-in booby trap for the whole war on poverty that should have been foreseen by the authors of the act.

Louis A. Zurcher studied the community action program in Topeka, Kansas (1970). The book is a good account of community action in social and geographic middle America. Feathers were ruffled in Topeka, as one might have expected. The book concerns the problem of building bridges between the poor and the established members of the community, who largely had ignored the poor's existence. It is not an unusual case; having participated in a similar program in another southwestern city, I could fill in a different set of names and leave the substance essentially unchanged.

Zurcher's book substantiates the claims of Levitan, Kershaw, and Levine, namely, that community action did help the poor make their presence known to those who had been ignoring them. In fact, the war on poverty probably did much to rid the poor of the notion that they should be quiet and mind their places; community action gave many their first experience in social action. As a matter of fact, this part of the war on poverty probably justifies the conclusion of Levine that we have three alternatives: "*either* an end to poverty and the establishment of far greater equality of opportunity; *or* a revolutionary degree of chaos; *or* a system much closer to totalitarianism than we would like to contemplate." No longer do the poor believe they are such by virtue of some innate ineptness. The mythology which justified the status system in which the poor kept their place is no longer accepted by its immediate victims; the preferred positions of the establishment are no longer secure or tenable.

If the war on poverty has left its permanent mark upon the poor, whom we still have with us, it also has affected economics. Even the hard-shell economists at the University of Chicago are discussing the plight of the poor. Economics, like sociology in the 1940s and 1950s, has, for the past two decades, been caught up in methodological purity and intellectual immaculate conception. It also has been divorced from the other social sciences. The war on poverty has forced the economist to become what is modishly referred to as relevant. The economist may be reluctant, but he is being directed to the question: Economics for what? At least, that is my impression of the focal point of a collection of essays edited by George F. Rohrlich (1970), which contains a foreword by Alvin Hansen.

In an introductory essay, Rohrlich extends the function of the economist far beyond the narrow marketplace definition. The economist must concern himself with the quality of life and the social performance of the economy. The collection deals with manpower, health delivery systems, social security; and other large social problems with which the economist in an industrial society must come to grips. It seems odd that economics must be prefaced with the seemingly redundant word "social," but the authors believe it necessary to emphasize the goals to which the economist must address himself in the 1970s. Perhaps if he had done so earlier, the war on poverty could have been handled with more finesse and with a greater sense of direction.

In summary, all of these books indicate that we have yet to solve the poverty problem. In fact, we may be about to change strategy once again from individual salvation through education and training to income maintenance. At least, that appears to be the meaning of the discussion of the guaranteed annual income and the negative income tax in Kershaw. As presently proposed, it too will not eliminate poverty. Despite the grandiloquent claims that poverty would be eliminated by 1976, we do not seem to be about to eliminate it, although we could. The economic possibility is not the problem, however. As Sar Levitan expressed it, "the crucial question is whether the American people consider the elimination of poverty a high priority goal."

Note

1 For Ayres' most recent statement see Robert Theobald, ed., *The Guaranteed Income* (New York: Doubleday, 1966), pp. 161–74. See in the same volume the chapter by Ben Seligman, pp. 59–80.

References

Kershaw, Joseph. *Government against Poverty.* Washington, D.C.: Brookings Institution, 1970.

Levine, Robert A. *The Poor Ye Need Not Have with You: Lessons from the War on Poverty.* Cambridge, Mass.: Massachusetts Institute of Technology Press, 1970.

Levitan, Sar. *The Great Society's Poor Law: A New Approach to Poverty.* Baltimore: Johns Hopkins Press, 1969.

Moynihan, Daniel P. *Maximum Feasible Understanding: Community Action in the War on Poverty*. New York: Free Press, 1969.
Rohrlich, George F. *Social Economics for the 1970s*. New York: Dunellen, 1970.
Zurcher, Louis A. *Poverty Warriors: The Human Experience of Planned Social Intervention*. Austin: University of Texas Press, 1970.

15 Welfare reform in the Reagan years

An institutionalist perspective

Journal of Economic Issues, vol. 24 (March 1990), pp. 49–56

COMMENTARY BY WILLIAM M. DUGGER

David Hamilton makes an important distinction here, a vital distinction that provides a critical edge to institutionalism. Reform, Hamilton points out, has two contradictory meanings. On one hand, it refers to the efforts begun by progressives to solve the social problems that accompanied the industrial way of life. That is the institutionalist meaning of reform. This kind of reform dealt largely with new kinds of insecurities and evolved into the programs of the welfare state. However, on the other hand, reform refers to efforts to return to the uncorrupted times of some idyllic past way of life. This is the ceremonial meaning of reform. This kind of reform dealt largely with identification and condemnation of those who violate the mores and taboos of the ancestors, and these reform efforts evolved into the elimination of the welfare state as an immoral and harmful growth.

How prescient he was, but surely Hamilton could not have known that only a few short years after his article critiqued President Reagan's reforms because they were based on a wrong-headed ceremonialism, even worse ones would be implemented. President Clinton, following the same ceremonial line as President Reagan, basically eliminated the welfare state altogether.

WELFARE REFORM IN THE REAGAN YEARS: AN INSTITUTIONALIST'S PERSPECTIVE

Welfare reform in the years of the Reagan administration was a product of the joint efforts of the Reaganites and the neo-liberals. One might readily assume that it was a product of the meeting of the minds. But such is not the case. The seeming meeting of the minds was in fact the product of a contradictory interpretation of the meaning of the word "reform."

"Reform" has at least two different contradictory connotations. Within this [twentieth] century, reform incorporated the efforts of the early progressives to develop social instruments to cope with the industrial society. This is the meaning that comes through in Richard Hofstadter's *The Age of Reform* (1955). The industrial discipline that had come to overshadow the older agrarian system subsequent to the Civil War, while contributing to a general rise in the level of living, introduced some new economic insecurities that had not been so glaring in the economy that preceded it. Machines that had an inability to distinguish between the raw material being processed and the human hands feeding the raw material into the machine left a long string of injured workers. Disruptions in the interstitial areas of the industrial system provoked periods of mass involuntary unemployment that greatly increased that consistent unemployment that seemed to be endemic to the system and to which the economist attached the names "frictional," "seasonal," and "technological." Frequently, dependent children, as was true of those responsible for their procreation, had no visible means of support. The nuclear family, characteristic of industrial society, did not have the economic elasticity of the extended family that characterized agrarian society. Children were nuclearized as well as their families. Reform in Hofstadter's age of reform meant not the return to some pre-existing idyllic time, but the creation of new social instruments to cope with problems that supposedly did not exist in the mythical idyllic state (Hamilton 1984).

From this meaning of reform as progress, as solving problems that were largely a function of the onward rush of the industrial way of life, came such things as workmen's compensation, social insurance, supplemental income programs, both in cash and in kind, unemployment compensation – in short, the welfare state. The latter in general terms was a system to establish a stream of income independent either of ownership of some part of the means of production or of direct participation in the productive process. This third stream of income would cover all of those voids in the system that left individuals without "visible means of support."

But reform has always, among its many meanings, also had a connotation of going back to some uncorrupted time in the past. Today's problems are interpreted as a function of having slighted the eternal ways of the ancestors. Reform means restoring adherence to the mores and taboos that circumscribe and define moral (status) behavior.

Any such problem-free ideal time, of course, is sheer mythopoeic imagination. Life itself is and always has been just one series of problems. As John Dewey once put it, we solve one problem so that we can get on to the two that follow the solution of the first.

Nevertheless, one time-honored way in which to address the chain of problems that define the life process is to appeal to the ancestors for guidance in resolving today's problems. And since every tribe has such a set of mythopoeic and not so mythopoeic ancestors who are alleged to have established this faultless life-way sometime in the past, great temptation exists for every people to reach back for such guidance. This temptation leads away from the actualities of the current problem that lies awaiting resolution. Instead of approaching it directly and employing new instruments to resolve it, the way of the ancestors says to do something else. Back off, do nothing directly. Reform daily practices by adhering to the eternal mores and taboos. Lead a moral life, that prescribed by the ancestors, and troubles will disappear. Perform ancient ritual; engage in incantation! So it was with the Ghost Dance, the Cargo Cults, the Ayatollah, and Pol Pot.

The Reagan meaning of reform carried this second connotation. The welfare system, largely referring to AFDC [Aid to Families with Dependent Children], but incorporating food stamps, rent supplements, and Medicaid as well, was in itself the problem because it violated the self-help morality of the ancestors. In the collective representations of our economist ancestors, as well as their moral philosopher colleagues, there was an original state of nature in which human beings existed as wholly self-sustaining entities. Adam Smith especially among the ancients, but not exclusively, was fond of invoking the original state of nature, before the appropriation of land and the accumulation of stock, which, in effect, means before society. Sometime in the immemorial past, wholly self-sufficient individuals apparently "gathered together by the river" in a sudden overwhelming spirit of good fellowship and harmony and established society. This concept of early society and its creation by autonomous, self-sustaining individuals, wholly false though it may be, was firmly held to and served as the basis for a philosophy of individualism and for its practical application in economics in the form of the free market.

From the time of the development of AFDC in the mid-1930s as a means of addressing the problem of children without financial support (all children are dependent – some just exercise greater pre-natal intelligence in the choice of their parents), conservatives have been concerned about the violation of the eternal mores of the tribe. Since traditional opinion contended that in a free-market system everyone would receive in accordance with the effort exerted, it followed that people would live on a level commensurate with their exertion. This, of course, extended to the children. The richness of the rich was testimony to their worthiness and virtue; obviously the absence of richness was evidence of slackness and irresponsibility. The sins of the father were visited upon the progeny.

To be fair, upholders of the ancient verities always did concede, even though grudgingly, that there were certain adverse circumstances that could thwart the best-laid efforts of worthy individuals. For the needy poor, Ronald Reagan's favorite contemporary appellation for Elizabeth I's "worthy poor," in contrast to the "sturdy beggars," there should be some provision. The provision was best if rendered privately, because private charity was voluntary and ennobled the giver at the same time as it clearly made the point that the recipient had no rightful claim on such largesse. Along with ennobling the giver, the recipient was not corrupted. It was understood that when the adversity warranting the charity passed, the no-longer-needy recipient would resume the path of the righteous and now receive bread by the sweat of the brow.

In more modern times the upholders of the private way, although somewhat reluctantly, have conceded that some public action might be necessary.[1] They did acquiesce in the continued existence of welfare (AFDC, etc.), but were most concerned that it not be established as a permanent way of life. It should always be so administered that life on the dole was a notch or two below the meanest of life in the "paid work force." It is perhaps a bit uncivil to call attention to the fact that large incomes from inheritance or from proper marital connection, all wholly "unearned," have never been considered to be corrupting. As a matter of fact, such income, which might irreverently be referred to as an "invisible means of support," is highly honorific, especially if it frees the individual from daily cares in order to patronize the arts or encourage civic uplift. Such "unearned" or "invisible" income supposedly enlarges the freedom of the individual to achieve noble ends; but enhanced "unearned" income to the poor has an overwhelming tendency to corrupt the individual.[2]

Today's welfare problem, as perceived by the upholders of the status quo, was that public welfare violated all the principles of welfare. The principles were quite straightforward and obvious. The recipient should remain contrite and not view payment as a right. The benefit should not be of such a dimension that it encourages slackness, procreation, or licentious living. It should be stigmatized so that only those desperately in need, the truly needy or the worthy poor, would resort to it. In the perception of the Reaganites, the current public welfare system (AFDC) failed on all counts. Such an organization as the National Welfare Rights Association was obviously evidence of welfare recipients viewing welfare as a right. This perceived failure of the welfare system is precisely the meaning of the stories concerning the affluent welfare recipients that seemed to enthrall Ronald Reagan. All that has thus far been written about this perception is contained in the bogus telephone conversation with which Reagan regaled his well-placed audiences in his 1966 campaign for governor of California that allegedly took place between a welfare recipient and the case worker (Levy 1978, p. 349). On its own it is unworthy of repetition, but it nevertheless bears mention because of what it reveals about the preconceptions of the "storyteller." The welfare recipient is alleged to have asked for special assistance in order to buy a crib for a new baby. The caseworker inquires about the present sleeping accommodations of the baby and is informed that they are the carton in which a new color television arrived. Welfare reform conducted in the state of mind of the believer of such a story is almost certain to become a sham (Abramovitz 1988).

And sham welfare reform most certainly it has become. It reflects all of the fears that have long obsessed the upholders of the eternal verities of the tribe. Welfare has corrupted the work ethic of the recipients, encouraged licentiousness, encouraged procreation, and created its own necessity (Murray 1984). When the subsequent President of the United States, then campaigning for governor of California, sees fit to tell such stories on the campaign trail, more is revealed about the mindset of the conservative critics of welfare than perhaps even they intended. Some individuals might possibly construe this mindset as the cynicism of the establishment. But I think that such an interpretation misses the mark by a long distance by participating in a common error: attributing too much intelligence and knowledge to the opponent. Reagan and his followers were not cynically using such stories. To them the stories were metaphors for the truth. They knew no better.

The welfare reform that was enacted embodies all of these preconceptions. It is a backward-looking program attempting to establish an ideal society in which we make sure everyone "sings for their supper." The alleged derelictions of the guardians responsible for the care of dependent children commanded primary attention. The children were in such a predicament because the elders were slack and lacked diligence. Instead of helping the children, the system in fact worsened their predicament by catering to the slackness of the elders. Welfare had so failed, according to Charles Murray, that it perpetuated its own necessity: Had it not been for the welfare system, presumably there would have been no need for welfare.

Because of these alleged failures, the cost of the system was alleged to be growing by leaps and bounds – the most frequently used and usually unchallenged term for this phenomenon being "our burgeoning welfare rolls." It is interesting to note that AFDC recipients in 1986 received 26.3 billion, including food stamps, while veterans' outlays were almost identical at 26.4 billion. The latter also have been growing, but no one draws attention to the "burgeoning veterans' rolls."

The facts were almost wholly contrary to the beliefs concerning welfare. Most of those who used welfare did so for three to four years at most; the children of welfare mothers were not absolutely destined to make up the next generation on welfare; given an opportunity for day care and a job that did provide equal amenities, such as health care, most of those on welfare would go for the job. Ironically, the notion that people were on welfare generation after generation had been around almost from the beginning of the program, at a time when it was impossible for at most more than one generation of welfare recipients to have been graduated. Most of the mythology concerning welfare had preceded the program and represented hold-overs from the myths concerning the behavior of the poor that had been around since the times of Elizabeth I. Some of the reasons given for the repeal of the British Poor Law in 1834, which also was called reform, were identical to those used in the 1980s to justify welfare reform (Trattner 1974, chap. 4).

To note the mythological character of these beliefs is not to argue that myth was inconsequential and non-functional. All myth functions as an explanation of the differential treatment accorded the members of society – the system of differential status. Nor is it to argue that no facts existed to which critics might point as justification for the myth. In one sense the system and its accompanying myth were self-fulfilling. A life on welfare, given the meanness with which the system was administered, was one that very well might be self-perpetuating and socially destructive of some individuals. Some recipients came to fit the welfare stereotype. But by pointing out the ineptness of the poor, one is able in the same stroke to point to the capability of the rich. This is all a part of the myth and legend whereby the overall pattern of rather extreme income and wealth inequality are justified (Holman 1978, chap. 5).

All of this is not to contend that the welfare program of the 1980s did not have faults. It most certainly did if one viewed the program from the standpoint of the first, or Hofstadter, meaning of reform. If we view reform as progressive and as solving problems, not as adhering to myth or the mythological past, there were plenty of problems to be solved. Welfare was in a sense too little and too late. In order to qualify, one almost had to be a serious battle casualty already. In fact, in order to demonstrate need one had to demonstrate existing, overwhelming economic incapacity; one had to demonstrate almost total inability to cope. This is what I mean by being too late. But once need had been established, the relief was too little. In 1986 the average annual family payment in California, the highest in the continental forty-eight states, was $6384, which was below the poverty line for a family of three.[3] Critics from the right are fond of pointing out the supplemental elements – food stamps, rent supplements, and Medicaid – but when these are looked at in the amounts received, the welfare child is still at or below the poverty line. And in order to benefit from Medicaid, recipients require some kind of medical problem. In other words, you must be sick to benefit.

Real welfare reform would recognize the fact that the aim of the program is to provide for children, not to punish their guardians for real or imagined moral derelictions. Second, it would look at the facts rather than conventional opinion, newspaper gossip, rumor concerning outlandish exploitation of the program, and political stump speeches using abuse of the poor as a means to public office. It would eliminate the meanness of welfare administration. It would take as a given that an industrial economy with the capacity possessed by the industrial economy of the United States could invest in the future of even the poorest of its younger members. Further, it would realize that not to do so is a loss to the whole society, not just to those who have been denied the "generous" protection of the welfare system.

It is unfortunate, but on the matter of welfare reform, progressives were taken in by conservatives calling reaction "reform," just as they were taken in by conservatives calling regressive taxation "tax reform."

Notes

1 As usual, an exception must be made for Milton Friedman. Our Nobel laureate in his *Capitalism and Freedom* states that in addressing the matter of poverty, "One recourse, and 'in many ways the most desirable, is private charity" (Friedman 1962, pp. 190–1). He goes on to state that private charity once flourished as a means of dealing with poverty, but that it has been largely displaced by the establishment of public programs. The statement is wholly contrary to the facts, but that never deterred an economist bent on justifying an ideology (Bremner 1964; Trattner 1974; Patterson 1981).
2 Actually one might observe, based on this anomaly, that great unearned income is apparently non-corrupting and conducive to good deeds. But small unearned income has the potential of corrupting. Then one might reasonably argue that today's poor are corrupted by the miserliness characteristic of welfare. The corruption hazard could be avoided by a large, munificent enhancement of benefits somewhat on the order of those that accrue to the heirs of the rich.
3 U.S. Bureau of the Census (1988).

References

Abramovitz, Mimi. 1988. "Why Welfare Reform Is a Sham." *The Nation* 247 (26 September): 221, 238–41.

Bremner, Robert H. 1964. *From the Depths: The Discovery of Poverty in the United States*. New York: New York University Press.

Friedman, Milton. 1962. *Capitalism and Freedom*. Chicago: University of Chicago Press.

Hamilton, David. 1984. "The Myth Is Not the Reality: Income Maintenance and Welfare." In *An Institutionalist Guide to Economics and Public Policy*. Ed. Marc R. Tool. Armonk, N.Y.: M. E. Sharpe.

Hofstadter, Robert. 1955. *The Age of Reform*. New York: Alfred Knopf.

Holman, Robert. 1978. *Poverty: Explanations of Social Deprivation*. New York: St. Martin's Press.

Levy, Frank. 1978. "What Ronald Reagan Can Teach the United States about Welfare Reform." In *American Politics and Public Policy*. Ed. Walter Dean Burnham and Martha Wagner Weinberg. Cambridge, Mass.: MIT Press.

Murray, Charles. 1984. *Losing Ground*. New York: Basic Books.

Patterson, James T. 1981. *America's Struggle against Poverty, 1900–1980*. Cambridge, Mass.: Harvard University Press.

Trattner, Walter. 1974. *From Poor Law to Welfare State*. New York: Collier Macmillan.

U.S. Bureau of the Census, *Statistical Abstract of the United States, 1988*. Washington, D.C.: U.S. Government Printing Office, 1989.

16 What has evolutionary economics to contribute to consumption theory?

Journal of Economic Issues, vol. 7 (June 1973), pp. 197–207

COMMENTARY BY WILLIAM M. DUGGER

This article is Hamilton's presidential address to the Association for Evolutionary Economics at its annual meeting held in Toronto in December 1972. In economics, Hamilton explains, "all theories of value are theories of consumption." In traditional theories, including neoclassical ones, values come from some sacred authority. In faith-based theories the authority is heavenly. In neoclassical economics the sacred authority is the individual. The values contained in an individual's utility function or in his or her preferences arise spontaneously from inside that individual. Institutionalists, starting with Veblen, disagree. They point out the inconvenient fact that all human behavior, including consumption behavior, is learned. While Veblen explained conspicuous consumption and much else, Hamilton correctly points out that Veblen's lasting theoretical contribution was his construction of a theory of consumption based on socially learned behavior instead of sacred inspiration. Furthermore, Hamilton emphasizes, if human wants are socially learned, they are not infinite. The scarce resources–unlimited wants definition of economics is discredited.

For more on consumption, see David Hamilton, *The Consumer in Our Economy*, Boston: Houghton Mifflin, 1962.

The importance of this Hamilton article is hard to overemphasize. Among other things, it clears the way for Allan Gruchy's redefinition of economics as the study of the social provisioning process.

WHAT HAS EVOLUTIONARY ECONOMICS TO CONTRIBUTE TO CONSUMPTION THEORY?

To many students of economics the suggestion that institutional or evolutionary economics might make some contributions to theory may seem a bit presumptuous, if not preposterous. The institutionalists are those economists who emphasize the study of social institutions and abjure theoretical activity. In the popular myths concerning the institutionalists, the latter are composed of individuals who once, long ago, objected to the rationalism of the classicists, especially that of David Ricardo. They insisted that the phenomena supposedly austerely defined and analyzed by the theory be described. They were, in other words, verbal virtuosos who wished to add a descriptive element to economics. They were "literary economists."

Unfortunately, some of the early institutional economics was of this character and lent credence to the belief. But this was never true of Thorstein Veblen and John R. Commons, even if one might gain this impression from some of their followers. But such a notion of institutionalism merely serves to obscure the theoretical contributions that institutionalism has made to a theory of consumption and of consumer behavior.

The mainstream of economics, to a certain extent, largely has ignored the theory of consumption. This is not wholly true, but certain historic circumstances in the development of our economy and in the development of economic theory make it essentially true.

No one could argue successfully that the workingman in the late-eighteenth and early-nineteenth centuries actually did live at some subsistence level which demarcated life from death. Subsistence in the Malthusian sense always contained something more than an elemental minimum to sustain life. Yet studies of living conditions at that time indicate the limited nature of the levels of living of workingmen. Jean Fourastie in *The Causes of Wealth* clearly indicates their "butcher's meat and bread" level of living in the mid-eighteenth century. In fact, as he shows, this level showed no startling changes until well into the nineteenth century.[1]

When, in addition to the level of living common at the time of formalization of economic thought, one considers the long cultural history of the level of living of mankind, which undoubtedly left its historic impact, one can understand the obsession with production. The affluent society was still a long way off. Today's lunch rather than tomorrow's food was of vital concern.

Certainly new products did enter the consumer budget during the time of the classical economists, but those budgets altered so slowly that they could be taken pretty much for granted. (Think how easy it would have been to run the Consumer Price Index on the eastern seaboard of the United States in the decade 1790–1800.) That being the case, it was quite logical to give little concern to consumptive activity. Adam Smith, in his *Wealth of Nations*, of course, treated consumption as the end-all of productive and exchange activity. It was consummatory, and since it was such, little could be said about it. It was an ultimate end beyond analysis.

But whether or not economists are conscious of it, all theories of value are theories of consumption. The consumption element may not be apparent, but it is implied. To be valued, the presumption is always made that the object of value possesses some inherent good or contributes in some way to human well-being. Traditionally, all values have been held to come from some sacred authority, heavenly or earthly. In some theories man himself has become the locus for that sacred authority.

In the conventional economics two theories of value have held sway for about equal amounts of time. Each has had a run of approximately one hundred years. We might, of course, argue that the labor theory precedes the year 1776 by many centuries. John Locke's justification of private property most certainly did lean on an early version of the labor theory, and evidence of the longevity of the labor theory is to be found in the Bible's admonition that bread shall be eaten in the sweat of one's brow. In so-called primitive societies the rudiments of the whole concept are to be found in the mixture of the personality of the creator with that which has been created.[2] But as an economic theory specifically it had a run of about 100 years.

The same thing might be said about the utility theory with its Epicurean background. But in saying so we are merely pointing out that ideas are seldom as new as we think when first applying them to new problems.

In any event, the labor theory can very well be looked upon as a consumption theory, even though it is infrequently looked upon in this context. As it was used, however, it assumed that goods had value according to the blood, sweat, and tears that went into their production. Certainly there were several variations, including the labor command theory, but in each version goods were held to have value because of the putative worth of the "toil and trouble" that was involved in their production. It may be questionable whether such a concept could have had much operational meaning for a theory of consumption, and the inability to relate it to the so-called measuring rod of price probably deprived it of any consumptive meaning. Nevertheless, the labor theory does make the presumption that what makes goods worth the candle is the labor necessary to their production, whether embodied or not.

Utility theory, of course, is the direct product of Jeremy Bentham and his felicific calculus. According to the legends of the history of economic thought, utility was introduced as a concept to resolve the water–diamonds conundrum unresolved by Adam Smith and the labor theory of value. This is not exactly an accurate account of what occurred, and it is quite clear in Eugen Böhm-Bawerk's *Karl Marx and the Close of His System* that the utility theory had other than intellectual puzzles to resolve.[3]

Value theories also can be used as the basis of power claims. Although the labor theory of value was not developed into a full-blown theory of consumption, in the hands of Marx it became the basis for such a claim. If labor was the creator of all value, and if some status groups other than labor received income, the whole system was unjust. A hidden assumption lies at the base of the entire argument. It is the presumption that we should consume in the same magnitude that we produce, and that if someone is consuming less than or more than he produces and the first condition is involuntary, we have an unethical system. The marginal productivity theory today purports to show that in the long run, in the absence of disturbing forces, and with the existence of perfect competition the market system provides the most ethical of all possible economic worlds.

But no matter that economic theory sometimes does serve as tribal legend. Economics is no more guilty of this kind of hanky-panky than any of the other social sciences and perhaps even a bit less so. The point is that whether or not the introduction of utility theory was wholly innocent, it did serve and does serve today as the basis of what passes for consumption theory in the mainstream of economics. And it does purport to show that values, consumer and productive, are measured by price.

On the surface, utility theory seems to have been a great achievement. It serves as the basis for one blade of the Marshallian scissors. It eliminates Marx's use of the labor theory of value. It gives us a theory of human behavior which can be mathematicized and proliferated from cardinal to ordinal to no-utility (revealed preference). We can explain just why a cup of coffee costs ten, and not nine or eleven, cents. Or so it all seems.

It is probably no more ethically neutral than is the labor theory of value in the hands of Marx. Utility, along with its counterpart, marginal productivity, most certainly does have ethical connotations. In a condition of equilibrium the purport of these two workhorses is to indicate that in the unfettered market system man will receive satisfactions exactly equal to the toil and trouble in producing the commodities in which those satisfactions are embodied, and that the equality of these is certified by price. Pleasure and pain reign supreme. Bentham rides again.

But the theory of human behavior, implied if not stated, is that of hedonism. (No one today is as brazen as was Stanley Jevons, who endorsed hedonism in an unqualified fashion.) It very well may be true that imaginative things can be done mathematically with infinitesimal increments of pleasure and pain. But when Veblen and others of the early institutionalist critics attacked this point they were on very solid ground. Unfortunately, conventional economics was responsive to only one of these. It was contended that no one could calculate utilities in the fashion presumed in the cardinal utility version of the theory. This, of course, was easily remedied by introducing ordinal utility. But even in this version calculation was presumed to the extent that the consumer was able to identify a condition of indifference. He might not be able to tell just how much one bundle of goods differed from another in utility yielding capacity, but he could tell when two bundles were equal. Revealed preference theory could be used to the same end without mentioning utility, but in this event any concept of value would have to be dropped. Consumers sought goods and attempted to maximize their take, whatever *maximize* could mean in the absence of any value concept. Those who clung desperately to cardinal or ordinal utility seemed on better grounds.

But none of these responses met the main criticisms of the early institutionalists or any others who rejected Bentham's theory of human behavior. The problem is that it is a rather meaningless theory, whether we use the words *pleasure* and *pain* or the allegedly more neutral ones, *utility* and *disutility*. The whole concept presumes that human behavior is almost genetic, that pleasures are something that spring from the inner yearnings of the human heart. But such is not the case. We do know that what one likes or dislikes is a function of the cultural process, or that when one enters this world as a piece of palpitating protoplasm one does not come programmed with a set of preferences. All consumption behavior is socially learned.

It is rather meaningless to state that man maximizes pleasure (utility) and minimizes pain (disutility) and to take this as a basic premise. Starting in this fashion, the null hypothesis is impossible. Whatever man does is assumed to maximize pleasure and minimize pain. In other words, man is as man does, and whatever he does is the result of a maximization effort, whatever that means.

No other social science continued with this type of human psychology into the twentieth century with the exception of economics. In fact, micro theory is saturated with Benthamism, on the supply as well as on the demand side. Indeed, the Marshallian scissors appeared to have been constructed by Jeremy Bentham.

But if the institutionalists were critical of consumption theory, they did have an alternative. Sometimes institutionalists are attacked as a dissident group who never hesitate to criticize but who have nothing positive to offer. If this is the usual criticism that they do not have an alternative theory of price, it is well taken and correct. Not viewing the price system with the same awe that is characteristic of the conventional wisdom, they never will have an alternative theory of price. What they do have is an alternative theory of consumption, the larger dimensions of which have been around for a long time.

Veblen's *The Theory of the Leisure Class* in a way has been too popular. It is one of those books that every educated individual is supposed to have read. It is accessible currently in several editions, including a very inexpensive one sold in popular news and book racks. The study has suffered in somewhat the same manner as Upton Sinclair's *The Jungle*. The latter attempted to produce a socialist tract, but ended up prompting food and drug legislation. Veblen wrote nothing other than a serious theory of consumption and ended up giving people the impression that he was satirizing the consumption habits of the rich.

Nothing could be further from the truth. If one keeps in mind the popularity and newness of the utility theory in economics in the late 1890s, it is quite apparent that *The Theory of the Leisure Class* is an alternative theory to that which was newly being introduced to economics. The traditional theory then taking formation considered the consumer a rational, independent individual with a set of unique preferences, who always attempted to maximize his satisfactions or utilities. He was the directing force of the economy, for he made his preferences known to the producer, who, always on the alert for the main chance in his profit calculations, delivered the goods in the quantity and quality the consumer desired.

Veblen's consumption theory, of course, was quite dissimilar. We must bear in mind the time and place in which he was formulating his ideas. The United States had been undergoing rather rapid industrialization in oil, railroads, steel manufacture, food processing, and other industries subsequent to the Civil War. This was a period in which many new fortunes were established as a result of having control of this new technology. A steady parade of newly established millionaires was arriving in New York from the steel and coal region west of the Appalachians, from the meat packing areas of the Midwest, and from the oil regions of western Pennsylvania. In New York they displayed their new pecuniary success. Chroniclers of the social mores of our society have found a gold mine of stories about the graceless manner in which these newly rich evidenced their wealth. Among these is the famous scene in Delmonico's when the guests, sitting on horseback, were given cigars wrapped in one hundred dollar bills which were lighted by waiters, dressed as grooms. This was the last event in an evening devoted to a demonstration of total indifference to wealth.

No one could observe these events and read, simultaneously, the works of Franz Boas and others on the Northwest Indians and the potlatch phenomenon without beginning to find some similarities. Reading further in the anthropology of the time, one could hardly miss the point that here was a universal principle of consumption. In Veblen's view, in all societies there are tasks which are honorific and those which are less so, and even demeaning. The first are fraught with magic and exploit and cannot be accomplished without what the Polynesians and Melanesians refer to as *mana*. But the success of those in high places must be evidenced through conspicuous consumption and conspicuous leisure. This leads to the development in industrial society of pecuniary standards of taste and esthetics which affect even higher learning. In fact, higher learning has as one of its functions the perpetuation of just such alleged taste.

Today we refer to the use of goods as status symbols, and our consumption is directed to the greater glorification of the status roles we happen to occupy. This is not simply a matter pertaining to the rich. It holds for all status roles and means only that the rich have a wider margin of conspicuous consumption, as they do of all consumption. Certainly we are not forced as in feudal times to obey sumptuary laws so that we do not outconsume those in more genteel status positions. Certainly we do not so rigidly fix our consumption that a man's station in life can be determined with certitude by observing his life style. But some of our common phrases do betray the identification of consumption with status. The terms *blue collar* and *silk stocking* in our vocabulary testify to this phenomenon.

Unfortunately, some of the recent popularization of these Veblenian ideas has not enhanced the credibility of this part of Veblen's consumption theory. One reason is the failure to realize that Veblen did not maintain that consumption was irrational or that it was wholly directed by status considerations. Obviously implicit in Veblen's theory of the leisure class was some criterion by means of which the wasteful and nonwasteful elements could be differentiated. He stated that "nothing should be included under the head of conspicuous waste but such expenditure as is incurred on the ground of an invidious pecuniary comparison."[4] But he went on to state that it is not necessary for the consumer to be able to identify any such waste. Goods establish their own necessity and in the eyes of the consumer may be utterly necessary for well-being. Such social necessity does not exempt an item from being classified as wasteful. "The test to which all expenditure must be brought in an attempt to decide that point is the question whether it serves directly to enhance human life on the whole – whether it furthers the life process taken impersonally."[5] Further developing the criterion on which waste is determined, he stated: "An article may be useful and wasteful both, and its utility to the consumer may be made up of use and waste in the most varying proportions."[6] Implicit in all of this is the instrumental theory of the American pragmatists Pierce, James, and Dewey. In fact, implicit throughout the volume is an instrumental basis on which Veblen distinguished between the meretricious and the meritorious in goods.

All goods not only are status symbols but also are instruments to achieve some end in view. Consumers are not irrational in their choices either when making largely status-oriented decisions or when making largely technologically oriented decisions. In any event, the consumer has a problem of the moment. An immediate consumption decision is actually a hypothetical decision. The consumer is saying that if he uses the good in the problem situation then he will achieve some desired end in view. To the extent that the good does achieve that end, it tentatively is certified as good. In the light of subsequent activities its effects will call for repeated rejudgment and assessment in all of the identifiable consequences.

Perhaps the most explicit statement of this position was made by C. E. Ayres in *The Theory of Economic Progress*, where he used it as a general theory of valuation. He maintained that all decisions are interrelated and that actions are judged in terms of their effect upon the whole evolving life process. All judgments are evaluated in terms of their consequences – not solely immediate ones but all identifiable consequences revealed now and in the course of events. But over forty years ago Hazel Kyrk, in *A Theory of Consumption*, used the instrumental theory of valuation as a theory of consumer judgment.[7] She made a rather clear demonstration that goods are not valuable because of some mystic labor power embodied therein, nor because of some equally mystic spine-tingling sensations experienced from their consumption. At the time, this was intended as a theory of consumption, and one which did have a theory of value.

Of course, if one accepts this institutionalist theory of consumer behavior, one is not able to relate the valuation process to market prices as revealed on the market. But then neither can any other of the valuation theories that have prevailed within the mainstream of economics. The utility theory can be related to market price only by imputation. The whole complicated apparatus can no more demonstrate a relationship between market price and subjective feelings than can the labor theory relate market price and the so-called labor content of goods. The economist probably would be well advised to cease the quest for the identification of market price and true value. The mystery of market price has become the economist's search for the Holy Grail.

The institutionalist, however, does raise some other questions with his theory of consumption behavior. A major tenet of modern conventional wisdom is the idea of scarce resources and infinite wants. The whole economic problem is held to center around the dilemma caused by the juxtaposition of the finite and the infinite. This seems to be a very plausible paradox if looked at in the traditional sense. But if we accept the notion that wants are socially conditioned (and, in the light of modern social science, how could we think otherwise?), then they are finite. As a matter of fact, the position of Veblen would lead one directly to the conclusion that wants, being defined by status position, are rather fixed at any one time. Certainly consumption does increase with the passage of time. We do know that levels of living expand, and as they do so wants expand, but this is an example of technology making its own necessity.

As technology proliferates, there appears to be no limitation on man's ability to make use of it. In the long haul, new technology does provide novel and more effective ways of resolving old problems, and it does provide new ways to achieve things not previously possible. Can anyone doubt that the conquest of Mount Everest was made possible by oxygen bottles and other new mountain climbing gear? [Some years after Hamilton wrote this essay, Reinhold Messner and others subsequently succeeded in climbing Everest with oxygen bottles.] But once developed, these new devices provide their own demand. Technology implies the human skill to use it; without the concomitant human skill, technology is meaningless. Since such is the case, the human animal seems able to create the necessary demand and the necessary means of satisfying this demand.

One situation does exist in which it is reasonable to contend we have infinite wants: In our fantasies – in our secret dream worlds – wants are infinite. But most of the time we are able to distinguish between fantasy and actuality, and in actuality we are confronted with concrete situations. We have an aching tooth and a want for its mitigation. We are hungry at noon and have a want for lunch. A car has a flat tire and we have a want for a repair job. In other words, wants in actuality, in contradistinction to the dream world, derive from specific problem situations in the on-going life process. Here our wants, although expansible, are rather finite in each problem situation from which they derive.

The means to satisfy our wants are not quite as limiting as the conventional outlook would have us think. Technology determines resources. What was a resource to Paleolithic man may not be a significant one today, although we still may possess and make use of it. Things which are highly significant as resources to us today may have been beyond the ability of man's technology to define them as such even a few decades ago. This concept of expanding resources has been developed elsewhere by institutional economists. Given these facts, the outlook of economics is less dismal. Most certainly the nature of the questions asked about the economy would largely change from ones concerning static equilibrium to ones on how the expansion and change may be guided in more favorable directions.

If we take the position that wants are socially derived, other problems also follow. There is an element of mystery in the assumption that wants are unique in each individual. Unique individuals are made in heaven, and it is not for man to tamper with man's wants. If wants are made on earth, then they no longer are sacred, and this also means that the restriction or reshaping of wants is not a mortal sin. One is not intruding into God's or even Nature's work. Looking at wants in this fashion means that the market can be conceived as a useful device for certain purposes, but not as a divine creation. The substitution of other rationing devices –

public, cooperative, or what have you, if they function in certain areas – has an equal validity and claim on the economist's attention.

All of this also would spell the end of consumer sovereignty, that is, in economic theory. The advertiser and the marketeer already have eroded that sovereignty rather thoroughly, if it ever existed, as John Kenneth Galbraith has so lucidly demonstrated. When I hear the term *consumer sovereignty* I always remember a roundtable discussion of ancient and honorable economic concepts at a "clandestine" meeting of this group's forerunner, the Wardman Group, at Chicago about ten years ago. George Zinke said that when he heard the term he was reminded of the sovereign queen, who, upon being handed a speech by the prime minister on a public occasion, turned and said to him: "Oh, this is what you want me to read?"

Of course, it would not mean the end of consumer judgment. As we stated earlier, the instrumental theory of value contends that the consumer does have some judgmental "sovereignty," if you wish. But it does rid us of the notion that the consumer is in the position of the feudal landed gentry, at the apex of the whole social system, and it does recognize that wants are socially derived and not the simple aggregation of each individual's inner yearnings of the heart.

All of this may not seem to contribute much to consumption theory as traditionally conceived. It would appear that much is being drummed out without a replacement. To that thought I can only refer to a passage in Veblen's *Imperial Germany* in which he listed a number of ancient and rather useless institutional encumbrances, including royalty and the Monroe Doctrine, and stated that their replacement would be as foolish as applying to the German ersatz bureau for a replacement for a wart lost from the end of one's nose.[8]

Notes

1 Jean Fourastie, *The Causes of Wealth* (Glencoe, Ill.: The Free Press, 1960), chaps. 1, 2.
2 Ernest Beaglehole, *Property: A Study in Social Psychology* (London: Allen & Unwin, 1931).
3 Eugen von Böhm-Bawerk, *Karl Marx and the Close of His System* (New York: A. M. Kelley, 1949).
4 Thorstein Veblen, *The Theory of the Leisure Class* (New York: Modern Library, 1934), p. 99.
5 Ibid.
6 Ibid., p. 100.
7 Hazel Kyrk, *A Theory of Consumption* (Boston: Houghton Mifflin, 1923), chaps. 6, 7.
8 Thorstein Veblen, *The Nature of Peace and the Terms of Its Perpetuation* (New York: Viking Press, 1945), p. 216.

17 Institutional economics and consumption

Journal of Economic Issues, vol. 21 (December 1987), pp. 1531–54

COMMENTARY BY WILLIAM M. DUGGER

Hamilton adds his middle initial to his name and considerable detail to his exposition in this article on institutionalist consumption theory. The article appeared
in a two-part symposium on institutional economics. The articles solicited for
the symposium, including this one, were then published under the title *Evolutionary Economics* by M. E. Sharpe in 1988 as a two-volume work. Marc R.
Tool was the editor.

Hamilton starts out by explaining how conventional economics largely avoids
consumption theory, and falls back on the utilitarian hedonism of Jeremy
Bentham to conjure up a world of "rational" consumer calculating machines.
Institutionalists, on the other hand, starting with Thorstein Veblen's *Theory of
the Leisure Class*, work up an instrumentalist theory of consumer behavior in
which consumers buy goods to help them achieve ends-in-view and also to help
them signal their status to other consumers. In institutionalism, consumer behavior is learned in a specific cultural context. Today, that context includes John
Kenneth Galbraith's revised sequence and it includes the industrial economy's
need for progress to be made in achieving ever higher mass consumption if progress is to continue in ever higher industrial production.

INSTITUTIONAL ECONOMICS AND CONSUMPTION

Conventional economics has given major attention to the production process.
Consumption has been given a rather minor position in the classic perception of
the economy. This is not to say that consumption has been wholly ignored, for it
most certainly has not. All economic theories of value have consumption implications. But these are often only implicit, rather than explicit, and hence
obscured. Further obscuring the matter that classic value theory does address
consumption is the fact that the utility substitution was introduced more to avoid

the political embarrassments caused by the labor theory of value than to further our understanding of the consumption process.

The institutional interpretation of the economy has given consumption greater significance. As a matter of fact the first major work in what is recognized to be institutional economics, Thorstein Veblen's *Theory of the Leisure Class*, lends itself readily to a useful analysis of the consumption process, something of which contemporary marketing science is only too well aware (Tucker 1964, 1967). In what follows, these differences will be brought out in the course of presenting the institutional analysis of consumption.

Jeremy Bentham and his ghost

In a chapter entitled "Economics and the Tradition of Despair," J. K. Galbraith argued that economics in its classic mold was one of despair (Galbraith 1984, chap. 3). Ironically, the despair was created at just the time that the rise of the industrial economy was beginning to make itself known by a long sustained growth in the general level of living. He attributed the despair to the long human experience of living close to the line of subsistence. And although this concept of a primitive ancestor constantly digging and grubbing for a living may be contrary to established fact, as Marshall Sahlins argued, the perception the classicist had of early man was unencumbered by anthropological fact (Sahlins 1972, chap. 1). The perception, correct or not, was firmly held and did color economic thought. Thomas Carlyle's sobriquet "the dismal science" was most certainly warranted.

More surprising than the fact that this despair was created at just the time that things were beginning to look up, is the subsequent continued, rather glum, outlook of the economist. With some two hundred years during which per capita income in the industrial economies has increased at a prodigious rate, not much has changed in the general perspective of conventional economics. The favorite saying of the orthodox when indirectly alluding to a general condition of scarcity involves a declaration of the non-existence of a free lunch. This allusion to scarcity and the meanness of life, usually said with a certain archness, is meant to convey in small compass what is defined as the fundamental problem of economic existence, infinite wants and scarce resources.

If this is accepted as the fundamental economic problem, and it goes largely unquestioned among the orthodox, then a notion of an "affluent society" or of an "economy of abundance" is preposterous. That being the case, who could possibly take the matter of consumption seriously when the needs of production remain so urgent?

Reinforcing the general downgrading of consumption in mainstream economics is Adam Smith's perception of consumption as a kind of final end-all of economic activity. As he put it in *The Wealth of Nations*:

> Consumption is the sole end and purpose of all production; and the interest
> of the producer ought to be attended to, only so far as it may be necessary

for promoting that of the consumer. The maxim is so perfectly self-evident that it would be absurd to attempt to prove it. But, in the mercantile system, the interest of the consumer is almost constantly sacrificed to that of the producer: and it seems to consider production, and not consumption, as the ultimate end and object of all industry and commerce.

(Smith 1937, p. 625)

That this is still the mindset from which conventional theory approaches consumption is testified to by the opening words of a chapter on the consumer in a very enlightened present-day introductory textbook: "The end result of nearly all economic activity is consumption" (Mings 1987, p. 79).

If consumption is the end-all of economic activity and nothing is subsequent, then, of course, nothing can or need be said. The consequence of viewing the general human condition as one of scarcity, combined with the notion that consumption is the end of all activity, left the study of the consumption process largely untended.

Further consigning the process of consumption to an obscure corner of all economic treatises was the adherence to Say's law. Anyone who dared toy with the notion that consumption as a part of aggregate demand just might be weak enough at times to provoke a bit of unemployment was ruled incompetent and beyond the pale. Lord Lauderdale, Thomas Malthus, John Hobson, and even Karl Marx (although the bill of particulars against the latter was so extensive as to make the underconsumption dereliction a minor offense) all bore the scarlet letter. Since any reduction in aggregate consumption would be offset by an equal increase in investment expenditure and vice versa – all by virtue of the magic of the interest rate – consumption on this count got no attention.

In terms of aggregate economic well-being, the only consumption worthy of attention was deferred consumption, or savings. Current consumption was a constant threat to growth in aggregate output. Consumption should be discouraged by a highly uneven distribution of income. The greater the savings of the rich, the greater would be aggregate output in the future. And since this great truth held at any point in time, it also held for all subsequent points in time. The long-run salvation of the poor was the current richness of the rich. Richness was a convenient social virtue, as J. K. Galbraith would have put it. If more current income went to the lower elements, very little would be accomplished to raise their level of living, and there was reason also to doubt the wisdom of their expenditure patterns. After all, John Wesley and his followers devoted their lives to saving the poor of England from the evils of gin!

To point out that consumption was treated rather shabbily in traditional theory, to some extent, overlooks the fact that the whole theory of value is related to consumption. A major aim of conventional economics has always been to demonstrate that the ratio of the prices of commodities is equal to the ratio of the true values of those commodities, whether the locus of that "true" value be in embodied labor or in subjective feelings. But whatever the locus of value, the whole value issue has a consumption dimension. The very word used to designate the objects of economic activity – goods – begs the question, good for what? And that question directs our attention to the consumptive implications of goods.

For the reasons already enumerated and also because of the obsession with price as a measure of value, the consumptive side of economic theory has largely been obscured even from the theorist. Yet both the older labor theory and the contemporary utility theory of value have implicit consumption implications. Demand theory, even though it purports only to help explain price, is the conventional theory of consumer behavior.

The shadow of Jeremy Bentham hangs heavily over all of this traditional consumption theory, even that of classical economics, if we mean by the statement the spirit as well as the disembodied formal ideas. Although Bentham was a contemporary and intellectual companion of some of the major classic theorists, only one half of the hedonist felicific calculus encumbered classic theory. And it did not get even that one foot – and the left foot at that – in the door, thanks to Bentham. The same climate of opinion that influenced Bentham influenced the early classical economists. Hedonist ideas have an ancient lineage, and identifying the valuable with that which is associated with either pleasurable sensations or painful creation has apparently always been quite tempting.

Psychological egoism, of which psychological hedonism is the Benthamite version, characterized most social thought of the seventeenth and eighteenth centuries and got itself into classical economics by way of the labor theory of value. Work was held to be irksome and painful, and those products representing its physical embodiment then were construed to have value because of the sweat and tears that were byproducts of that creative process. If it takes two days to capture a deer and one day to capture a beaver, obviously the former represents twice the value represented by the latter. To the eighteenth-century gentleman-philosopher that was a self-evident truth.

Despite the non-existence of "self-evident" truths, the labor theory of value did have a consumption meaning (Galbraith 1986, pp. 42–5; Veblen 1945, pp. 78–96). What made goods good was the labor embodied therein. Since the goods that one produced by blood, sweat, and tears would exchange for goods in which an equal amount of blood, sweat, and tears was embodied, the consumption implication was that one literally ate bread in the sweat of one's brow, even though the bread embodied someone else's sweat.

However, the labor theory of value entailed certain social hazards even though it might satisfy some ethical questions concerning the equality of effort and subsequent consumptive enjoyment. Present-day conventional consumption theory is largely a derivative of an effort over a century ago to retrieve classic theory from the grip of Karl Marx, the innocent legends concerning water and diamonds notwithstanding.

Any theory of authorship, whether in behalf of land, capital, labor or what-have-you, can easily be construed as an ownership claim. Any labor theory of value can readily be turned into a power claim. If labor is the ultimate author of all things, then it seems only reasonable that the author should also be vested with ownership. This proposition suggests itself to even sluggish minds; those with more nimble minds can do all sorts of things with it. As Max Beer once wrote, "Locke used it as an argument in favour of private property; while the socialists used it as an argument against capital" (Beer 1938, p. 57). Some of these latter possibilities were taken advantage of by the Ricardian socialists Thomas Hodgskin and William Thompson (Stark 1944).

Contemporary standard consumption theory is largely a response to Marx's later employment of the labor theory to lay a much more powerful claim to the whole product of labor for labor. This turn of events is often brushed aside in accounts of how Bentham's utilitarianism, and only his right foot now, came to be the base upon which contemporary consumption theory was built. Most accounts of the borning of modern orthodox consumption theory attribute it wholly to an innocent attempt to resolve a knotty problem that Adam Smith had left unresolved and that subsequent classical economists had apparently found embarrassing. As mentioned above, conventional economics has spent an inordinate amount of time attempting to show that the ratio of the prices of commodities is equal to the ratio of their real value. And although it was assumed that the ratio of the labor embodied in two commodities was equal to the ratio of the prices of the two, this was not taken without question.

Smith himself raised doubt in his water and diamonds question as to why some things having great value in use – water, for instance – had little value in exchange (price), while other things having little value in use commanded a high price. With his usual good sense, Smith dropped the matter and went on about his work. But according to the legends that pass as history of economic thought, this question kept economists awake at night until the whole conundrum was resolved by the shining lights of economics of the 1870s, Stanley Jevons, Carl Menger, and Leon Walras.

It is conceded that these latter were "anticipated" – the usual word used for the work of predecessors upon whom later innovators build – by such as Hermann Gossen and Richard Jennings.[1] But these "anticipators" went unappreciated until the same ideas were arrived at by almost immaculate intellectual conception by the "innovators" of the 1870s. These latter solved the water and diamonds problem with finality.

Guy Routh in his *Origin of Economic Ideas*, however, contends that, while the sequence of events is correct, the interpretation lacks something in veracity (Routh 1977, chap. 4; Hamilton 1970, p. 35). While it is true that Gossen, Jennings, and others had earlier versions of the utility theory of value, their failure to make a significant dent in economics was not because of a lack of clarity in exposition; nor was the success of their successors ascribable to any enhanced clarity of exposition. Changed social circumstances probably explain the more charitable treatment of the exponents of hedonism in the 1870s than had been the case twenty and thirty years earlier.

As a means to showing that price measures something called real value, the labor theory of value is no worse off than the utility theory. The utility theorists, in rejecting the labor theory, have always contended that no independent measure of embodied labor existed other than that of price. Hence, price measured embodied labor, and embodied labor was that stuff that price measured. But exactly the same tautological objection can be made to any meaningful relationship between utility and price. No one has yet come up with a utilometer, so that price as a measure of utility, a subjective feeling about which little can be known, is no better off than it was in its attempt to measure labor. Hence every reason and quite a bit of evidence suggest that the substitution was for other than the advancement of the frontiers of knowledge. The reason is not hard to locate.

By the 1870s, Marx's *Das Kapital*, in its first and most useful part, Volume One, was available and had an influence on the socialist movement. It represented as formidable an interpretation of the Western world economy as any of the works of the received classical economists. In fact, it was classical in every way and merely represented Ricardo in reverse, as Marx contended. By the 1870s there was a handbook for socialists and there were Marxists ready to carry out some of its propositions, as events in the early 1870s in Paris and elsewhere in Western Europe were ample testimony. Twenty years before, no such formidable challenge to the established institutions of capitalism existed. And all of this derived from the labor theory of value (Böhm-Bawerk 1949).

That the appeal of utility theory had much to do with its usefulness in getting rid of the troublesome labor theory of value is now well established. But the triumph was not one that was instantaneous. Guy Routh wrote:

> Menger and Jevons published their books in 1871, Walras his in 1874, and the doctrine spread, not by teachers of economics crying "Eureka!" and casting aside their lecture notes, but, as befitted the new creed, marginally but continuously, creeping into the texts, syllabuses and examination papers until, by 1890, the metamorphosis was complete.
>
> (1977, p. 198)

The substitution of the utility theory for the labor theory did, of course, get rid of the specter of the Red Baron and undoubtedly retrieved classic theory from the jaws of defeat. But what is not often fully appreciated is that it gave to classic theory a consumption theory that was pure Jeremy Bentham. The "first neoclassical synthesis" was engineered by Alfred Marshall, who brought Bentham into economic theory now with both feet. Demand represented pleasure (utility) and supply represented pain (disutility).

The psychology that snatched victory from the Red Baron was itself flawed, however. Hedonism was not acceptable in any other area of social inquiry except economics (Girvetz 1963, chap. 7). Rather than rise to the defense of Bentham, an impossible task, some economists began to deny that psychology was relevant to the theory. This is the route taken by Lionel Robbins in the 1930s and this is the meaning of the phrase "We take wants as given" (Robbins 1949, pp. 83–4). 'Tis not for the economist to ask why! If the consumer is willing to pay a price, then that is taken as evidence that the object of that purchase is a desired thing and hence valued. As Bentham said, "Pushpin is as good as poetry" (Mill 1962, p. 123).

Of course, there is no secret about the origin of wants. They are most certainly not a reflection of the inner yearnings of a pre-programmed human heart. Any marketeer worthy of his pay knows this not to be the case. And most certainly J. K. Galbraith, when he developed what he called the "dependence effect," was saying that wants are not made in heaven (1984, chap. 11).

Such a concession to social reality as Galbraith made is wholly unacceptable to a theory that contends that the market reflects the inner yearnings of the human heart. If wants are made in heaven, and if those wants can only be expressed in the free market, then that expression is very significant. Wants are precious to each individual. Thus, any theory that suggests that wants may, in fact, be made culturally here on earth suggests that there is nothing sacred about them. To the avid believer in the virtues of a free market, such a suggestion is heresy of the worst kind. Galbraith committed the unforgivable. He suggested that to want is to be human and that being human is a culturally conditioned expression.

To the larger criticisms of hedonism, the conventional economist has been singularly unresponsive. Indifference analysis proliferated in the 1930s as a response to the rather minor criticism that no one could be counted upon to calculate cardinal utilities in the manner the theory presumed. And Paul Samuelson rushed in with revealed preference so that the word "utility" could be wholly unsaid, while still retaining the geometric and mathematical apparatus and, purportedly, also giving to the whole apparatus empirical verification. The consumer, by purchasing any particular combination of goods at a specified total price, revealed by that purchase that all other possible combinations at the same total price had been rejected. He/she revealed thereby his/her preferences. To many observers this seemed, however, to say no more than that we choose.

Today, even minor questions and self-doubts seem to have been shoved under the rug as we go about our appointed tasks as though Benthamism had been established with great finality. Rehabilitation is by way of reassertion. As one contemporary theorist wrote:

> There is little to be added to the doctrine of Jeremy Bentham, a nineteenth century English philosopher, who postulated that utility is power in goods which creates satisfaction, and that the happiness of the individual is the sum total of his or her satisfaction.
>
> (Gisser 1981, p. 15)

In short, the classic theory of consumption has viewed the consumption process as wholly consummatory, a final end to economic activity. What theory does exist is largely concerned with explaining why the consumer is willing to pay so much for the whistle. After substituting the value theory of Jeremy Bentham in order to avoid the social implications of the labor theory of value, the economist was only minimally responsive to the inadequacies of utilitarianism as either a theory of consumer behavior or a theory of value. Those minimal concessions today go largely unspoken as Benthamism is simply reasserted. This, of course, does leave the theory of consumption without much theory.

The simultaneity of goods as symbols of status and as instruments to achieve an ends-in-view

That the first major work in institutional economics was written as a theory of consumption is frequently missed even by those who profess sympathy for the institutional approach. But it was in a time when the slow incorporation of marginal utility into mainstream economics was still under way that Veblen published *The Theory of the Leisure Class*. This work should be viewed as a positive alternative to the hedonist invasion of what passed for consumption (demand) theory in conventional economics. That this work, however, is not frequently so interpreted is attributable to two circumstances.

The first of these is the manner in which the book was received at the time of its publication. There were reviewers who indicated no tolerance for an analysis of present-day economy analogous to that one might make of the Hottentot. Others, who appreciated this cultural analysis, treated it as though it was satire. Comparing us to the Hottentot! What wit! In neither case, as unappreciated satire or as appreciated satire, was it accepted as a serious attempt to develop a theory of consumption (Dorfman 1940, pp. 191–7).

Second, the book has subsequently been interpreted by many to refer to the foibles and follies of the rich engaged in excessive consumption. Those who take this interpretation then superimpose Veblen upon utilitarianism. In other words, "conspicuous consumption" and "conspicuous leisure" are terms that refer to an exceptional consumption and a peculiar form that it sometimes takes. A few years ago an English economist took this interpretation in a book entitled *Conspicuous Consumption: A Study of Exceptional Consumer Behavior* (Mason 1981). Rational consumption was guided by the old felicific calculus; conspicuous consumption represents a form of irrational behavior, a kind of social aberration. This, of course, is not what Veblen was saying.

It is quite clear that Veblen rejected any kind of hedonist explanation of consumption behavior or, for that matter, any kind of hedonist explanation of any aspect of behavior (Veblen 1942). To Veblen, human behavior was social behavior, one that took its form from cultural conditioning. His *Theory of the Leisure Class* was a theory of consumption in cultural, rather than individual, terms. It rejects the basic premise of conventional theory that wants are unique to each individual, that wants must be taken as givens – things about the origin of which we can know nothing. In fact, we know very much about their derivation, as any student of marketing well knows.

Conventional theory operates from the premise that the normal state of any individual is an equilibrium one. Human beings are always attempting to reach a static state, but are constantly thwarted in this quest by disturbing (exogenous) forces. Quietism is the normal human state. We become active only when aroused from our quiet state by a disturbed equilibrium. This contrasts sharply with the position of Veblen, and with contemporary behavioral theory, for that matter.

It might be said in contrast that the institutionalist contends that any attempt to establish any kind of individual or social equilibrium would be an impossibility given the active nature of human beings (Girvetz 1963, pp. 162ff.). As John Dewey stated the case long ago:

> The idea of a thing intrinsically wholly inert in the sense of absolutely passive is expelled from physics and has taken refuge in the psychology of current economics. In truth man acts anyway, he can't help acting. In every fundamental sense it is false that a man requires a motive to make him do something. To a healthy man inaction is the greatest of woes. Any one who observes children knows that while periods of rest are natural, laziness is an acquired vice – or virtue. While a man is awake he will do something, if only to build castles in the air.
>
> (Dewey 1930, pp. 118–19)

In *The Theory of the Leisure Class*, human beings are viewed as active, not passive, receptors of sensations, as is characteristic of hedonistic interpretations. Veblen views the human animal as engaged in an ongoing life process, producing goods, consuming goods, and the latter activity contributing to the subsequent production of more goods. In fact, in an institutional analysis, it would be difficult in many circumstances to differentiate production from consumption. Is the worker's lunch a part of the productive or consumptive process? Does not the re-creation engaged in by the worker in off-work hours contribute to subsequent production? Is the birthday cake at noontime in the office consumptive or productive? Is the handsome, smart corporate headquarters in the "right" location a matter of conspicuous consumption or conspicuous production? To answer these questions would be to indulge in the kind of taxonomic exercise of which Veblen accused conventional theory. Life is an on-going active process with nothing that can be substantively distinguished as a consummatory end from a productive means. Means and ends are such only in a temporal sequence. Life is an active continuum.

In conventional hedonistic theory, people, of course, do act as they are driven to do so by circumstance (disturbing forces); the sum total of those actions is the social. The presumption is that meaningful human behavior would take place in the absence of any social dimension. Culture as a shaper of human behavior is totally absent. As a matter of fact, people act first, and in acting they somehow manifest culture. Culture is nothing more than the actions of people. A solitary individual somewhere in the Australian bush, if it is not preposterous to conceive of such an individual, in his actions is building culture. In other words, culture, somewhat like a coral atoll, is the sum total of human accretions (Mayhew 1987).

However, today it is realized that all behavior is both individual and social at the same time and that the form that it assumes is a culturally conditioned and derived one. In fact, there is no such thing as a solitary individual who is not the product of the acculturation process. Those economists who are fond of alluding to Robinson Crusoe as an illustration of solitary economic behavior seem to wholly overlook the fact that that fictional hero was a thoroughly acculturated

Englishman (Gisser 1981). And that presumes that at some time he participated in a socially organized learning process. What we are treated to when we deign to look at the real world is people eating, working, recreating, meditating, traveling, loving, and always in socially organized motion. And, simultaneously, they maintain their biological individual identities.

In viewing consumption from this activist standpoint, Veblen noted that all of the actions can be viewed as having two dimensions – one being ceremonial and one being technological or instrumental. We use goods in two ways. We use goods as symbols of status and simultaneously as instruments to achieve some end-in-view.

In one sense, our consumption honors the distribution of income. According to common belief, as well as high economic theory, the distribution of income reflects the differential contribution that individuals have made to the production of the total yet-undistributed income. It is commonly believed that there is distributive justice. What disagreement does exist over the matter is over whether in specific cases that distributive justice inherent in the system has somehow been violated. Some particular individual or particular group is alleged to have acquired some income over and beyond the contribution made or vice versa. But few, indeed, question the justness of the system itself.

This differential receipt of income is required to be put in evidence. The interpretation of this phenomenon is, however, never blatant. It is commonly contended that one must observe the amenities in consumptive behavior. One must "dress for the occasion," maintain a "decent" house, live in a "decent" neighborhood, eat with "proper decorum," neither be "tight" nor "profligate," belong to the "right" organizations and clubs. And what is "decent" or "right" or "proper" at any moment is a function of the role we occupy at the moment.

Veblen made this quite clear in *The Theory of the Leisure Class*. But this point has frequently been misinterpreted both in scholarly and in popular usage. Popularly, and sometimes in scholarly presentations as well, the phenomenon is referred to as "keeping up with the Joneses," as though consumption were a pell-mell race to outspend one another and that prestige accrued to the victor. But nothing could be further from the facts. The racketeer who put ill-gotten gain on display in vast quantities to the shame of the banking millionaire who had inherited large sums would not surpass the latter in status. Of course, it behooves the racketeer to spend on a level commensurate with one of his status within the racketeering world, likewise the banker of substance within the banking world. And so it goes from the most prestigious position to the most lowly. And the most lowly cannot elevate themselves by spending, perhaps by a deft use of credit cards, to a level commensurate with the most prestigious. The canons of conspicuous consumption, as well as demanding "adequate" expenditure, also put limits on that expenditure. Again, what is fit depends upon the role at the moment. To exceed what is called for will attract an unwanted attention, as will inattention to the status-defined amenities. Status defines what is adequate expenditure, not vice versa.

All of this is not to assert that an entire status group cannot symbolize an advance in rank by altering consumptive habits. But a particular group can do so only if the larger society has already acceded to this advancement. Within the last three generations in the United States, the status of the veterinarian has been markedly advanced by circumstances that have little relation to the direct action of the major beneficiaries. At the opening of this [the twentieth] century, veterinarians took care of farm animals and worked largely in the barnyard. Horses were a major part of their clientele. As motorized vehicles displaced the horse, the move from rural to urban living was a part of the larger industrial transformation of which the horse was a victim. At least rural veterinarians were being technologically displaced.

In small town and rural America, as well as in cities, dogs and cats were not likely subjects for the veterinarians' attention – not when larger and more important animals called for the services of the veterinarian. Dogs and cats had to earn their keep, such as it was, guarding the house and controlling rodents. When ill they were dispatched rather quickly, if not by the owner, most certainly with the aid of the town constable.

With increased urbanization and apartment living, dogs and cats were bred as ornaments to be kept within the household, assuming human names, and being taken to the veterinarian when ill just as all family members were taken to the medical doctor. They were expensive ornaments and no longer the product of casual liaisons. Veterinarians have risen to the occasion. Diplomas from prestigious universities are framed and displayed on the walls of their examining rooms that resemble those of the more prestigious MDs. Soft music is played in the waiting room and the veterinarian is no longer addressed as "Doc," an appellation that always conjured up the distinct odors of horse liniment and the barnyard, but is now accorded the title "Doctor." They have, in other words, with changed circumstances, elevated their consumption habits much as the subcastes, the jatii, in India Sanskritize their behavior when moved up within the caste ordering. But no one veterinarian could so elevate himself; the whole order moves up in union, with some, of course, more equal than others.

Tangential to this phenomenon is that of style and fashion. Veblen contended that the leisure class set styles that were then emulated by the lower orders. He also insisted that style, heavily laden with the mark of conspicuous consumption, lost touch with function. In a rather short period, what had been appreciated as attractive began to be viewed as awkward and perhaps dingy and ugly.

This probably has it only half right (Hamilton 1962, pp. 70ff.). What does in the latest in fashion is the emulation by the so-called lower orders. When milady's maid arrives in an inexpensive imitation of milady's original, the original is no longer in style. When the Cadillac tail fins appear on the Chevrolet, they have already disappeared from the Cadillac. Style is a necessary part of conspicuous consumption; without style there is the suspicion that today's suit may have been purchased with yesterday's income.

Style is a factor in just those items most prominent as major symbols of status. It is very apparent in transportation, where in yesteryear a fine brougham was a symbol of status as is today's latest imported sports car. In matters of dress, housing, and gourmet food, styles come and go with almost rhythmic regularity. And these are all items that serve as conspicuous status symbols.

Actually, the ceremonial requirements for consumption do not differ greatly in their functioning today from those of medieval times. The just-price doctrine that required that one charge no more for a product than a price that would enable one to live on a level commensurate with one of that calling incorporated the canons of conspicuous consumption. It linked income received with consumptive outgo. We today do not have sumptuary laws such as those that reinforced the medieval just-price doctrine; but we do not need them. Much of our early childhood and early adulthood is involved with knowing what is decent consumption on any occasion, and what is decent is defined by that which is commensurate for one in a particular role. We internalize the values of the tribe and police our own consumption. No overt social action will be taken against us for violating the prescribed standards. But we, through Charles Horton Cooley's looking-glass self, see ourselves as we think others see us (Cooley 1964). That is sufficient to keep our consumption within the requirements of one of our rank. As it was in the twelfth century, 'tis today and ever shall be! Ah, institutions!

The judgment of the worthiness of any consumptive item or practice institutionally hangs on the matter of authenticity. Given the role in which the participant is engaged, wife, bride, groom, minister, priest, carpenter, salesperson, banker, the question is, what is authentic dress under the circumstances? Given the occasion, a wedding, Thanksgiving, Easter, a funeral wake, a business lunch, a worker's lunch, a clubwoman's luncheon, what is appropriate food? We are all well aware of these demands at the time of marked and infrequent rites. But the same governs everyday life. Our casual dress at casual occasions does not indicate an indifference to authenticity. A tuxedo or a wedding gown would be "out of place" at a summer tennis match. And the casual dress of the bank clerk at a Wimbledon tennis match is not the same as the casual dress of those occupying the royal box. Casualness in consumption is no less attentive to role behavior than is that which we recognize as more formal. There is nothing casual about casual dress.

When attention is called to these cultural complexes, one is apt to conclude that the attention-caller is meaning to say that we give great thought to these matters on each occasion. But nothing could be further from the fact. Certainly a full-blown wedding requires much attention on the part of the major parties and those anxious parents off in the wings. But that is because of its infrequency. The invited participants, having been to many weddings and knowing what is expected in their minor role as participants, do not have such anxieties. As we move through life we have become so habituated to respond to the consumptive role requirements that we are practically no more aware of the demands of role and status behavior than is a fish of the water in which it swims. Conformance seems to be "natural" once acculturated; we can walk and chew gum at the same time.

Ironically, it may well be that this conformance is what gives credence to a hedonistic interpretation of behavior. Conformance begets certain self-satisfaction. To adhere to the mores and taboos that define role behavior gives to the adherent a certain feeling of righteousness. Bentham was right. There is emotion in human behavior. But the emotion is not the cause of the behavior, nor is behavior some maximizing quest for this emotion. It accompanies and may even follow the behavioral pattern. And it may also be that there are feelings that could be defined as painful when one does not comply with the requirements of role and status. We feel that we have attracted an unwanted attention, we feel shamed and diminished in stature. So strong is the acculturation process that these feelings of expansiveness and of being diminished may be experienced even when no one is present to register either approval or disapproval. But action is not a quest to secure or avoid these feelings – nor to maximize or minimize them. Action needs no such motive. Action is its own motive; feelings are a derivative (Dorfman 1940, pp. 130–1).

The utilitarian interpretation of human consumption behavior as a quest to maximize pleasant feelings and minimize the unpleasant has been construed as rational behavior in contemporary economic theory. The use of goods as symbols of status contrasts to this rational maximizing behavior. Of course, in an uninhibited hedonistic interpretation, conspicuous consumption would simply be said to be the means by which some human beings maximize their pleasure. No possible form of behavior would be excluded from the first premise, that of a maximizing individual. But to a more cautious hedonist, conspicuous consumption would remain exceptional or anomalous behavior. Some students of these matters, such as Roger Mason, who accept the concept of conspicuous consumption, have construed it in this manner (Mason 1981). In this view, Veblen was only pointing out some irrational anomalies that live on, in contrast to the rational system of choice based upon strong feeling.

This interpretation of Veblen and the institutional theory of consumption is faulty for two reasons. One, to place the locus of valuation in feelings is to place it on an extremely ephemeral base. Nothing is more mercurial or illusory than feelings. First you have them, then you don't. How frequently good feelings turn to bad and bad feelings turn to good! And how frequently immediate good feelings turn out to reflect something that in longer perspective has pernicious effects. This seems most certainly to be the case with the cigarette smoker and the cocaine user. And the negative judgment is not based on subsequent pain exceeding pleasure, which in some cases it never does.

To get out of this predicament, the economist has usually resorted to Bentham's way out. Pushpin is as good as poetry. 'Tis not for the economist to ask why, but to accept as good anything for which the consumer is willing to forgo something else. Valuation is purely subjective. There is no disputing tastes since they are unique to each individual, and to judge such subjective feelings is to impose those of the judge upon those being judged. Such is the route of the dictator. Applied to consumption this is merely a specific application of a more general position in which it is contended that it is impossible to assess the outcome of the valuation process – values. Judgments of value are unique to the beholder.

This values nihilism gets reinforcement from the position of the sociologist and anthropologist in the form of mores nihilism and cultural relativism. Thus, the hedonist theory of consumer behavior seems to have authentication in the other social sciences in which a blatant acceptance of Bentham's eighteenth-century notions would provoke nothing but mirth. The cultural relativist, in a worthy effort to avoid ethnocentrism, sometimes gets into the position of arguing that judgment other than on a ceremonial basis is impossible. All truth is unique to the culture in which it is held. And although this is something quite different than contending that all truth is dependent upon the individual who holds it, it does seem to sustain the notion that nothing can be said about values.

In any event, that behavior that has no more to be said for it than that it is guided by a singular quest for pleasure would appear to warrant classification as irrational. As a guide to life and living, nothing could be a more fatal Lorelei than the whimsicality of pleasures and pains, whether they be referred to as utility and disutility or merely satisfaction.

A more important criticism of the conventional interpretation of Veblen's consumption theory is what it ignores, rather than what it accepts. If goods were used solely as symbols of status, most certainly the theory could be interpreted as one of irrational behavior. Some institutionalists have actually taken this view. They have conceded that rational behavior is hedonistically guided self-interest. What they find objectionable to traditional theory is that it ignores the irrational in the form of socially induced conspicuous consumption. Their objection boils down to arguing that people are creatures of social convention as well as of self-interest. Their only fault with conventional theory is that it ignores what they feel is a most important element, the socially induced irrational.

This latter position both participates in what is wrong with a hedonistic egoism and fails to appreciate all of Veblen's theory of consumption. Veblen did not contend that conspicuous consumption was an irrational struggle among people to outstrip one another (Hamilton 1973). As noted above, the consumer maintains a modicum of decency given a certain status and role position. Consumption neither falls much below nor much above. Both conditions would attract unwanted attention, or so it would seem to the mind of the consumer. But, more importantly, goods are used in two ways simultaneously: they are, of course, used as status symbols, but, more importantly, they are used as tools or instruments to achieve some end-in-view, one of many way stations in the continuity that is the life process.

Throughout *The Theory of the Leisure Class*, Veblen alludes to a standard of function in distinguishing between the use of goods to satisfy conspicuous consumption (waste) and the use of goods to achieve some end-in-view. The goodness of goods is their contribution to the continuity of the life process. "The test to which all expenditure must be brought ... is the question whether it serves directly to enhance human life on the whole – whether it furthers the life process" (Veblen 1931, p. 99).

Many readers of Veblen slight the value theory that is not everywhere explicit, although it most certainly is explicit in the concluding paragraphs of the chapter entitled "Conspicuous Consumption." His judgment of the usefulness or value of anything is an instrumental one.

We most certainly do judge goods on the basis of authenticity. Conspicuous consumption mandates that an item be authentic for the occasion and for the role of the consumer. But this is not the exclusive basis for judgment. At the same time that goods are used as symbols of status and as marks of the occasion, they are also used as instruments to achieve some end-in-view. Automobiles are excellent examples of this dual purpose. We use our cars as symbols of status and simultaneously as instruments of transportation to get from one point to another. And when we state that we need a new car, elements of both are intertwined. The need may refer to a ceremonial need at the same time it refers to a technological need. The physical deterioration of the car, which makes it unreliable as an instrument to reach an end-in-view – work, for example – may simultaneously render it weak as a symbol of status or as representative of the ability to pay.

Most certainly this dual use of goods makes their judgment all the more difficult. But more importantly the goodness ultimately of any consumption item is determined in the same manner in which we judge the goodness of a wrench. Goods are used in problem situations, in the continuity of living. If, for the moment, my attention is focused on the removal of a series of hexagonal nuts of varying sizes, I may for the moment value an adjustable wrench. My judgment of its goodness is how effectively it functions in conjunction with my skilled use of it in removing the set of nuts. I do not choose a pipe wrench because it would score the heads and render unfit any kind of wrench for their removal in the future. We judge according to present and future known consequences.

The use of goods takes place within an "if–then" context. If I use this snark in this fashion, then.... If the "then" represents a desired outcome, then the judgment of the employment of the snark in the context will be contingent upon achievement of the desired outcome. If left at this point, however, it would represent nothing but crude pragmatism. But there is no necessity to leave it at this point, nor in our behavior do we do so most of the time (Hamilton 1962, pp. 76–81; Kyrk 1923, chap. 7).

Asbestos was once judged on the basis of its qualities as a fire-resistant material. On the basis of the knowledge then at hand concerning the consequences of its employment, it did retard fires in public buildings, theaters, schools, and homes. As a fire retardant it was deemed "good." Subsequent experience indicates other consequences not desired, namely lung cancer. We have, thus, reassessed the employment of asbestos and would no longer classify it as a good for the purposes once used. Fiberglass, used in a variety of consumer goods, is currently under the process of rejudgment because of possible health hazards. Historically, the same can be said for the smoking of cigarettes, a product once rejected for women on status considerations. Ladies did not smoke – pseudo-social consequences were cited as sufficient reason. Prostitution was held to be one of the consequences of smoking. When the bogus nature of all of this was uncovered, the matter of "to smoke or not to smoke" was considered to be a personal decision. Today no one, outside those dependent for income on the tobacco industry, would argue that cigarettes represent a "good." This new judgment is based on subsequent evidence relating smoking cigarettes to lethal consequences.

To observe this valuation process in action we need but look at the operations of consumer testing organizations within the United States as well as within most of the other major industrial nations. These organizations simulate the instrumental usage to which we subject consumer goods. Their criterion for judging the goodness of the goods is how effectively the good contributed to the simulated end-in-view. They do not test on the basis of institutional authenticity or on the basis of feelings, whether defined as pleasure, utility, or satisfaction. Tires, when tested, are placed on automobiles, driven under controlled conditions, and the results as carefully measured as they can be under the circumstances. The tread wear is measured, the ability of the carcass to withstand the exigencies of the road is noted, the performance in wet weather is tested, and all detectable influences on driving characteristics are recorded. The published ratings provide these matter-of-fact experiences along with a rating on the basis of overall performance. Most certainly no single consumer can go through such processes in making everyday consumer decisions. As a matter of fact, it is precisely because of such an impossibility that consumer testing organizations survive. But in a rough and ready manner and within the limitations imposed on individuals, this is the way we choose. Again, this is not to argue that questions of authenticity do not intrude themselves insidiously into this judgment process. As we noted above, they most certainly do. But, in the long haul, what makes things good is an instrumental efficacy and efficiency.

Judgment is never absolutely certain, nor is it eternal. It is always uncertain and temporal. It is based on the evidence now at hand, and with the understanding that very likely future evidence will require rejudgment.

There is, in other words, no certainty whereby we could link price and value. Prices, as perceptive readers of consumer testing reports know, are sometimes a deceptive guide to the good. And over time even items that commanded a price, and almost all do, are found to be deleterious. Over time, the bad as well as the good commands its price. No institutional theory of consumption would attempt to link value and price. That is not to say that the institutional analysis does not recognize the problems of consumers in allocating cash income to procure a way of life. But that is something other than contending that price measures meaningful value.

Aggregate consumption expenditure does matter

In institutional economic theory, aggregate consumption and consumption expenditure are significant determinants of national income and employment. As we mentioned earlier, conventional economic theory is interested in consumption in its postponed dimension. Saving represents postponed gratification. That postponed gratification is a vital necessity if the economy is to grow. It could be said without much distortion that the conventional version views savings as a dynamic force and consumption as a deterrent to savings. Currently, much concern is expressed over what is viewed as a low rate of saving; some attribute the lagged growth rate to this low rate.

In the institutional view of the overall economy, we are all technologically interdependent. Our technologically oriented behavior is related to both that which is precedent and that which is subsequent. It is complementary, not competitive. The work of the sanitation specialist, including sanitation workers who tote refuse, is complementary to that of the medical doctor. And the work of the medical doctor is complementary to that of the sanitation worker. Our technological behavior is complementary to all other technological behavior in the same manner that the various technological operations in a factory complement one another – both those that precede and those that follow. The economy is one huge factory.

But granted this fact, ours is not an industrial economy only; it is also a pecuniary one. Complementarily linked as we are in our tool-oriented behavior, we are reciprocally linked in our pecuniary behavior. If one had aerial photos of the countryside, as used during World War II for selecting bomb targets, one could see the technological linkage that bound all of those living within the photographed area. Bombing targets were chosen to disrupt these linkages. But one could not see the pecuniary linkages that punctuate the passage of goods through the system. Nor was the bourse a prime bomb target, testifying to the primacy of the technological activity. As goods pass in one direction, money, symbolizing a change in ownership, passes in the reverse direction. We recognize these counterflows of goods and money in what we refer to as the "great wheel of wealth." The continuity of technological activity is punctuated periodically in the process of transfer of ownership and investiture of status all of that require some pecuniary transfer (Hamilton 1984).

Institutionally, money serves as a permissive agent in giving access to the technological process. Any disruption of the flow of funds will inhibit the full use of the technological process; any expansion in the flow of funds will allow the technological process to be more fully utilized and expanded. Technology, however, is primary; the pecuniary reflection is secondary. For the society as a whole, anything technologically feasible can be funded. Whether the society will allow this to take place is institutionally determined.

To the institutionalist, none of the conventional flows of funds – consumption, investment, or government – is any more important to the total flow other than in relative size. A stoppage or reduction in any one or several can have a devastating effect on the technological process and on employment. The notion that in order to enhance the investment flow, consumption expenditure must be reduced is contrary to historic fact. Historically, within the United States, as well as within other of the industrial nations, consumption expenditure increased *pari passu* as investment expenditure increased. There is no record of any people having starved themselves into economic advance. As a matter of fact, full utilization of expanding technological possibilities, given the institutions, requires an expansion in permissive pecuniary flows.

Technologically, it is rather difficult to differentiate between those activities that constitute consumption and those that constitute production. On the pecuniary side, consumption expenditures are usually those emanating from a household, but not exclusively, and investment expenditures are those emanating from some business, but also not exclusively. The government flow has always been treated ambivalently, being called government investment but being treated as wholly consummatory.

Only in this second half of the [twentieth] century has conventional economics recognized that consumption expenditure such as that for education can be treated as an investment in human capital. That such an obvious matter should have taken so long to have been recognized is a source of wonderment. But even more startling is the fact that all the other items in the consumer budget have yet to be so treated. But if we treat the technological process as one of continuity, it then becomes apparent that health and nutrition (food) are most certainly on a par with education. And if we can go this far, we can surely see that transportation to get children to school and to the doctor is no less related to production. But then so is recreation, which, when looked at etymologically, points to its relation to the productive process. When it is realized that what is commonly recognized to be consumption is directly related to production, it becomes apparent that real investment cannot be expanded without a concomitant increase in consumption.

Most certainly it is true that we had the "guns or butter" problem during World War II when the neat "trade-off" phrase first became prominent. Its very neatness in application in the form of production possibility curves in elementary texts has a tendency to obscure its rather trivial meaning and its lack of general application. Indeed, if a certain metal was absolutely critical to the production of military aircraft and its current output was limited, it might have to be restricted in its usage for home refrigerator production. But home refrigerator production, given the state of the domestic arts, could not be eliminated. Substitutes were resorted to. It is often noted that total consumption within the U.S. economy reached, up to that time, an all-time high in 1944 at the height of war production. If it is kept in mind that war workers had to be fed, had to be housed, had to be clothed, it is no anomaly that all-time production and consumption heights were reached simultaneously. Further confounding the conventional wisdom is the fact that the military output was one hundred percent consummatory in the conventional sense. It did not contribute to further production, but to further destruction.

From this view of the interrelationships between production (investment) and consumption, the institutionalist would not view them as antithetical. On the other hand, the institutionalist would argue that our system of distribution of pecuniary income is such that it consistently inhibits the expansion of consumption warranted by the potential increase in production. As Hobson contended, we do have periods when income is transferred from lower to upper income groups, provoking both a surfeit of funds at the upper level and a shortage at the lower level. Various stratagems are created to circumvent this hiatus. We use what is referred to as "creative finance" in the form of ingenious devices to postpone the ultimate day of reckoning. At the same time, the excess of savings is absorbed in "paper" creations, corporate takeovers, stock speculation, and foreign adventures, giving the impression of a shortage of savings, and reinforcing the notion that savings is a dynamic force, the shortage of which limits production.

The institutional position would be one endorsing the welfare state within which consumption would be underwritten by income maintenance and excess savings reduced by progressive taxation. These devices would get around the great "capitalist" flaw, long ago cited by John Maynard Keynes – economic instability along with great inequality of income distribution. To the institutionalist, the great problem of the modern industrial economy is ever-rising consumption to underwrite the ever-rising production potential.

Summary

In summary, it can be said that the conventional theory of consumption is a static one. The primary concern is with an equilibrium situation in which some maximum condition of well-being, based on Bentham's felicific calculus, could be achieved. To the institutionalist, with emphasis on the dynamic character of technology, interest in consumption is first in its expansive nature, and second, in utilizing that expansive potential to eliminate utter degrading poverty. The conventional theory sees consumer well-being as a function of Bentham-derived feelings. The institutionalist identifies well-being as a function of a valuation process, no different than how to choose the right wrench. It is what we do most of the time in choosing the good, here on Earth.

Note

1 Erich Roll, for example, wrote, "But there is at least one other author whom one is obliged to mention in company with them (Jevons, Menger, and Walras). Gossen was not dealt with in the preceding chapter because he is an anticipator rather than a forerunner" (Roll 1946, p. 412).

References

Beer, Max. 1938. *Early British Economics*. London: George Allen & Unwin.
Böhm-Bawerk, Eugen von. 1949 [1896]. *Karl Marx and the Close of His System*. New York: Augustus Kelley.
Cooley, Charles Harton. 1964 [1902]. *Human Nature and the Social Order*. New York: Schocken Books.
Dewey, John. 1930 [1922]. *Human Nature and Conduct*. New York: Modern Library.
Dorfman, Joseph. 1940 [1934]. *Thorstein Veblen and His America*. New York: Viking.
Galbraith, J. K. 1984. *The Affluent Society*. New York: New American Library.
———. 1986. *A View from the Stands*. Boston: Houghton Mifflin.
Girvetz, Harry, ed. 1963. *The Evolution of Liberalism*. New York: Collier Books.
Gisser, Micha. 1981. *Intermediate Price Theory Analysis*. New York: McGraw-Hill.
Hamilton, David. 1962. *The Consumer in Our Economy*. Boston: Houghton Mifflin.

——. 1970. *Evolutionary Economics*. Albuquerque: University of New Mexico Press.

——. 1973. "What Has Evolutionary Economics to Contribute to Consumption Theory?" *Journal of Economic Issues* 7 (June): 197–207.

——. 1984. "The Myth Is Not the Reality: Income Maintenance and Welfare." *Journal of Economic Issues* 18 (March): 143–58.

Kyrk, Hazel. 1923. *A Theory of Consumption*. Boston: Houghton Mifflin.

Mason, Roger. 1981. *Conspicuous Consumption: A Study of Exceptional Consumer Behavior*. New York: St. Martin's Press.

Mayhew, Anne. 1987. "Culture: Core Concept under Attack." *Journal of Economic Issues* 21 (June): 587–603.

Mill, John Stuart. 1962. "Essay on Bentham." In *Utilitarianism, On Liberty, Essay on Bentham*, ed. Mary Warnock. New York: Meridian Books World Publishing.

Mings, Turley. 1987. *The Study of Economics: Principles, Concepts, and Applications*. Guilford, Conn.: Dushkin Publishing Group.

Robbins, Lionel. 1949 [1932]. *An Essay on the Nature and Significance of Economic Science*. London: Macmillan.

Roll, Erich. 1946. *A History of Economic Thought*. New York: Prentice-Hall.

Routh, Guy. 1977 [1975]. *The Origin of Economic Ideas*. New York: Viking Books.

Sahlins, Marshall. 1972. *Stone Age Economics*. Chicago: Aldine.

Smith, Adam, ed. 1937. *The Wealth of Nations*. New York: Modern Library.

Stark, Werner. 1944. *The Ideal Foundations of Economic Thought*. New York: Oxford University Press.

Tucker, W. T. 1964. *The Social Context of Economic Behavior*. New York: Holt, Rinehart & Winston.

——. 1967. *Foundations for a Theory of Consumer Behavior*. New York: Holt, Rinehart & Winston.

Veblen, Thorstein. 1931 [1899]. *The Theory of the Leisure Class*. New York: Modern Library.

——. 1942 [1919]. "The Limitations of Marginal Utility." In *The Place of Science in Modern Civilization*. New York: Viking.

——. 1945 [1934]. *Essays in Our Changing Social Order*. New York: Viking.

18 Thorstein Veblen as the first professor of marketing science

Journal of Economic Issues, vol. 23 (December 1989), pp. 1097–103

COMMENTARY BY WILLIAM M. DUGGER

In this article, Hamilton explains another element common to all institutionalist thought. Institutionalists consider human behavior to be learned and to be instrumental. They reject the hedonistic maxims of human behavior worked out by Jeremy Bentham over two centuries ago and used to purge Marx and his application of the labor theory of value from economics. Hedonism is outmoded, but it still is the foundation of neoclassical consumer theory. In neoclassical theory, hedonism is rational because hedonistic consumers maximize their pleasure and minimize their pain. But actual consumers are not led around so cavalierly by their feelings of pleasure and pain, explains Hamilton. They are far more rational in their instrumental pursuit of ends-in-view than the mechanical calculator of pleasure and pain found in neoclassical theory.

Hedonism is still the base of neoclassical theory, Hamilton explains, because it supports the myth of consumer sovereignty, which, in turn, supports "the sanctity of the free market."

Veblen is the first professor of marketing science because he rejected all this silliness and explained consumer behavior in a straightforward manner. Veblen did the theoretical work necessary for John Kenneth Galbraith's revised sequence to replace consumer sovereignty. Consumers use goods and services to achieve some end-in-view and to display their status. They do so in a cultural context, including manipulation by commercial advertisements.

THORSTEIN VEBLEN AS THE FIRST PROFESSOR OF MARKETING SCIENCE

To the economist, consumption is the end-all of economic activity. From the time of Adam Smith, at least, to the present, consumption ends with a satiated consumer as a kind of globule of hedonistic contentment. This goes along with a theory of production that contends that these satiated hedonistic globules must be somehow driven or, in modern-day lingo, "bribed" by a wage, to undertake the exertion involved in productive activity. That bribe is a ticket to further satiation as a consumer.

That the hedonist conception of human behavior prevails in economics today is one of those constantly puzzling aspects of so-called modern economics. The position was at one time the center of much of the attack on conventional economics. But much of that criticism seems spent today and the maxims of Jeremy Bentham, that strange eighteenth- and early nineteenth-century savant, are taken as intellectual coin of the realm. At least, this seems to be the case within economics, and to the extent that the seeming scientific rigor of economics impresses itself on the other social sciences, it is beginning to impact in areas once reasonably immune from the Benthamite philosophy (Etzioni 1989).

Historically, the formal introduction of Bentham into economics was intended to scotch the artful use of the labor theory of value by Karl Marx to lay a power claim for labor within a social system in which capital reigned supreme (Routh 1977; Hamilton 1970). That is sufficient to explain the initial injection of Benthamite hedonism, but the Marxian pall in its weakened form today is insufficient to sustain such a faulted bit of social thought. That hedonism is invalid as a theory of value, as a theory of esthetics, and as a theory of behavior should be well understood.

First of all, it is premised on the notion that the individual is a primary datum and that society is secondary. Surely by now we know that human beings and society are coterminous. We take as evidence for the existence of early human beings the presence in archeological finds of both fossilized skeletal remains and tools. The fossilized skeletal remains of human beings cannot be distinguished from those of our simian ancestors. The dividing line between "man" and his ancestors is taken to be the existence of tool remains. The latter imply culture conveyed from one generation to another and organized society.

Of course, all human behavior is manifested by individuals; but in their manifestations they reveal socially conditioned individuals. No one, all on his/her own, designs the language they speak, nor for that matter any other aspect of behavior. And to attempt to differentiate within behavior that which is unique to the individual from that which is unique to the society is a hopeless and meaningless exercise. Analyzing the "unique" psyche of an individual is analyzing a socially conditioned or, perhaps, flawed psyche.

Secondly, hedonism is premised on the notion of individual feeling. This is not only a precarious, mercurial base on which to pin such matters as valuation and behavior as well as esthetics, it has very little meaning. If we state as a first premise that human beings in their behavior are guided by calculations of net pleasure and pain, and that at all times they attempt to maximize the first, no possible human behavior is excluded. The whole exercise says no more than that we do what we do. If someone persists in stating that they do what they do because it maximizes their pleasure, otherwise they would not be doing it, they say no more than that they are behaving. All the rest is purely gratuitous.

All of the efforts of the economist to shore up the jerry-built system of Bentham have been of no avail. Some critics have made the minor criticism that no one can calculate pleasures and pains in the rational manner that marginal utility analysis presumes. To save the theory from this criticism, the economist resorted to indifference, which still assumes that the individual can know within him/herself more or less feeling. In revealed preference we throw out the nasty word "utility," but drag back the essence by assuming that individuals in revealing preferences are revealing that they know themselves – in a kind of Descartian self-embrace.

All of this is not to deny that we experience feelings. We most certainly do. But even these are socially conditioned. The Hindu abhorrence of eating beef and the Big Texan's delight in seventy-two-ounce steaks in Amarillo are not a function of the genes. Nor are we saying that feelings do not play any role in our behavior. Feelings are causes for examination and reexamination of on-going activity.

But they are a result of socially conditioned on-going activity, not the cause of that activity.

But how could such a theory survive in this industrial age? Hunting for a logical explanation is probably as futile as hunting for the Holy Grail or, perhaps, the Loch Ness Monster. It is argued that hedonistic egoism is rational, meaning reasoned, behavior. Yet nothing could be more irrational, meaning lacking in reasoning, than behavior predicated on the emotions and feelings. Nothing is more ephemeral or mercurial than feelings. To argue that reasoned behavior is a function of emotional states seems almost to elevate the irrational as a way of life. Assuming that the calculation of feeling states was even possible in the precise fashion predicated by Bentham, it would not seem to be a rational guide to behavior, either ex ante or ex post.

But hedonism serves a sociological function, not a logical one. And when we examine it as a sociological matter it becomes clear that hedonism is part of the myth, mathematically expressed utility functions notwithstanding, by virtue of which we uphold consumer sovereignty and hence the sanctity of the free market. It is testimony to the justness of a system that supposedly delivers the goods in just the quality and quantity that consumers desire them.

If, as the hedonist insists, wants are unique to each individual and spring from the inner yearnings of the human heart and that those wants can be made known only through bids in the marketplace, then the market, unsullied by interference on the part of anyone, is synonymous with freedom of expression. The theory upholds a policy of laissez-faire, which, given the structure of the market, says no more than that the market is the best of all possible worlds. Such flawed logic is often sufficient to justify social practices. Myth is notoriously tautological, defining two things in terms of one another.

Given this position, it is clear why Veblen was such a threat to economic doctrine. He was not merely trying to correct a bit of broken logic, he was a threat to a whole large part of the mythology that sanctified the ceremonial practices. Even the seemingly obvious point made by John Kenneth Galbraith that wants were not necessarily made in heaven, that the advertising fraternity might have some influence, was enough for him to once again be drummed out of the fraternity of economist and into that of sociologist (Galbraith 1958).

Unfortunately for many readers, Veblen was not a solemn ass. The ironies and eccentricities of human behavior did not escape his attention. In *The Theory of the Leisure Class* the posturing and role-playing aspect of consumption in other cultures was compared with that which, to the practitioners, was not so self-evident in our own. As a consequence, many of the readers assumed that the book's major message was a satirical one. Comparing us to the Hottentot; how droll! But, while not missing the humorous aspects of our consumption, he was offering a serious alternative to the utilitarianism which, by the late 1890s, was viewed as a newly arrived scientific theory of demand. In contrast to the latter, which took the individual as its primary datum, Veblen elevated consumption analysis from the one-dimensional level to the cultural level. In other words, he long ago recognized the truth of Walter Goldschmidt's much later statement that "anthropology has removed Western man from the pinnacle and quintessence of human perfectibility and placed him with the Australian aborigine and the Hottentot as one of so many diverse cultural beings" (Goldschmidt 1966, p. x). Western culture was no longer viewed as singularly rational in contrast to all others. Our way of life had no more going for it than did that of the Arunta of Central Australia. Both participated in the foibles and follies that, along with "rational" behavior, make up a cultural whole.

The hedonist would, however, respond that lying behind cultural diversity is the felicific calculus. But to note that the New Guinea Papuan maximized utility while consuming dog, and that we reached the same height of emotional excitation by eating the frankfurter, leaves the process of consumption in either culture or between the two cultures wholly unexplained. The observation tells us no more than that people of diverse cultures get their kicks in diverse cultural ways. A milk-drinking culture gets its kicks from drinking milk and a rice-eating culture gets its jollies from eating rice. All of which says that people of diverse cultures do as diverse cultures direct. And we are back to the observation that people do as people do.

However, once having resorted to the cultural level of analysis, it becomes quite apparent that consumption has two dimensions. We use goods as symbols of status and simultaneously as instruments to achieve some end-in-view in the continuity that Veblen referred to as the life process. So it is in all cultures. The taros, such an obviously essential element in Trobriand society, in great abundance at a feast and on display through the interstices of each yam house, are symbols of the great generosity and the great productive potency of the chief of the village of Omarakana; simultaneously they satisfy the nutritional demands for producing more yams and fishing in the lagoon. They are used both ceremonially and as nutritional instruments – and all at the same time. Even wedding cake and caviar have some nutritional value.

This dual function of consumption in our own culture is evident in our automobiles, university architecture, clothing, eating regimen, and every other aspect of consumption. We use goods in two ways and do so simultaneously. No one could possibly come up with a list of goods that are wholly ceremonial and honorific symbols and another consisting wholly of tools and instruments. That is not to contend that in some consumption instances the first element is not predominant, nor to contend that at other times instrumental aspects are not overwhelming. But both aspects of behavior are always present.

If we go one step further it becomes rather difficult to distinguish between what we refer to as consumption and what we refer to as capital goods. If we would once and for all view life as a continuous process, as having continuity, rather than as one of constantly thwarted attempts to reach social stasis, it would become quite clear that consumption contributes to and makes possible the continuity of production and vice versa. The valuable in goods, then, is not the feelings that one experiences in their use, but their contribution to the continuity of the life process. If I use this wrench, then ...; If I use this toothpaste, then ...; If I use these tires, then .... . Goods would have goodness in the sense in which consumer testing agencies find them good. They are good for something, and that something has to do with the continuity of the life process. To my knowledge, no consumer testing agency in the whole industrial world possesses a utilometer and rates goods on the feelings generated in the process of testing them. Again, not that feelings are not present, but feelings, positive or negative, are not what generates or governs the choice of a particular good in a specific problem situation.

Then what has all of this to do with marketing "science" and what has Veblen to do with the profession of marketing? Within a highly technological society, marketing, meaning the physical distribution and coordination of the distribution of essential elements, as capital or consumption goods, to the continuity of the life process, is itself essential. What is critical is how the marketeer sees that function and how the marketeer performs the function.

There is no question that the marketeer is aware of one half of the Veblen message in *The Leisure Class*. Anyone saturated with today's advertising and other market stratagems knows of the blatant appeal to status and conspicuous consumption. Today's message is that you owe it to yourself to indulge yourself. You should want it all! The appeal is to blatant hedonism, the expansive feeling that one undoubtedly experiences when fulfilling all of the consumption requirements of an upwardly mobile life way. That, of course, misses any technological aspect of even the grossest forms of conspicuous consumption. It misses wholly the nutritional element of caviar.

It is most certainly true that we use goods in the industrial economy as the Trobriander uses taros – as symbols of status and simultaneously as instruments to achieve some end-in-view. But just as business impedes industry, so does the technological function of the marketeer. As we noted, the marketing function is one of getting goods to the right place at the right time. We can envision an assembly line being fed essential elements at way stations along the line. If we view the whole life process as a never-ending assembly line then it is obvious that the marketing process is an essential element. That is true if we concentrate on the technological side. But to the extent that business uses marketing as a stratagem to overtake rivals in a game of economic warfare, to capture brand loyalty, to lead consumers to choose by emotion, it represents a disservice to the continuity of life.

And here is where the marketeer can find the hedonistic calculus useful. It is surely obvious by now that marketing operates in fact on a theory of consumer behavior essentially in agreement with that of Veblen. In answering the beck and call of their business employers, caught up in maximizing pecuniary returns, the marketeer can exploit all that Veblen indicated governed consumer behavior in the area of conspicuous consumption and conspicuous leisure. On the other hand, they can convey useful and reliable information to make a wise choice between alternatives essential to solve one of life's many problems. In consumer magazines – and the higher-toned ones seem sometimes to reveal the worst – the marketeer appeals to conspicuous consumption. In trade magazines going to a knowledgeable, specialized group we see marketing at its best. But, of course, both do exhibit information tailored to conspicuous consumption and simultaneously to the use of goods as instruments.

At this point Jeremy Bentham is useful to the marketeer. Not to help the marketeer in a legitimate function, of course; Bentham is wholly irrelevant to any useful social function. But Benthamism is helpful as justification for the more questionable practices of marketing. If it can be said that the goodness of goods is in the eye, or perhaps the soul, of the beholder and that the consumer reveals this inner knowledge by bids in the marketplace, then the marketeer is absolved of any responsibility for even the grossest appeals to conspicuous consumption. It is not advertising that bears any responsibility for people smoking. Smoking is an expression of the inner yearnings of the human heart. All the advertiser does is get them to one brand rather than another. And after all, the brand of cigarette that got the patient to the lung surgeon is a matter of indifference to the outcome of the treatment. It was the smoking, not the brand, that got the patient there. And as Jeremy Bentham said, and he said it all, "Pushpin is as good as poetry." Jeremy would be delighted. Veblen, as the first professor of marketing, would give them [promoters of conspicuous consumption] an "F" (Veblen 1935, p. 64).

References

Etzioni, Amitai. 1989. *The Moral Dimension: Toward a New Economics*. New York: The Free Press.

Galbraith, John Kenneth. 1958. *The Affluent Society*. Boston: Houghton Mifflin.

Goldschmidt, Walter. 1966. *Comparative Functionalism*. Berkeley: University of California Press.

Hamilton, David. 1970. *Evolutionary Economics*. Albuquerque: University of New Mexico Press, p. 35.

Routh, Guy. 1977. *The Origin of Economic Ideas*. New York: Vintage Books, chap. 4.

Veblen, Thorstein. 1935 [1904]. *The Theory of Business Enterprise*. New York: Charles Scribner's Sons.

19 On staying for the canoe building, or why ideology is not enough

Journal of Economic Issues, vol. 23 (June 1989), pp. 535–43

COMMENTARY BY WILLIAM M. DUGGER

Hamilton excels at both instructing and entertaining the reader. In this article he uses three different allegories to teach an important institutionalist truth. He talks about flying airplanes, building canoes, and observing human behavior. However, the truth he teaches is a simple one: much of what we have been taught about the modern industrial economy is of the same scientific standing as superstition. We have been taught to believe in the efficacy and beneficence of the market, in spite of what our own eyes and ears tell us about the realities of the life process. Hamilton's allegories urge us not to disregard our own matter-of-fact knowledge and accept, as a matter of faith, what we are taught. Instead, we should disregard the ceremonial teaching and have a look around for ourselves.

ON STAYING FOR THE CANOE BUILDING, OR WHY IDEOLOGY IS NOT ENOUGH

Over sixty years ago, Stuart Chase in a now long-forgotten book, *The Tragedy of Waste*, mused about what would have happened had the World War I control of industry been continued after the war in the form of a war on poverty.[1] He started off his musings with a statement concerning what relevant considerations would have been necessary. In a passage worth quoting he noted that they would need what he called the "aeroplane view" of the economy:

> As in the war with Germany, the General Staff would be forced to regard the industrial process in terms of manpower, natural resources, physical plant, stocks of goods, transportation load, and consumptive requirements, rather than in terms of money. Money after all is not very digestible. It has its uses and it has its abuses, but greenbacks under a boiler never raised a pound of steam.

What are the relevant physical facts? They are essentially those which an aeroplane pilot equipped with quite celestial eyesight would see as he cruised and re-cruised over the continent of North America. He could hardly get near enough to see bank ledgers, promissory notes, or certificates of capital stock. He would only see the farms, the forests, the mines, the railroads and highways, the rivers, canals, transmission lines; the factories, warehouses, stores, schools, libraries, theatres, golf courses, and homes; and the behavior of some 100,000,000 of men, women and children in relation to these things. Men digging and plowing, pulling the throttles of engines, balancing on steel girders, painting signboards, holding steel under a drill, wrapping up packages, driving trucks, bending over desks, talking through telephones, jamming people into elevated train doors, fishing on the high seas, fighting forest fires, pumping oil wells, reading newspapers, yelling at ball games, sleeping, love making, going to church, dancing, swimming, climbing mountains, pacing, in a striped suit, through prison corridors. Women minding spindles and babies and cook stoves, playing Mah Jong, drinking tea, smoking cigarettes. Children answering the school gong, twisting in their seats, rushing through the playground, working in cotton mills, tossing with fever.... A vast conglomeration of human activity.[2]

Granted that any airplane pilot seeing all that Chase specified would be in violation of the fourth amendment and that the stereotypical roles violate today's sexual revolution, what Chase is presenting are the realities of the economy, the industrial aspects of the economy, both domestic and factory. Pecuniary activities are not readily visible.

During World War II we did get just such a view of various economic landscapes in aerial photos that were used to trace the various technological interrelationships of the economies of those we were attempting to defeat. Hopefully, but frequently not too successfully, we would pick points to disrupt the technological interrelatedness by bombardment. We did not pick the bourse as a significant target.

From either Chase's highly imaginative description or the actual wartime aerial photos, it was impossible to determine whether the steel mills and oil refineries were capitalist, socialist, or cooperative in ownership or whether, like Harvard University, they were so private that the corporate body owned itself. From the air, if you have seen one university or one steel mill, you have seen them all. Also, as Chase noted, exempt from view would be all of those pecuniary transactions which, somewhat like the musical banks in Samuel Butler's Erewhon, give a certain ceremonial adequacy to the transfers of ownership and control (power) that take place at rather invisible points in an otherwise wholly integrated net of industrial activity.

Staying for the canoe building

In an article entitled "The Past and the Present in the Present," the anthropologist Maurice Bloch, otherwise concerned with the matter of social change, brings out rather elegantly a distinction between what he terms knowledge and what he calls ideology.[3] He gives credit to Emile Durkheim, A. R. Radcliffe-Brown, and others for recognition that many of our collective representations spring from the social order itself. Our perception of the universe reflects the social order from which we perceive it. This being the case, the anthropologist has accounted for the fact that peoples with different social organizations perceive the same natural phenomena in varying ways. As Bloch points out, much has been made of the fact that the Balinese supposedly have a different conception of time than the linear concept that characterizes western culture. Life is lost in a permanent nirvana, and the past and present merge in time. The past is present in the present. Ceremonial performances are explained as deriving from the practices of the cultural ancestors and carry out a recreation of the past in the present. Clifford Geertz, especially, has emphasized that the Balinese have a wholly cyclical sense of time. The social order is eternal.

With the Geertz interpretation, Bloch takes exception. He contends that it is only half true. Balinese are perfectly aware of the sequence of events in Indonesia whereby the Dutch were superseded by the Japanese, in turn to be succeeded by the Dutch and the latter to be displaced by Sukarno. They have a concept of linear time in the world of everyday affairs. It is in that dramatic activity honoring hierarchical social arrangements only that the sense of time is endless.

He contends that anthropologists have a tendency to capture the exotic in any culture and to emphasize it wholly out of proportion to the role it plays in the entire culture. All peoples have an ideological belief that has to do with the hierarchical structure of ceremonial behavior bound by the past. But they also have a body of knowledge bounded by the realities of the life process, or what Thorstein Veblen referred to as matter-of-fact knowledge. In the workaday world, conceptions and beliefs are bounded by physical realities.

In what Bloch calls the long conversation in which anthropologists engage with those being observed, they get all of the dramatic action and ideology that reinforce one another; the practice reinforcing the belief, the belief authenticating the practice. But their eyes and ears have been diverted from the matter-of-fact activity and belief by virtue of which the tribe secures a livelihood. They get only part of the long conversation. As he put it,

> Radcliffe-Brown, like Geertz, not using a long conversation view of society, simply forgot all about the other parts of the discourse. Unlike Malinowski, when the magician had stopped incanting his spells, they did not stay to watch the canoe building.[4]

Somewhere in her autobiography, *Blackberry Winter*, Margaret Mead lamented the fact that in her work with Reo Fortune in the Sepic River valley of New Guinea she was given the onerous and non-honorific task of recording the daily round of activities and employment of tool skills whereby the observers secured a livelihood. In other words, she had to "stay to watch the canoe building."[5] Whether this incident contributed to the foreshortened marriage with

Fortune or not, it is obvious that at the much later date at which the autobiography was written, she was still piqued that Fortune took for himself the recording of the more dramatic aspects of the culture. As Bloch contends, it was apparently not uncommon among anthropologists to take the canoe building as secondary.

In one sense the anthropologist, not staying for the canoe building, gets a view of a culture that ignores that part that is so apparent in the airplane view. Flying over the Owen Stanley Mountains of New Guinea during World War II, one got the airplane view of a Neolithic people and saw just those parts that Margaret Mead, in her irritated state, was left to record. One saw the life process and the technological integration apparent at even that elemental level. One saw the canoe building.

We can take exception with Bloch's sharp distinction between what he refers to as ideology as distinct from knowledge, as in fact does his fellow anthropologist Donald Brown.[6] But like Brown we can agree that these two aspects of human cognition can be analytically distinguished, as did Bloch. In actuality, human cognition is a mixture of ideology and knowledge in a kind of intellectual symbiotic relationship. We have ideology supporting a hierarchical system authenticated by the past and we have knowledge by virtue of which we build the canoes, make the steel, educate the children, wash the clothes, and bake the bread, and do all of those interrelated things so apparent from the airplane.

Aeroplane views, canoe building, and the theory

But what, pray tell, have airplane views, canoe building and ideology to do with economics? Surely modern economics is the epitome of science among all of the social sciences. After all, we have all of those utility and production functions so elegantly expressed in mathematical notation. What I am arguing, however, is that economics is a mixture of ideology and of knowledge, or a mixture of what might be referred to as high theory and low theory, the high theory's function being to give meaning to those actions largely concerned with conveyancing, honoring, and taking away status. It is concerned with the dramatic events of the marketplace; the low theory deals with the canoe building and how that is linked to steel making and how that impacts on the making of automobiles. In another way of putting it, high theory records the dramatic aspects of our economy much as the anthropologist participant-observer dutifully records the dramatic events of the observed culture. On the other hand, low theory records all of those tedious, non-honorific, but most essential events that both precede and follow the excitement of the market.

Lester Thurow, when expressing his concern over the rigidity of today's economic theory, is right on when he writes:

> Both then and now all honor is reserved for those who can explain current events in terms of "The Theory," while anyone trying to develop new theories to explain recent developments is regarded with suspicion at best. In economics today, "The Theory" has become an ideology rather than a set of

working hypotheses used to understand the behavior of the economy found in the real world.[7]

I would disagree with Thurow only as to the time and place that "the theory" became ideology. Economics from its inception has been a mixture of ideology and knowledge. Sometimes we get the impression that Adam Smith invented modern economics de novo; we ignore that much of his theory was built upon the works of the very mercantilists he insisted upon beating over the head. As Guy Routh in his *Origins of Economic Thought* showed, what I have designated as high theory originated 100 and 200 years before Smith. It was an expression of the collective representations of the newly rising merchant class, which purported to show that their pecuniary activities, unbridled, led not only to their own enrichment, but also worked to the public good.

At no time can one state that economic high theory in its origin was the product of intensive research. For one thing, the tools, such as statistical information, for establishing the invalidity of hypotheses were not available. The newly rising merchant class simply used convenient hypotheses to project what was good for the individual or class of merchant to the society as a whole. As the wool merchant goes, so goes the nation. In other words, the social structure was projected to the universe. In its origin it was what Bloch calls ideology.

Routh insisted that Adam Smith's *Wealth of Nations* contained both types of economics. But we took the high theory and ignored that which pertained to canoe building. As Routh put it,

> In due course, Smith the doctrinaire was installed as the Father of Economics, while Smith the empiricist and skeptic was forgotten, and the curious legend fostered that he had invented or discovered it all. Perhaps it would have strained credulity if people had been asked to suppose that a theory developed long before the industrial age was relevant to problems to which industrialism had given rise? And the fact that, as we have seen, the main corpus of theory ante-dates the industrial revolution by a hundred years and lives on in the textbooks of today is, indeed, a testimony that it is remote enough from reality to be impervious to those substantial changes, for better or worse, to which reality has been prey.[8]

The Theory today justifies "the market" way of doing things. But the market is rather vaguely defined so that it accommodates almost any arrangement of things so long as it has the blessing of private ownership. The only remaining meaning that "the market" has currently is one of private ownership. Even a prison may disappear into the market system if someone is given a private patent to operate one as the exclusive agent of the government. As used by Smith, the market had some delineating features; today it means no more than the status quo in that part of the economy that is rather euphemistically referred to as the "private sector."

The irony of modern national income accounting, which shows so clearly and overwhelmingly the interrelated nature of the government and industry, is that it has contributed a terminological water-tight bulkhead separating the private from the public sector. It is always rather amusing when someone, for the moment a public figure, announces, like a stage figure, that he/she is about to step through the bulkhead to the private sector. Those from the petroleum, airline, automobile, food and fiber, and communications industries, to name only a few more notable ones, have found that bulkhead in actuality is about as watertight as a sieve.

It seems to me that institutional economics has been emphasizing that economists should focus on knowledge, not ideology. When both Commons and Veblen made a distinction between business and industry, Veblen using these specific terms and Commons using the terms "business efficiency" and "engineering efficiency," they were making the distinction that Bloch found in all culture. No separation can be made between belief and practice. The two are an integral part of all behavior; in fact, behavior in the absence of belief is impossible, and belief in the absence of behavior is meaningless. On the cognitive side rather than the practices side of human behavior the bifurcation took the form of ideology and knowledge.

One reason that it seems to be so difficult even today to make these distinctions register is what can only be held to be the preposterous belief that for some strange reason we are remarkably rational and free from such cultural legerdemain. Sometime – the exact time remains unspecified – we, like a snake sloughing its skin, left behind all such belief and practice. But all peoples participate in this form of self-deceit. It is those others that practice magic and believe in myth. Any anthropologist who approached a group of people by insisting they record their myth would totally botch the job – that is, presuming that this anthropologist used the word in their language that connotes what myth does in ours. The researcher would be asking them to reveal their most emotionally held beliefs and indicating, by the word choice, that he/she thought them to be dispensable.

The return to ideology

Ideology is at its height at those times in which a group of people, for whatever reason, feel most threatened. That is the meaning of the Ghost Dance of the Plains Indians, the cargo cults on the north shore of New Guinea in post-World War II days, and of Pol Potism in Cambodia or Kampuchea. And that just may help explain the turn to Reaganism and all it connotes in our society today.

What used to be referred to as the East–West split has created an atmosphere of fear both in the United States and in Russia. That fear is intensified by the existence of the atom bomb. There are individuals in the United States, such as the Identity Christians, who believe in a literal apocalypse coming in the form of an atomic war. The survivalist cult is one that sees imminent disaster.[9] Admittedly these groups are manifesting extreme forms of fear. But even among less extreme groups, there has been a sense of anxiety and ennui ever since the end of the Vietnam War.

Under these conditions we find that ideology, fundamentalism if you wish, plays a larger role. Is it any surprise that the same condition exists within the economics profession? What else would sustain a Mont Pelerin Society?[10] The seeming triumph of marginalism in economics today is not a function of prodigious new research. Nor is it an adjustment in theory to accommodate the startling technological change transforming the workaday economy; far from that, it attempts to shape and form the rather awkward actualities to conform to the theory. It construes the airline industry, operating $125,000,000 747s, as no different than Adam Smith's berry merchants and wonders why deregulation means only that necessary regulation has shifted from the public to the private. As Guy Routh has shown, its basic premises were well in place as the collective representations (ideology) of a newly rising merchant class three hundred years ago. Bloch's past is in the present.

Even Keynes has been brought within the ideology. Keynes represented a break from faith in the unbridled market. The consequences of Keynesian analysis of the economy were some very practical governmental measures that to the faithful meant intrusion into the market, a blurring of the private and public sectors. This threat was taken care of by the neo-classical synthesis so that today bastard Keynesianism has become part of the ideology. It is so interpreted to demonstrate the futility of any policy other than that of laissez-faire. Of course, we must exempt the post-Keynesians, but they represent low theory.

One of the more interesting far-reaching consequences of The Theory (ideology) is the creation of a stock exchange in China under the impression that such a creation will promote industrial efficiency.[11] In the United States this has been greeted with enthusiasm. In China it has been promoted by an economist, Li Yining, no doubt trained in The Theory in the United States, perhaps even Chicago. In some mysterious way a stock market will promote technological efficiency in steel, power, aircraft production, and perhaps sewage disposal. Such is the power of ideology parading as scientific economics.

It seems to me that the job of the institutionalists, as well as other economists not enamored with The Theory, is to look and see, to stay to watch the canoe building. Do all of those things that galled Margaret Mead. Gather knowledge, not perpetuate ideology.

I will conclude with one more quote, this one also from Guy Routh:

> I do not for a moment underestimate the difficulties that lie ahead, for blocking the way are powerful vested interests with the qualities of a self-perpetuating religious order. On the other hand there is no way forward from this order except to abandon it. We have to identify and study the ills of society with the meticulousness of virologists, and the devotion of anthropologists studying a primitive tribe. I firmly believe that the economy is susceptible of understanding by those who are willing to look and see, and that the appropriate paradigm will tell us what to look for, where to look, and how to find answers.[12]

Notes

1 I do not know whether Chase was ever given credit for such a phrase as a "war on poverty," but I have never found any earlier use of the phrase.
2 Stuart Chase, *The Tragedy of Waste* (New York: Macmillan, 1925), pp. 17–18.
3 Maurice Bloch, "The Past and the Present in the Present," in *Man* 12 (August 1977): 278–92.
4 Ibid., p. 286.
5 Margaret Mead, *Blackberry Winter* (New York: Washington Square Press, 1972), p. 223.
6 Donald E. Brown, *Hierarchy, History and Human Nature* (Tucson: University of Arizona Press, 1972), pp. 330–2.
7 Lester Thurow, *Dangerous Currents* (New York: Random House, 1983), p. xix.
8 Guy Routh, *The Origin of Economic Ideas* (New York: Vintage Books, 1977), p. 104.
9 James Coates, *Armed and Dangerous: The Rise of the Survivalist Right* (New York: Noonday Press, Farrar, Straus & Giroux, 1987).
10 Sidney Blumenthal, *The Rise of The Counter Establishment: From Conservative Ideology to Political Power* (New York: Times Books, Random House, 1986). Real events, of course, such as simultaneous inflation and unemployment, as well as unsettling problems of the Near East and elsewhere, graphically depicted daily by television on the evening news, prepared the way for the return to fundamentalism. That economics is not immune to these influences is made quite clear in the chapter entitled "Capitalism and Friedman" in Blumenthal. What is happening in economics is only a part of what is happening on a much broader front. Economists, like the members of the Supreme Court, are not immune to the newspapers. Not that economists generally go with the wind, although some do seem to be very fashion conscious. But how the wind is blowing will affect which economists are generally heard at the moment. This most certainly does have an influence on young economists engaged in the "long conversation" called graduate education. Who is worth listening to is partially determined by who for the moment is being heard outside the classroom. Robert Eisner responded to a note of praise for a non-fashionable op-ed piece on savings in the *New York Times* in the midst of the 1988 presidential campaign by writing, "I shall keep trying to influence politicians and our colleagues, but it is not always easy."
11 Nicholas D. Kristof, "China, Seeking More Efficiency, Looks to a Stock Market System," *New York Times*, 5 December 1988, p. CI.
12 Routh, *The Origin of Economic Ideas*, p. 311.

20 Ceremonialism as the dramatization of prosaic technology

Who did invent the *coup de poing*?

Journal of Economic Issues, vol. 25 (June 1991), pp. 551–9

COMMENTARY BY WILLIAM M. DUGGER

This essay is one of the most succinct critiques ever written of the great man theory of economic history. Hamilton explains that new technology is not invented or discovered by great men. It is not a product of individual genius. Instead, new technology is a product of the community's existing body of matter-of-fact knowledge about how to do things. Technological progress is not a poetic struggle of great heroes as they battle against communal ignorance. Technological progress is the life process of the community as its working members go about the everyday activity of making a living.

As he explains one of the major themes of institutionalism, Hamilton also illuminates ceremonialism and the great neoclassical fallacy of treating the factors of production as products of the natural world rather than products of the social world.

By "*coup de poing*," Hamilton does not mean giving someone a direct punch with the fist. That is the common meaning of the term. However, it is also the name of an early tool, a hand-held tool with a sharp edge that was used in Paleolithic times as an ax. Hamilton uses the latter meaning of *coup de poing*.

CEREMONIALISM AS THE DRAMATIZATION OF PROSAIC TECHNOLOGY: WHO DID INVENT THE *COUP DE POING*?

The technological process, in current application as well as in advancement, is an impersonal one – not one of heroics or histrionics. As one examines the actualities of past technological development, it becomes clear that inventive possibilities and probabilities displace specific individuals as primary actuators. The progression of technology is perfectly explicable in the absence of knowledge of the specific individuals under whose supposed suzerainty the advancement took place. Who did invent the *coup de poing*? What was his/her name? And who was responsible for the first scraper, the first arrowhead, the first fire drill, the first bow, the first blow gun? Who invented the fish hook? What are the names of those stalwart and unsung heroic individuals who gave to us those rudiments of technology on which all the rest is built? Who wert thou, O heroes and heroines of old? Who were the neglected Nobels of the past?

If such questions seem irrelevant today, so are today's quests to enshrine the individuals supposedly responsible for today's particular way stations on what is otherwise a continuous impersonal technological process. Disputation sometimes becomes quite fierce over the true authors of specific technological innovations. And concern is expressed over providing sufficient incentive to individuals to keep the process going. Can we sustain inventive genius? This is the kind of question of which great conferences and symposia are made. This outlook, however, is one generated by the false view of the technological process that asking such a foolish question as who invented the *coup de poing* is meant to help clarify.

Such exercises to establish praise, if not blame, are partially attributable to the conventional manner in which invention is perceived. In the traditional account of inventive advance, the individual is primary and the invention is secondary. All innovation is no more than the sum total of unique individual creations that at any time make up the totality of technology. Individual inventors contribute to the totality of technology somewhat in the manner that individual coelenterates contribute to the totality of the coral atoll – by discrete individual accretions.

Without raising once again the nineteenth-century preoccupation with the ontological and epistemological questions of idealism versus materialism, this whole notion of the individual basis of the inventive process is fueled by an outlook that is essentially idealist. The invention of the steam engine really did have its conception in the mind of a precocious young James Watt intently watching that steam kettle lid! It is also manifest in Alexander Graham Bell's first telephonic message concerning the technological intentions of God. All such anecdotes, of course, contribute to the perpetuation of the notion that the advance of technology is nothing more than the arithmetic sum of all unique individual creative acts.

If, for understanding the technological process, this conception of invention being a function of immaculate intellectual invention is a pestiferous one, so is the further misconception of technology to which it almost certainly leads. Even institutionalists participate in this latter, although they usually warn against the intellectual hazards that follow from just such a view. Perhaps, since all technology does manifest itself in some physical presence, the misconception is almost inevitable. But it is almost fatal to the understanding of the technological process, or what Veblen called the life process, to view technology as a collection of inanimate things that human beings must somehow master. Both of these views or preconceptions concerning technology, that it is a function of individual genius and that it consists of a heap of physical things that go ultimately as archaeological remains to furbish present and future museums, misinterpret what is the most significant aspect of the human enterprise.

It is perhaps a trite point to make once again, but man is distinguished from fellow primates by a singular ability to manufacture and use tools. Most certainly R. M. Yerkes and subsequently many others have contrived situations so that some of the higher apes, aided by other than natural biological means, have been able to retrieve bananas from without their cages. They thereby demonstrate elementary tool behavior, at least to the satisfaction of their benevolent tormenters. But human beings compose the only species that is able to advance the process and build on previous banana retrieval devices. As a matter of fact, it is human beings who obligingly supply the instruments for their fellow creatures to retrieve bananas. One might even go so far as to argue that it is the tool-making capability of human beings that, through the creation of the experimental setting, makes it possible for fellow sapiens to demonstrate their rudimentary tool-using potential. Hence, what is being demonstrated primarily is the tool-making capacity of *Homo sapiens* when the caged animal retrieves the banana with the artifacts conveniently provided (White 1949, p. 35; 1987, chap. 17).

The tool process is a human function, not a function of ants, guppies, antelopes, or zebras. Tools have no meaning in the absence of human beings. And in ancient digs in caves, alluvial washes, and river gorges, we identify the fossilized skeletal remains of *Homo sapiens* when there is clear and unmistakable evidence of tool behavior and tool making.

In any culture the technological process by virtue of which human beings secure a livelihood is most certainly an impersonal and prosaic one. Not impersonal or prosaic in the sense that its outcomes are a matter of indifference to humankind, but in the sense that the contribution of any one specific individual is largely a matter of indifference to the technological system and one that cannot be differentiated from the whole (Hobson 1909, pp. 109ff.). Certainly it is individuals who make use of the cultural heritage of scientific and matter-of-fact knowledge. But in taking advantage of such opportunities to use the social heritage of the group, they do so as fully acculturated individuals and, hence, not as authors of that of which they make use. If we may be excused from a verbal circumlocution, it can be said that they are themselves a product of that of which they make use.

In his essay entitled "On the Nature of Capital," Thorstein Veblen made rather clear this impersonality of technology when he wrote:

> Yet it might be argued that each concrete article of "capital goods" was the product of some one man's labor, and, as such, its productivity, when put to use, was but the indirect, ulterior, deferred productiveness of the maker's labor. But the maker's productivity in the case was but a function of the immaterial technological equipment at his command, and that in its turn was the slow spiritual distillation of the community's long experience and initiative.
>
> (Veblen 1919, p. 339)

The impersonality of the technological system is especially manifest in the process of invention, the very one point in the technological process where authorship claims might seem warranted (White 1987, chap. 18). It is not because heroes, all on their own, do their inventive stuff that technology is advanced, popular myth to the contrary notwithstanding. Invention consists of the combination of pre-existing technological traits into a new combination. In order for some one individual to make a contribution to the inventive process, the state of the industrial arts must have already advanced to the point that invention is possible. Heroes are not such by advancement of the state of the industrial arts; the state of the industrial arts makes heroes. In the vernacular of those who specialize in these matters, invention takes place when technological conditions are "ripe" for such an occurrence.

As testimony to this point, we have numerous examples of more or less simultaneous and independent inventions and discoveries, some of the more outstanding and oft-cited being the calculus by Isaac Newton and G. W. Leibnitz and evolution by Charles Darwin and Alfred Wallace, as well as more mundane matters, such as the invention of the automobile in the late nineteenth century. This latter event has quite a number of claimants and most with an element of legitimacy that could not adhere to any claimant prior to the advent of the relatively compact internal combustion engine. In other words, the opportunity to become an accredited inventive hero is a function of the impersonal advancement of the industrial arts.

In short, we cannot assign to individual responsibility the advance of technology because the individual actions that we might isolate as evidence are themselves a function of that continuous technological process. The technological process is a social, not an individual, one. New Guinea highlanders do not invent microchips, just as Grecian philosophers of old strolling about the Acropolis did not invent printing from movable type – not because of a lack of something called basic intelligence or, perhaps, initiative and enterprise, whatever they happen to be, but because they did not live within a technological milieu that made such inventions possible.

If we view technology as behavior rather than as things to be created and then mastered as an ongoing behavioral process, then there is no place for individual heroics. So-called inventors are themselves a product of that which they allegedly invent. Their inventions are a part of what is a social process. Of course, individuals as such do make use of technology, if one wishes to put it this way. That was the point of the fingernail painting controversy that agitated anthropologists at mid-century and earlier (White 1949, p. 143). But an individual separate from technology is an individual separate from culture, a mere piece of palpitating protoplasm. In other words, the inventive process is one in which it is impossible to separate the unique individual contribution from the total context within which that contribution takes place. Inventors work with tools. And that alleged unique personality, to which it is so tempting to assign responsibility, is itself a creation of the tool process.

We have a total situation. We have an inventor and we have an invention. We have an inventor working within a continuous process of development and we have an advance in that process. Does this deny that individuality? No. It merely acknowledges that within the total situation it is impossible to distinguish what was contributed by the inventor and what by the technological possibilities or opportunities, both past and present. The advance of technology is a prosaic one, not a poetic one.

Within the cultural analysis of the institutionalist, however, another, poetic dimension is most certainly present. Although we might agree that the life process, or the technological process, is an impersonal one, no culture, no people has been satisfied to let it go at this. As we are well aware, this impersonal process is associated with other social activity, to which Veblen referred as rendering ceremonial adequacy. Ritual invidiousness seems endemic in every culture from the hunter and gatherer, such as the Arunta and the Andaman Islander, through the Melanesian Neolithic taro raiser, down to industrial culture of today. From the witchety grub gatherer to the space-age astronaut, the answer to the question of who invented the *coup de poing* seems to be of overriding importance.

Sometimes we are apt to note that the ceremonial aspect of culture seems to simulate the technological (Ayres 1944, chap. 8). When so noting, we are also apt to look for a one-for-one relationship. With every stroke of the drop forge, surely someone else must strike a blow with a small, ineffective ceremonial counterpart. But no such literal meaning can be attributed to the notion of the simulated nature of ceremonial behavior. The ceremonial aspect is actually the recounting of impersonal technological events in personal terms. It is an account that, while not excluding technology, treats it as a minor necessity, as "mere" technology, an assortment of physical things manipulated and directed by cultural heroes.

Within the capitalist system, to which most economic analysis has been directed, production and technology and the advance of technology are accounted for in the theory by other than prosaic means. A society composed within its economic dimensions of landlords, laborers, and capitalists gets projected to the whole universe of production as land, labor, and capital (Hamilton 1987). And somehow the prosaic processes of steel production, aircraft construction, oil refining, and sewage disposal get transformed into rather interesting combinations and recombinations of substances called land, labor, and capital. In any treatment of any one of these technological processes, two explanations exist. One is very prosaic. Steel is produced by the mundane processes of mining coal, iron, and limestone, converting the coal to coke, combining these elements within a blast furnace, converting the resultant iron into steel through other technological processes and on to further finishing. Each step of the way can be detailed in very matter-of-fact terms. But within the analysis of conventional economics this can all be described as the combination of land, labor, and capital by a foresighted entrepreneur or personalized corporation so as to turn out steel in just the quantity and quality that consumers have indicated, through their bids in the marketplace, that they desire. And that disposes of the matter of production of any commodity or service, be it the production of clams or space flight.

Clarence Ayres insisted that analyzing production in terms of substances called land, labor, and capital "is an odd way to summarize the blessings of civilization" (1952, p. 354). And yet we seem to be able to shift back and forth from one system to the other in a remarkable show of classificatory virtuosity.

Ceremonialism is a dramatic presentation in terms of human potencies of the same technological prosaic events by virtue of which a tribe actually does secure a livelihood. Ceremonialism supposedly establishes personal authorship within an impersonal productive system. It constitutes a personification of an impersonal social process.

The chief of Omarakana in the Trobriands is ultimately responsible for the outcome of the mundane grubbing care by virtue of which the tribal members actually raise tubers (Malinowski 1935). By virtue of his manipulation of land, labor, and capital, Donald Trump really does erect all of those buildings. Just as the taros that are produced in fields in which the chief has never set foot are attributable to his productive potency, so are the buildings on land on which Donald Trump has never, or only fleetingly, and then only on ceremonial occasions, set foot. If one cared to be facetious and risk the charge of being frivolous, one might refer to this as "the Trump effect."

Such attributions of personal productive potency in differential amounts sanctify and justify a differential flow of income. In the absence of such a communally held belief in differential productive potency, the wide discrepancies that exist in income distribution, and hence in levels of living in almost all societies, would be intolerable. The success in the technological activity is attributed to the "instituted hierarchy," as the eminent French anthropologist Maurice Bloch referred to the status system (Bloch 1977). By projecting the status order to the impersonal productive system, the former is authenticated. Most certainly the well-being of any people, taken as a whole, is a matter of the state of the industrial arts available to them. This is no less true of the hunter and gatherer and the early Neolithic manipulator of the digging stick than it is of those peoples with access to today's industrial arts. But by projecting the "instituted hierarchy" to the productive process and by establishing claims by imputing authorship, the well-being of the tribe seems to be contingent on the preservation of that system of authorship (ownership?).

And, ironically, by attributing success in the industrial arts to this hierarchy, the latter is authenticated by the real source of human well-being, the industrial arts. To the extent that a tribe does eke out an existence, however precarious, since it attributes its success to the moral order through which it dramatizes the productive process, the real success of the latter authenticates the relevance of the moral order. There are flocks and crops, there are steel ingots and kilowatts of electricity, and their very existence evidences the truth of the moral order. If other peoples seek similar success, they too need to lead such a moral life. Free enterprise über alles! Theology reigns supreme.

Nowhere in economic literature is this way of thinking more devastatingly clear than in Joseph Schumpeter's *Capitalism, Socialism and Democracy*. Therein he claims that all of modern science is attributable to the profit system and that, in the future as in the past, all victories over "cancer, syphilis, and tuberculosis will be as much capitalist achievements as motor cars, pipe lines or Bessemer steel have been" (Schumpeter 1947, pp. 125–6).

The ceremonial elements in the modern economy have attracted the major attention of conventional economics. Economists have devoted their major efforts to what might be called the shadow economy. Of course, the significance of technology is grudgingly conceded, but it is always acknowledged as a secondary element within today's capitalist economy. It is "mere" technology –not the very life process of human beings, the real thing that distinguishes *Homo sapiens* from other primates. And much effort has gone into rationalizing through such concepts as marginal productivity, marginal utility, real rates of interest and natural rates of unemployment and price, and, of course, equilibrium, the instituted hierarchy and attributing to its functioning the real cause of human well-being. The effect of this effort has been the creation of a Platonic economic universe within the bounds of which reality is invisible and the visible or experiential is not real. That whole endeavor misses the connection by relegating the primary source of human well-being to the position of a silent partner.

I assume this observation to be the major thrust of Veblen's oft-quoted statement to the effect that "there is the economic life process in great measure awaiting theoretical formulation." Surely he was not saying merely that there was much work yet to be done. By his time, economists had already done much work. What he was saying is that the major source of human well-being and progress, the technological process, or the economic life process, had been taken for granted – more or less as a given. He was well aware that much theoretical economic work had been done, as his critical essays testify. What he was saying is that we have done the wrong work. We have spent our time rationalizing what constitutes the poetic and dramatic aspect of economic behavior; how we earn our daily bread still remains largely obscured.

References

Ayres, C. E. 1944. *The Theory of Economic Progress*. Chapel Hill: University of North Carolina Press.

——. 1952. *The Industrial Economy*. Boston: Houghton Mifflin.

Bloch, Maurice. 1977. "The Past and the Present in the Present," *Man* 12 (August): 278–92.

Hamilton, David. 1987. "A Theory of the Social Origin of Factors of Production," reprinted in *Alternatives to Economic Orthodoxy*. Ed. Randy Albelda, Christopher Gunn, and William Waller. Armonk, N.Y.: M. E. Sharpe.

Hobson, John. 1909. *The Industrial System*. New York: Longmans Green.

Malinowski, Bronislaw. 1935. *Coral Gardens and Their Magic*. New York: American Book Company.

Schumpeter, Joseph. 1947. *Capitalism, Socialism, and Democracy*. New York: Harper.

Veblen, Thorstein. 1919. *The Place of Science in Modern Civilization*. New York: Viking.

White, Leslie. 1949. *The Science of Culture*. New York: Farrar, Straus.

——. 1987. *Ethnological Essays*. Albuquerque: University of New Mexico Press.

21 Economics

Science or legend?

Journal of Economic Issues, vol. 18 (June 1984), pp. 565–72

COMMENTARY BY WILLIAM M. DUGGER

As an institutional economist, Hamilton challenges the validity of conventional theory. He shows that conventional or orthodox economics is a religion, not a science. Its basic arguments are tautologies and truisms. It is impervious to logical and empirical attack. It is a ceremonial belief system that gives spiritual legitimacy to our economic practices. It is not a set of tools and skills that furthers the technological process of social provisioning. It is a belief in the entrepreneur as the fountainhead. Hamilton concludes the article with "To challenge the validity of conventional theory is to challenge the validity of capitalist society itself."

ECONOMICS: SCIENCE OR LEGEND?

The enduring powers of conventional economic theory are legendary. Guy Routh, in his study of the durable nature of conventional economic theory, noted that substantial criticism originated almost simultaneously with the rise of the conventional doctrine. As Routh put it:

> Heresy accumulated, but the heretics did not succeed in bringing about the changes that they sought. They did, nonetheless, establish an impressive critical literature. Indeed, if one were to assemble the writings of the heretics and add those of the faithful during their lapses into heresy, a body of doctrine would emerge as impressive, in its way, as the orthodoxy itself.[1]

But as Routh shows, despite the formidable nature of the heresy the conventional wisdom continues rather undisturbed by the trenchant criticism. C. E. Ayres has remarked on this matter. He noted in his *Theory of Economic Progress* the ability of the orthodox body of theory to absorb its critics:

Furthermore, the critics themselves are continually reabsorbed into economic orthodoxy, in many cases apparently without their being aware of this singular conversion. If the axioms and theorems of the classical tradition could somehow be tabulated, it would be found that there is no one of them which has not at some time or other undergone critical demolition. Even today critics of classical orthodoxy complain bitterly that it is a sort of Hydra. Classical theory presents no one head upon which a lethal blow might be delivered; instead, wherever criticism scores a stroke the particular expression that is under attack is forthwith abandoned and two more are straightaway developed to virtually the same effect.[2]

The extreme durability and immunity to criticism of conventional theory has led some observers to liken it to theology. John Kenneth Galbraith stated in his *American Capitalism*, in reference to the tenacity with which the simplistic Smithian model of the economy is held, that "man cannot live without an economic theology – without some rationalization of the abstract and seemingly inchoate arrangements which provide him with his livelihood."[3] C. E. Ayres, in his *Toward a Reasonable Society*, in commenting on Smithian economics and the conviction with which it is held, stated, "In the six generations that have passed since the time of Adam Smith this doctrine has come to be held by the community at large with an intensity of conviction that approaches religious faith."[4]

In his latest book-length publication, Lester Thurow argues at considerable length that the conventional version of the economy, which he refers to as the price-auction model, is becoming a theology. He is worth quoting at length:

> But beyond a shift in ideas, something else has been at work: The profession, the discipline of economics is on its way to becoming a guild. Members of a guild, as we know, tend to preserve and advance traditional theories rather than try to develop new ways of thinking and doing things to solve new problems. The equilibrium price-auction view of the world is a traditional view with a history as old as that of economics itself; the individual is asserted to be a maximizing consumer or producer within free supply–demand markets that establish an equilibrium price for any kind of goods or service. This is an economics blessed with an intellectual consistency, and one having implications that extend far beyond the realm of conventional theory. This, in short, also a political philosophy, often becoming something approaching a religion.[5]

Further on, he adds:

> By analogy, once the Confucian scholars of ancient China passed a very complicated set of entrance examinations, they used the same examinations to keep others out. Both then and now, all honor is reserved for those who can explain current events in terms of "The Theory," while anyone trying to

develop new theories to explain recent developments is regarded with suspicion at best. In economics today, "The Theory" has become an ideology rather than a set of working hypotheses used to understand the behavior of the economy found in the real world.... All over the globe, we have recently witnessed a return to religious fundamentalism. In my view, the return to the equilibrium price-auction model in economics represents a parallel development – a desire for psychological certainty in a world that is, in the last instance, uncertain.[6]

It has become quite common to refer to the conventional model of the economy, in both its formal version and that more simplistic version collectively held and espoused on suitable occasions by highly placed corporate executives and highly placed journalists, as theology-like. Most certainly if we ever did attain the condition of equilibrium toward which the worldly economy is allegedly striving, but from which it is always distracted by disturbing (evil?) forces, it would indeed resemble a total state of grace. Consumers would be receiving satisfactions exactly equal to those rendered by the money forgone, producers would be receiving money incomes in direct ratio to the money value of the contributions made to the products being purchased, and price would measure both sides of the equation. All reciprocal obligations would be met; maximum well-being would prevail; we would have the best of all possible worlds. A system so articulated is indeed benign and whether one could say that, given laissez-faire, it is provoked by benign neglect, it most certainly would be one of divine grace. Thorstein Veblen's allegation that the economics of Smith was teleological most certainly alluded to its theological aspects.[7]

But suggesting that this classic model, which its proponents insist is the product of scientific endeavor, is truly theological in substance, as well as likeness, would be viewed even by many of its critics as pushing an analogy too far. Yet there is not one part of the whole train of thought that has not at one time or another been subject to successful attack, successful in the sense that the emperor has been shown to be without clothes. The tautological nature of utility and of productivity, the twin foundation stones of demand and supply, has been acknowledged frequently. Price measures utility, and utility is that stuff manifest in price. Wages are determined by productivity, and productivity is that stuff measured by wages. No separate measure of either utility or productivity exists other than one of price. One must take it on faith that there is such an equality. The explanation of price as being affected by two abstract forces, supply and demand, comes off no better. It too turns out to be a truism. And most mysterious of all is capital, which is neither money nor technology, yet is both and still yet neither. This defies even the mystery surrounding the trinity.

Most critics have concentrated on these tautologies and truisms, although some have concentrated on the unreality of the whole system. After Veblen, Frank Fetter, and Edwin Cannan, as well as others, exposed the logical problems in the meanings of capital, that should have been it; no more confusion.[8] Get on with the show. But even after the great exposures, the confusion remains. It would almost seem that economists are particularly susceptible to wrong-headedness, an unwillingness to mend their ways. Surely economics can be straightened out simply by pointing out its logical inconsistencies and internal contradictions.

But such has not been the case. The fallacy of composition that pervades what is now referred to as micro-economics, and to which much of Keynes's arguments were directed, is resolved not by abandoning the fallacy, but by engrossing Keynes and making him a party to the fallacy. Such is the great neo-classical synthesis. New terms for older ones are invented, all to the same effect. Pleasure and pain (W. S. Jevons) are dismissed for utility and disutility (A. Marshall), and the latter dismissed for revealed preference, all to the effect of showing the consumer in a state of Benthamite ecstasy. The problem of Say's law, that savings will flow back into real investment, is pointed out clearly, only to be resurrected in a new guise as "supply-side" economics.

Obviously we are confronted with something other than intellectual obstinacy. The conditions call for an examination of economic ideas and beliefs as cultural phenomena rather than as logical constructs in which contradictions will yield to cool reason. In other words, we need to examine economic theory, that part Thurow refers to as "The Theory," from the perspective of the anthropologist rather than from that of the logician. We need to ask ourselves first, what are the attributes of theology and practice? Secondly, we must ask ourselves whether "The Theory" and the practices that "The Theory" authenticates constitute our religion.

All religions consist of practices, or rites and ritual, to the efficacy of which the theology purports to testify. These are rites and rituals that propitiate, ameliorate, and extend a life force, belief in which is perpetuated by the practices. It is, in fact a self-fulfilling set of practice and accompanying belief. The belief sanctions the practice; the practice testifies to the truth of the belief.

All too frequently when we think of religion in our own culture we are drawn to those highly formal versions represented by the established churches, holdovers from an earlier agrarian and pastoral society, which have about as much to do with today's society as does today's spoken word with the ancient languages in which some services are still conducted. As a matter of fact, more than one study of these readily recognized religions have noted how they accommodated themselves to the new pecuniary society that overwhelmed the medieval society in which they had a day-to-day meaning. As scholars have insisted, the medieval church was integrated into society in a way that does not characterize the vestigial remains of that church today.[9] The secular and the sacred were an integrated whole.

Emile Durkheim showed in his *Elementary Forms of the Religious Life* that religion arises from social practice.[10] And A. M. Hocart indicated very effectively that all social practices and accompanying belief are coterminous.[11] But both practice and belief have two dimensions, an institutional or ceremonial one and a technological or instrumental one. As Bronislaw Malinowski demonstrated in the case of the Trobriand Islands, the construction of sailing canoes as well as the raising of taro involved practices and skills, some of which were instrumental and some of which extended to the whole technological process what Veblen referred to as ceremonial adequacy.[12]

This technology/institutions dichotomy is readily recognized in regard to practice. It is not so readily recognized in regard to belief. We have a tendency to view the social process as one of practice, some of which is ceremonial and some of which is technological, and concomitant belief. But belief can be similarly bifurcated for analytic purposes. The beliefs of the Trobrianders concerning the efficacy of garden or canoe magic are something quite different from those concerning the nature of adzing in hollowing a canoe or digging-stick cultivation in raising taro. The latter set of beliefs is very matter-of-fact. Manipulate an adz in such a fashion and one is able to hollow a log as one step in the construction of sailing canoes. This will be explained in terms of sailing properties of the resultant canoe, as will digging stick manipulation be explained in terms of the successful cultivation of tubers. But along with this belief exists in a symbiotic relationship a whole set of beliefs not subject to test by any possible operation. The justified practices are ones in which mystic forces are manipulated by properly authenticated individuals in properly authenticated roles. Proof of their efficacy lies in the myths and legends of the tribe that testify to the dire events that happened in the past when the practices were scamped and to the richness of life when they were meticulously observed. To the extent that the technological practices do produce canoes and taro, the mythological belief is confirmed. If the technological processes fail or uncontrollable adversity strikes, it is evidence that counterforces were at work, that perhaps some of the ritual was not properly performed. Technology can fail; magic and ritual can never go wrong.

It is a modern-day conceit that such ceremonial practices and beliefs do not exist in this matter-of-fact world. At some time – just exactly when has never been ascertained, although the date is vaguely associated with the eighteenth century – all such ceremonial and associated belief was dropped. People became creatures of pure reason. Other tribes have pre-logical minds; ours is wholly logical. Yet no other tribe believes in identified myth and legend either. Had the Trobriand Islanders translated the anthropologists' use of the word "ceremonial" into their Trobriand linguistic equivalent, they would have realized that a term that obviously indicates that its referents are dispensable was being used to refer to some of their most dearly held beliefs and practices. This being the case, perhaps we should begin to look at economic thought in our culture being this two-edged type of analysis.

When we examine the origin of economic ideas, as did Guy Routh and others such as Max Beer, we find that early economic thought was not the work of prodigious research into those inchoate social relationships that comprise a pattern of economic relationships.[13] The early economics, which lives on until today in general outline, was composed of the collective representations of a merchant community steeped in the virtues of buying and selling. These were the collective representations of the new merchant classes being propelled to dominance in a "frontier" society, being thrust forward by control over technological innovation in a society open to cultural diffusion.[14] Technological economic activity was ceremonialized by the cash nexus; it was authenticated by the creation of ownership equities. This, I take it, is why institutional economists have always insisted on the importance of the institution of private property.

In any event, as the merchants took hold of the new technology through the institution of private property, it became quite clear that money, the vulgar representation of the mystic force, capital, was also the basis of power. Without the possession of money or monetary power, no real economic activity would take place, just as in the Trobriands no boat building would take place in the absence of bullroaring. The reciprocal obligations, by virtue of which one trader was ceremonially linked to another, the ceremonial linkage simulating the real technological linkage, were settled by money funds. In a pecuniary society, money comes to have a coercive role that very readily lends credence to a belief in money power. Capital, the collective representation of this money power, is the mystic force from which springs human well-being, or so it is believed.

Many of the mercantilist writers were themselves merchants; these collective representations sanctioned their way of life and simultaneously were very congenial to contemplate. Their primary activities, buying and selling, were the source of human well-being, just as the ceremonial functions of the chief of Omarakana were the source of Trobriand well-being.

The fact that Adam Smith drew upon these earlier writers for many of his notions has been obscured by the emphasis placed upon his criticism of mercantilism. He has been viewed as resolving some of the logical inconsistencies of mercantilist doctrine in his "quest for truth." That misses the significance of Smith. Smith's great virtue to the merchants, who took up his thought almost as it was issued, was his clarification of the collective representations by which money and pecuniary activity were deemed to be the creator of all things. Adam Smith's merchant was primary; the artisan and technician were secondary. And this concept and belief was in conformance with the social ordering of such roles at that time. Although it is not relevant to the present article, the whole classical system was a projection of a society composed of landlords, laborers, and capitalists into an interpretation of the whole universe as land, labor, and capital.

To the present time the correspondence of the theory to reality, or its internal consistency, are wholly irrelevant to it as a belief. That is why critical examination on either of these two points sometimes turns into an exercise in futility. It is not the job of the theory to correspond with reality or to be internally consistent. The job of the theory is to sanction pecuniary activity, which in turn gives authenticity to technological activity. Those who have contended that we worship money have been closer to the truth than their flippancy and irreverence in the traditional sense would indicate. Capital is the representation of the mystic force that the compulsiveness of social life engenders, as Durkheim insisted. That mystic force may be represented as the witchety grub among the Arunta in Australia; in a pecuniary society it comes in the guise of capital and as such is held to be a first cause.

If we look at the social function of classic economic theory, the reason for its tenacity becomes apparent. We undertake no technological activity without its capitalization; and by virtue of capitalization of all technological activity we are constantly reassured of its beneficence. And no role is more beneficent than that of the manipulator of this life stuff, that of the capitalist entrepreneur.

But just as in the Trobriands it would be physically possible to construct sea-worthy canoes without bullroaring, so it is possible in our culture to develop atomic energy without capitalization. As a matter of fact, some of our most pro-digious modern-day technological feats have been without ceremonial adequacy or, in other words, without capitalization. Atomic energy and space flight and satellite activity are but two that come to mind. Of course, given our institutions, an appropriation of money was essential to permit access to the essential tech-nology. But this is something else again from a capitalization process testifying to the mystic efficacy of capital funds. We are ill at ease with such governmental activity, and ironically, when all of the dimensions of our ceremonial activity are recalled, we feel that such governmentally sponsored and budgeted activity lacks authenticity. Only businesspeople have the dynamic perception, the foresight, or what the Polynesians and Melanesians call *mana*, to undertake such technologi-cal activities – despite the fact that we accomplish them daily without such authorization. The research activities of the U.S. Department of Agriculture stand as a monument to the technological success of U.S. agriculture, although they would be the last thing to which an economic historian would allude when recounting agricultural success. Belief in the efficacy and primacy of pecuniary activity and the primacy of entrepreneurs and the entrepreneurial role is the essence of religion. To challenge the validity of conventional theory is to chal-lenge the validity of capitalist society itself.

Notes

1 Guy Routh, *The Origin of Economic Ideas* (New York: Vintage Books, 1977), p. 1.
2 C. E. Ayres, *The Theory of Economic Progress* (Kalamazoo, Mich.: New Issues Press, 1978), p. 11.
3 J. K. Galbraith, *American Capitalism: The Concept of Countervailing Power* (Boston: Houghton Mifflin, 1956), p. 17.
4 C. E. Ayres, *Toward a Reasonable Society* (Austin: University of Texas Press, 1961), p. 25.
5 Lester C. Thurow, *Dangerous Currents: The State of Economics* (New York: Random House, 1983), p. xviii.
6 Ibid., p. xix.
7 Thorstein Veblen, *The Place of Science in Modern Civilization* (New York: Viking Press, 1942), p. 118.
8 Thorstein Veblen, "On the Nature of Capital," in *The Place of Science*, p. 324; Frank Fetter, "Capital," *Encyclopedia of the Social Sciences* (New York: Macmillan, 1930), pp. 187–91; Edwin Cannan, "Capital and the Heritage of Improvement," *Economica* 1 (new series) (November 1943): 381–92.
9 R. H. Tawney, *Religion and the Rise of Capitalism* (New York: Penguin Books, 1947).
10 Emile Durkheim, *The Elementary Forms of the Religious Life* (New York: The Free Press, 1965); see also A. R. Radcliffe, *The Andaman Islanders* (Glencoe, Ill.: The Free Press, 1948), and also Guy E. Swanson, *The Birth of the Gods* (Ann Arbor: University of Michigan Press, 1974).

11 A. M. Hocart, "The Life-Giving Myth," in *The Life-Giving Myth and Other Essays* (New York: Grove Press, n.d.).

12 Bronislaw Malinowski, *Magic, Science, and Religion and Other Essays* (Boston: Beacon Press, 1948); see especially the title essay, "Magic, Science, and Religion."

13 Max Beer, *Early British Economics* (London: George Allen & Unwin, 1938); see also Beer's *An Inquiry into Physiocracy* (London: George Allen & Unwin, 1939).

14 Lynn White, *Medieval Technology and Social Change* (Oxford: Oxford University Press, 1962).

Critique of orthodoxy

22 The cure may be the cancer

Remarks upon receipt of the
Veblen–Commons Award

Journal of Economic Issues, 17 (June 1983), pp. 267–93

COMMENTARY BY WILLIAM M. DUGGER

This is a short and blunt article in which Hamilton explains that Reaganomics
was merely an application to our economic problems of more of that old-time
religion (neoclassical economics) when, in fact, the old-time religion is the cause
of our economic problems. His argument is pure institutionalism and is as applicable today as it was in 1983. Hamilton insisted, "There is no invisible hand."
Instead, Hamilton repeated a simple institutionalist insight: humans must come
together and collectively determine their own well-being in a "pragmatic,
problem-solving approach to the economy."

**THE CURE MAY BE THE CANCER: REMARKS UPON
RECEIPT OF THE VEBLEN–COMMONS AWARD**

Some fifty years ago, in a note on the author of *The Theory of the Leisure Class*,
Stuart Chase wrote:

> The collapse of orthodox doctrine during the years of the world depression
> has vindicated the keenly analytic and prophetic writings of Thorstein
> Veblen. The new point of view and method elaborated by him riddled the
> whole structure of economics as a pseudo-social science and created instead
> an entirely original set of economic categories, based on changing industrial
> conditions rather than an inflexible system formulated from so-called eternal
> principles.[1]

Would that that had been the case!

Sometimes nothing seems ever to change. The conditions I remember well
from my youth – long lines of people waiting patiently for some kind of handout,
private charity organizations such as the Salvation Army declaring they cannot

cope with the homeless, unemployment rates unthinkable in the preceding decade, pronouncements by prominent public figures that prosperity is just around the corner, a president assuring the country that he has heart while he announces he will veto a jobs bill, economists sitting in place and watching hopefully for signs of recovery much like weather observers looking for a break in the storm, the public resigning itself to whatever is in store – are all a part of life today. No one argues as lucidly as some did in the 1930s that we lived too high on the hog so that we are simply suffering the seven lean years that Biblically follow the seven fat, but there are those who take great joy in arguing that our present plight is the harbinger of permanent hard times. The hair shirt will replace the silk, or perhaps the polyester, but we must all knuckle down to austerity. The willingness with which the public as well as its guiders of conventional thought accept this truth rivals the apathy with which many people faced the 1930s great depression, especially in its early days.

One difference exists in the situation today when compared with that of the 1930s. That depression was one into which we blundered, although it was perhaps not unavoidable, as the Brookings Institution's four-volume study *Distribution of Wealth and Income in Relation to Economic Progress* indicated in the mid-1930s. But no one deliberately fingered us all in the late 1920s. That is not the case today.

Of course, the mild depression of the preceding decade – and I consider an average 1970s unemployment rate of 6.2 percent as malingering depression – was also fingered. But in those days the fingering was tempered with a bit of humanity. The gunmen indicated some true concern for the victims. But the depression today was deliberately provoked and we are told by those totally immune from such exigencies that it is the cost "we" must suffer in order to put our house in order.

But how can a nation with the technology we possess and still with resources available to provide well for its population, as well as the populations of a large part of the rest of the world, willingly consign 12,000,000 people to "no visible means of support"? It is interesting to view our present economic discontents from the perspective of Thorstein Veblen as well as that of John R. Commons. That declaration of the collapse of orthodox economics made by Stuart Chase fifty years ago may have been premature. And the failure of the theory to collapse may be at the root of our problems today. The proffered cure may, in fact, be the cancer.

If I interpret Reaganomics correctly, it is a return to the old-time religion, "supply-side" window dressing notwithstanding. Mr. Reagan's economic mind contains the copy-book simplicities of Adam Smith as modified by Alfred Marshall. This is the best of all possible worlds, for everything is working out to a good end. If each and every one of us pursue our own jack-rabbits and the government sees to it that we follow the rules of the hunt, the result will be a magnificent condition to behold. Consumers will receive satisfactions precisely equal to the money satisfactions given up for the products and services; producers will receive income precisely equal to the blood, sweat, and tears incurred in

producing those satisfaction-yielding goods. And price, in competitive equilibrium, measures both the satisfaction extracted and the blood, sweat, and tears
injected. And, of course, under the divine hand of J. B. Say, everyone will be at
work. We need but keep government in its place and the lazy fairy will see that
private anarchy becomes a state of public grace.

Richard Reeves, in his nationally syndicated column, indicated that in the fall
of 1982, when unemployment was rising, the president was quite content with
the successes his program had achieved. He depicted a smiling president vaca-
tioning in California who was convinced of the success of his efforts. To back
up his claim, Reeves quoted from a recent broadside of the American Enterprise
Institute done by a staffer by the name of Rudolph Penner, an economist, and a
Harvard (no less) political scientist by the name of Hugh Heclo. In view of the
sponsor of their "research," it is almost a certainty that the authors are sympathetic to the aims of the Reagan administration.

In any event, in their bulletin they explain the origin of the beatific presidential smile. Somewhat in the candid manner of the Director of the Bureau of the
Budget, they indicate that supply-side economics is a shell game. As a matter of
fact, they argue that Reaganomics is nothing more nor less than a compromise
among fiscal conservatives, monetarists of various persuasions, and supply-
siders, all of whom are doubtful of the others' mental equilibrium. They are
willing to go along, however, because each sees that the outcome of the others'
policy would be to restrict government. Fiscal conservatives, by going for a balanced budget, can reduce government expenditures and they interpret the efforts
of the supply-siders in this light. The supply-siders see virtue in the fiscal conservatives' willingness to curb government spending in the name of balancing
the budget as all to the good in curbing government. And the monetarists buy the
package because tight money (high interest rates) would kill inflation and restrict
government.

In other words, the workability of the economics is not the relevant matter.
What is important is the curtailment of government. It is government that
impairs the free working of the natural order and that inhibits the free spirits of
our entrepreneurs. And the worst of this government activity is that represented
by our expenditure for welfare.

Casper W. Weinberger, when Secretary of Health and Human Services, made
this philosophy clear in a speech before the Commonwealth Club of San Francisco in 1975. He alerted his audience of largely conservative and conventional
persuasion that our social and economic problems stemmed from disregarding
the maxim that government should be minimal for the market (natural order) to
function effectively:

> Federal spending has shifted away from traditional federal functions such as
> defense and toward programs that reduce the remaining freedom of individ-
> uals and lessen the power of other levels of government....
> The shift in federal spending has transformed the task of aiding life's
> victims from a private concern to a public obligation.... We are ... creating

a massive welfare state that has intruded into the lives and personal affairs of our citizens. This intrusion affects both those it seeks to help and those who do the helping. The entire human resources field is under the lash of federal law – doctor, hospital, teacher, college president, student, voluntary agency, city hall, and state capital....

It is also the propensity of welfare states to spend beyond their means, leaving the day of fiscal reckoning to another generation. The news today is that we are that generation.[2]

Having presided effectively enough over welfare in an earlier administration to earn the appellation "Cap the knife," Weinberger apparently now feels sufficiently at ease to assume direction of that aspect of government he indicated in that earlier speech to be government's major function. In any event, the philosophy expressed in that San Francisco speech is the unchallenged conventional wisdom of yesteryear and is apparently the revived received opinion today. That being the case, even those who suffer from the cutbacks in federal expenditure acquiesce in its alleged necessity.

Although Stuart Chase indicated that this way of thinking no longer prevailed in economics, the formal versions of economics that pass muster today as high theory are simply formal versions of the folk wisdom of the tribe. It seems to me that Mr. Weinberger and other highly placed individuals today, as well as their economic counterparts, the keepers of certified truth with a temple in Chicago, may be wholly wrong about where our problems lie. It just could be that our problems do not stem from alleged deviation from the abiding faith. Our problems may very well be the persistence of that abiding faith. To this audience I need not even indicate the author [Veblen] of the words about to be quoted, but this may be one more incidence of "the triumph of imbecile institutions over life and culture."

It seems to me that if Veblen could analyze our situation today he would undoubtedly argue the case other than it is now being argued. For one thing, I am sure that he would note that some of our problems stem from having held the technological lead. In the nineteenth century and in the early part of this century, we were heavy technological borrowers. As a matter of fact, most of American industrial culture is a borrowed and transported product, placed on a continent that, although fully occupied by the industrial arts available to the Indian peoples, offered little institutional resistance to the proliferation of industrial culture. This is in contrast to European culture, in which the industrial revolution occurred. There the new industrial discipline was encumbered by the actualities of an older way of life in place for many centuries. On the North American continent the industrial culture could spread uninhibited by ancient and honorable institutions. We experienced all of those advantages accruing to the borrower that Veblen analyzed in *Imperial Germany*; Europe in this [twentieth] century, relative to the United States, suffered from having taken the lead.

Our conventional view of our own economic development, however, is also an imported product. Classical or conventional economics represents a formalized version of the collective representations of a merchant-dominated society. And in this version development is not viewed as a case of advantageous borrowing. In the conventional account, classical economics and classical economic history come into their own. It was through the initiative, foresight, and enterprise of entrepreneurial cultural heroes that the prodigious events of economic development took place. In their quest for profits the entrepreneurs transformed capital funds by some mysterious process into steel mills, railroads, meat packing plants, sugar mills, and oil refineries. One thing was clear: commercial activity represented a first cause. Pecuniary enhancement of values was primary; industry or technological activity was derivative. In such a version, governments could do nothing but get in the way.

Of course, the actuality was something else. In all cases of industrial development in the United States the alleged prodigious feats of Joseph Schumpeter's innovative entrepreneurs were aided and abetted by the government. We need not go into the history of railroad construction, of tariffs, of an earlier canal building, of banking, or of ship building to illustrate the manner in which government welfare to the well-off was billed as incentive. We have always followed a policy of billing welfare to the rich as incentive and incentive to the poor as welfare.

In all of these cases industry was largely aided and abetted by some privilege, the cash value of which made the difference between bankruptcy and solvency. But what have eluded the economist imbued with the idea that government is a nuisance are the technological successes when government has taken a direct role in advancing technology. One of the bright spots technologically in the United States is our agricultural sector. But when we examine it carefully we find that lying back of the prodigious success is the research made generally available to agriculture and fostered by the United States government. Unlike industrial research, the results of which are often restricted to the patron, government research is available to all, gratis. Perhaps the real danger of the industrialization of agriculture is the possible capture of research by large agri-business units that would thereby be able to restrict and limit the use of the results of that research.

In contrast, in our private enterprise industrial sector, technological advance is restricted in its usage by the rights of private property. And in that industry where the market mentality prevails, a forthright and free use of technology is restricted by corporate hegemony. It is these trappings of private enterprise that Veblen insisted inhibited the free development of technology.

We suddenly find that our industries that led the world forty years ago [in the 1940s] are lagging behind those of other nations today. And industry by industry, from automobiles to steel and oil, we are being told that the solution to the problems of these faltering giants is a return to the free market – meaning, of course, absence of any public planning in areas already privately controlled for private purposes, but areas of such economic magnitude as to be affected with the public interest, as Walton Hamilton once put it.

And I am sure that Veblen would argue that this faith in the market is as much at the root of our problems as are the obvious troubles that befall those who happen to take the technological lead for a while. It appears to me that it is this theological aspect of conventional economic theory to which institutionalism is partially directed. It is an attempt to liberate all from this aspect of economics. Veblen referred to it as the received opinion; John Kenneth Galbraith refers to it as conventional wisdom. It is the kind of faith that Overton Taylor pledged himself to some thirty years ago [in 1952] at a meeting of the American Economic Association when he pledged his allegiance to "liberal capitalism or the system of free enterprise." He stated that his views on the subject were "beliefs or judgments of faith beyond strict knowledge."[3]

Beyond today's new-fangled economic terms lies that theology and faith in the market with no realization whatever that the market registers the values and social fabric of the society, but does not direct that society. There is nothing sacred about market mechanisms. The market is not the reflection of the workings of an invisible hand; it is the reflection of many very visible and busy ones and some not so visible but every bit as busy. Neither Veblen nor Commons could possibly believe that some benign order would come to prevail from the tugging and shoving of the economic behemoths dominant in today's economy. No one familiar with the hearings of the Industrial Commission at the turn of the [twentieth] century could hold to such a simplistic interpretation of economic events. Commons was a participant in those hearings; Veblen obviously had read them, as the notation in *The Theory of Business Enterprise* indicates.

The economics of Veblen and Commons was a problem-solving economics. In solving economic problems no possible approach would be barred because it did not pass the market conformance litmus test. Since the market is not a sacred device, public price controls would be useful devices in conjunction with a Keynesian stabilization policy, as they undoubtedly would have been with Keynes. Economic ideas would be open to amendment and emendation. Planning where necessary would be indulged. Income maintenance systems would be used not only as welfare devices, but as stabilization measures. Cooperatives would be looked upon as useful devices for organizing some of our economic affairs. In short, we would have an open system and a mixed economy.

We would approach problems with the same sense of high adventure that characterized the New Deal. What differentiated the New Deal from what went before was that sense of adventure – not the particular forms that attempted solutions took to existent problems. Those who identify the New Deal with specific programs miss the characteristic that differentiated that era from the preceding one and most certainly from the climate of opinion that prevails today. An absence of economic theology and faith only in human intelligence was typical of that earlier era. To those who insist on emphasizing the obvious fallibility of human intelligence one can only ask, What else have you got to offer?

Our problems today stem from the very faith in the free market that our leaders tell us is the road to our salvation. Institutional economics, in taking the market as non-sacred, as a cultural phenomenon, and as useful in some circumstances and not so useful in other cases, represents secularism in economics. It is an antidote to theology, from which even liberal economists sometimes suffer.

Institutionalism represents an attempt to liberate all from economic theology. I well remember C. E. Ayres one day expostulating to a student who insisted on asking what he suggested we put in its place, "If you need a religion, why not get a good juicy one!"

In the hands of Veblen and Commons, economics was secular, a way of approaching problems pragmatically with a minimum of preconceptions. If we are to save ourselves from a "precarious situation" it will only be by dropping our "imbecile institutions" (Reaganomics?) and following a pragmatic, problem-solving approach to the economy. There is no invisible hand!

Notes

1 Stuart Chase, "A Note on the Author of *The Theory of the Leisure Class,*" in Thorstein Veblen, *The Theory of the Leisure Class* (New York: The Modern Library, 1934), p. v.
2 Casper W. Weinberger, speech before the Commonwealth Club of San Francisco, 21 July 1975. Quoted in Campbell R. McConnell, *Economics: Principles, Problems, and Policies*, 8th ed. (New York: McGraw-Hill, 1981), p. 743.
3 Overton Taylor, "The Future of Economic Liberalism," *American Economic Review* 42 (May 1952): 1.

23 Is institutional economics really "root and branch" economics?

Journal of Economic Issues, vol. 25 (March 1991), pp. 179–86

COMMENTARY BY WILLIAM M. DUGGER

Hamilton begins this article by referring to what he believed to be the seating arrangements of the French Assembly at the time of the French Revolution of 1789. On the right, parties were seated according to their degree of support for the *ancien régime*, with the extreme right being occupied by the most loyal. They were the Royalists and, according to Hamilton, wanted to preserve all of the past. On the left, parties were seated according to their degree of disagreement with the *ancien régime*, with the extreme left being occupied by the most opposed. The parties on the extreme left, according to Hamilton, wanted to eradicate the old system, "root and branch." Hamilton argues that the thinking on both the left and the right were (and still are) dominated by ideology, and ideology is a particular orientation toward a hierarchical system. The left was against the existing one, the right was for it. The ideology of both the left and the right, according to Hamilton, is "root and branch" thinking.

Moving the whole seating arrangement or spectrum into the present day, Hamilton seats himself and institutional or evolutionary economics in the middle. He argues that institutional economics is not ideological, and by this he means that it is not oriented toward the preservation or the replacement of the existing social system. Instead, evolutionary economics is instrumental, and by this he means that it is oriented toward solving specific social problems. Institutionalism is not root and branch economics, Hamilton concludes.

IS INSTITUTIONAL ECONOMICS REALLY "ROOT AND BRANCH" ECONOMICS?

By accident of the seating arrangements in the French Assembly at the time of the French Revolution, the world, or at least the western world, has been afflicted by what can only be called "spectrum thinking." The habit of thought to which

we are giving this designation is so deeply ingrained that on social matters we find it extremely difficult to think without invoking it. All people and all ideas are graded as to being something called leftish- or rightish-oriented.

It is a spectrum and not a polarity because all peoples and ideas are ranged from one polar terminal to the other. There are no voids or vacant spaces in between the so-called polar opposites. To those holding to the leftist pole, all of those even slightly to the right of the extreme left polar position are contaminated to some extent by the right polar position, and vice versa. In our habits of thought we persistently rank ideas and people as to how far to the right and how far to the left they happen to be, the degree of contamination being a function of the square of the distance from the position of the observer. Unlike the degree of contamination, what we may refer to as the degree of detestation seems to vary inversely with the square of the distance from the position of the observer. Both the right and the left seem to be able to hold a contempt for those in the so-called middle far exceeding their mutual contempt for one another. Social ideas and individuals find it almost impossible to escape such invidious placement.

As we indicated in the opening of this piece, such a way of orienting our thinking came about from the French Assembly seating arrangements in which the various contending parties were seated according to their allegiance on the right to the *ancien régime* and on the left their degree of disenchantment with that same regime. Those on the right upheld the past; those on the left represented the new order. One's radicalism was defined by how thoroughly one believed in replacing the old order; if one was for "root and branch" elimination, for leaving nothing standing, as were the Jacobins, one was a radical. Those who wished to preserve all of the past, as did the Royalists, were conservatives. To the present time we more or less rank individuals and movements on how they perceive the present social order and social problems. Those who uphold the existent order usually approach social problems on an individual basis, resorting to personal moral salvation through exhortation. Those on the left usually contend that moral exhortation is futile, that our overwhelming social problems are endemic to the whole rotten system. Short of initiating an entirely new social system, nothing can be done. And, of course, if one assumes that the current ordering of social matters is well designed, it almost precludes any other approach than one on a personal level. And if one assumes that those personal problems that seem so massive in their totality are a function of a faulty social order, then "root and branch" eradication seems the only way to go.

Ironically, the laissez-faire policy typical of upholders of the right polar position joins in a full circle with the anarchist position of the extreme left, which, in its detestation of present society, turns easily into a detestation of social organization in general. Little distinction can be made between the anarchist sans society position and the conservative position that society is no more than the sum total of individual actions. Social individualism, however, in any form is actually an endorsement of the status quo. And on this level, rightists and leftists seem to revel together in reckless abandon.

Unfortunately for such easy classification, not all of human belief lends itself to such treatment. Maurice Bloch, the eminent French anthropologist, in an article "The Past and the Present in the Present," deals with the general problem of human cognition (Bloch 1977). He contended that human belief consists of knowledge and of ideology, the latter finding its authentication in the mythological past and serving as explanation and justification for what he called the current "instituted hierarchy." Bloch is, of course, following along the lines of Emile Durkheim's analysis of the interaction of social hierarchy and the projection of that same social stratification to phenomena of the universe,

For long, Durkheim was construed as contending that the categories in which we conducted social thought and our view of the social and physical universe were reflections of the social structure. We projected the social universe to the world at large, to all phenomena within the realm of experience. However, this overlooks a very significant footnote in Emile Durkheim and Marcel Mauss (1967, pp. 81–2), *Primitive Classification*, in which a distinction is made between those classifications that are based on hierarchicalized notions and those they categorize as "technological classifications." Although in the main text they infer that scientific classification stems from the hierarchical, given what is known about the interrelated nature of science and technology it is probably from the latter that scientific classifications spring. Technology rests on a matter-of-fact basis rather than on an ideological one.

In any event, Bloch insists that ideology constitutes the beliefs that uphold an instituted hierarchy, and they consist of a mass of myth and legend concerning their derivation from the past. Although Bloch does not get into the matter, their counterparts, those ideologies on the "left" that stand in waiting, also have their basis in myth and legend. If in contemporary society the supreme position of capital within capitalism is based on the alleged unique creativeness of capital in a legendary past, as the conventionalized account of the Industrial Revolution pretends, so do those systems that would thrust labor to the fore base their claims on some unique original creation of all things (Hamilton 1983). Both authenticate themselves by reference to events that occurred in some legendary past. Hence Bloch's use of the phrase "the past in the present."

Donald E. Brown in a recent volume, *Hierarchy, History and Human Nature*, while upholding Bloch in general, contends that the distinction between ideological beliefs and those that Bloch labels knowledge, in actuality cannot always be clearly made (Brown 1988, pp. 330–2). Since all belief, ideology, and knowledge exists in a kind of symbiotic relationship, as does all concomitant socially organized behavior, our beliefs in practice are intertwined, ideology and knowledge having a coexistence.

As belief is intertwined with knowledge and ideology, so are tool-oriented behavior and role and status-oriented behavior intertwined. The first, tool-oriented behavior, functions on matter-of-fact knowledge. The second, role/status-oriented behavior, is rationalized and intellectually justified by ideology. The two faces of socially organized behavior are ones in which the first is simulated by the second. Frequently it has been noted that ceremonial behavior appears to be a simulation of tool-oriented behavior (Ayres 1944, pp. 169ff.).

In all cultures, behavior manifests itself as a whole. Canoe building in the Trobriands accompanied by adzing as well as bull-roaring is an integrated one, explicable by reference to a mixture of matter-of-fact knowledge and ideology. The adzing assures a seaworthy canoe and the ceremonial conveys on all those who are participating authorship of the finished canoe. Much the same dual process can be observed in productive activity corporately organized in our own economy (Hamilton 1956, 1957). In other words, a social process based on Edwin Cannan's "heritage of improvement" is converted into one in which personal authorship and ownership rights by virtue of the conveyancing of mystic properties is held responsible for successful sailing and for the output of steel. The whole social/technological process, which, as Cannan pointed out and Thorstein Veblen before him (Ayres 1967), is wholly social, is given a dramatic flare, or what Veblen was wont to specify as "ceremonial adequacy." And the eventual technological success is taken as evidence of the success of the ceremonial vestitures. The latter dramatically simulate and personalize the technological, matter-of-fact, and even prosaic, activity.

But even though technology and institutions are so intimately intertwined, they can be distinguished as social processes. And nowhere does this become clearer than when we attempt to analyze them from the spectrum viewpoint. Ideologies can be easily arranged and sorted out as to how closely they uphold or deny the present status hierarchy. But knowledge is another matter. Is there a right and left way of adzing? Does the manufacture of steel lend itself to ideological classification? Could one ascertain from an aerial photo whether a steel mill was left (Russian) or right (U.S.)? Do the ongoing changes in Eastern Europe mean that current technology is obsolete? Obviously spectrum thinking in this realm is irrelevant.

As a way of resolving social problems, spectrum thinking has little to recommend it either logically or historically. In a perceptive volume three decades ago, William J. Newman (1961) analyzed the beginnings of the post-World War II conservative movement in the United States as it took form in the immediate two decades after the close of the war. Sidney Blumenthal in his more recent *The Rise of the Counter-Establishment: From Conservative Ideology to Political Power* covered the period dealt with by Newman, and as the title indicates also covered some of the political consequences of the rise of the new Conservatism (Blumenthal 1986). Newman, however, entitled his study *The Futilitarian Society*, the title coming from his observations that conservatism was unable to cope with change, which, in an industrial economy, is absolutely vital. It could not cope with the major realities and dynamism of the age within which we live.

On the other hand, revolution does not have a very good historical record of lasting innovation. Once getting over the heady excitement of the new dispensation, the old order seems to get itself reestablished, albeit with new names for those now serving in the same capacity as that in which the Czar's ministers previously served. W. Bruce Lincoln in his *In War's Dark Shadows* (1983), although it is not his intent, demonstrates clearly that the oppressive practices to which we objected in Bolshevism were foreshadowed by the quaint practices of the Czar. The Old Bolsheviks knew the route to the Gulag very well, having been there by the free transportation provided by the Czar.

So what has this to do with institutional economics? Or, for that matter, does it have anything to do with economics? Where does institutionalism fit on the spectrum? Or does it fit? If we are talking about social systems characterized by instituted hierarchy, then institutionalism just does not fit on the spectrum. It has no proposed instituted hierarchy "from whom all blessings come" – neither of the right, left, nor a bastard version. If we are talking about systems dominated by capital or labor or some other mystical force from the dim dark past, such as land, and of systems of economic thought upholding such instituted hierarchies, it is possible to place them and their adherents on the spectrum – according to the degree of fervor involved in upholding or denouncing an existent instituted hierarchy. But if the spectrum is a ranging of ideas by ideological intensity, then institutionalism has no place on the spectrum.

As a matter of fact, as I understand the main focus of institutional economics, it has been one long effort to get away from spectrum thinking, away from ideology towards knowledge. It is problem oriented and is not much interested in whether a proposed solution to an economic problem passes the test of ideological responsibility. Although I have problems with the Tool–Foster notion of building instrumental institutions, I have great respect for Marc Tool's *Discretionary Economy* (1979) for its dismissal of spectrum thinking and its emphasis on problem solving. To me the instrumental position precludes any acceptance of ideological thinking or any other form of theological exegesis.

Ideologies lend themselves to spectrum classification because they relate to systems of instituted hierarchy, what Veblen referred to as systems of "graded men." But these do not by any means exhaust socially organized behavior nor include all of social belief. There is also all of what Veblen called "the economic life process awaiting theoretical formulation." I take Guy Routh's eloquent call at the conclusion of his *The Origin of Economic Ideas* for economists to abandon the old doctrines and ways and to "study the ills of society with the meticulousness of virologists, and the devotion of anthropologists studying a primitive tribe" to be the same as that of Veblen (Routh 1977, p. 311).

Is institutionalism then radical or is it conservative? If the terms radical and conservative are used adjectivally, then if there is a radical institutionalism there must also be a conservative institutionalism, but what is being preserved and what is being torn down? In other words, just what are radical institutionalists rooting out and what are conservative institutionalists attempting to preserve? Put this way, I think the answers become apparent. An institutionalist approach is a problem-oriented one that concentrates on specifics. What to do about oil spills? How to maintain full and enlarging employment? How to get the homeless home? How to get income to dependent children? How to get health care already possible to those who need it? And so it goes. There is no overall instituted hierarchy, right or left, by virtue of which someday life will become a thing of beauty and a joy forever. No institutionalist ever promised that life would be a rose garden. Life is one series of problems. This is the only matter on which the phrase "as it was in the beginning, 'tis now and ever shall be" is meaningful. Institutionalism is godless economics. And that does not qualify it for a position on the classical right–left spectrum.

In recent decades, non-spectrum thinking in economics has been referred to as evolutionary as well as institutional. Perhaps the word "evolutionary" is much more appropriate to this way of thinking about economic affairs. Other forms of economic thought have concentrated on the instituted hierarchy aspect of social organization. C. E. Ayres insisted that

> [a]s a designation of a way of thinking in economics the term "institutional-ism" is singularly unfortunate, since it points only at that from which an escape is being sought. Properly speaking, it is the classical tradition that is "institutionalism," since it is a way of thinking that expresses a certain set of institutions.
>
> (1944, pp. 155–6n)

Within the distinction made by Bloch between ideology and knowledge, the classical way of thinking is ideological in that it upholds a particular instituted hierarchy. The same can be said about the Marxian version of classical economics.

Both classical economics and Marxian economics, have, of course, acknowl-edged the importance of technology. But in both instances, technology takes a back seat to the more dramatic affairs of "instituted hierarchy." Technology in the orthodox pantheon is a function of individual incentive and, therefore, of genius. And in the Marxian lexicon, the material forces of production, although important, play a secondary role to the class struggle by virtue of which change is actuated.

Perhaps no such evolutionary view of economic development was sustainable when classical economics and its Marxian derivative were first formulated. The evolution of technology throughout history was not clear before the archaeolo-gists uncovered the artifacts of ancient societies from under the shifting desert sands, the rough gravel in river washes, and the deep recesses of Aurignacian caves – all of which were products of late-nineteenth-century archaeology. In this way, the evolutionary nature of the tool process was exposed to view.

Before the record became clear, invention and discovery could still be easily attributed to individual genius. Its significance as a social process could also be easily overlooked, as history, including inventive history, was held to be a func-tion of the activities of heroic ancestors. However, after the archaeological digs, no longer could the history of technology be viewed as a series of discrete events.

Before the record became clear, however, invention and discovery could be easily attributed to individual genius. Each invention and each discovery could quite plausibly be treated as a discrete event unrelated to that which preceded and equally unrelated to that which was subsequent. That kind of interpretation is perfectly compatible with ideological belief that holds that today's heroes are reenacting the ways by which their heroic progenitors created such a successful way of life. And such interpretations of the social order uphold instituted hierarchies that can be arranged in accordance with the seating arrangements in the revolutionary French assembly.

In taking the tool process as of primary importance, institutional economics is of necessity evolutionary. That is to say, its evolutionary and problem-solving position is not the product of squeamishness over more forceful methods to effect change, nor a product of a soft-heartedness that lacks the steel to uphold the eternal verities against the barbarians from without.

Does rejecting spectrum thinking mean that institutionalism has no overall view of the economy? Not at all if we are talking about the economy in a Keynesian macro-sense, of interrelated and reciprocal flows of expenditure and delivery of goods. This does deal with the interrelatedness of the parts within the whole economy. But those interrelationships are matter-of-fact ones, not a system of hierarchical interrelationships by virtue of which authorship for all good things is assigned and claims laid.

References

Ayres, C. E. 1944. *The Theory of Economic Progress*. Chapel Hill: University of North Carolina Press.

——. 1967. "Ideological Responsibility." *Journal of Economic Issues* 1 (June): 2–11.

Bloch, Maurice. 1977. "The Past and the Present in the Present." *Man* 12 (August): 278–92.

Blumenthal, Sidney. 1986. *The Rise of the Counter-Establishment*. New York: Times Books.

Brown, Donald E. 1988. *Hierarchy, History, and Human Nature*. Tucson: University of Arizona Press.

Durkheim, Emile, and Marcel Mauss. 1967. *Primitive Classification*. Chicago: University of Chicago Press.

Hamilton, David. 1983. "The Conventional Account of the Industrial Revolution as Myth and Legend," paper read at the Western Social Science Association meeting, Albuquerque. April.

——. 1956. "The Ceremonial Aspect of Corporate Organization." *American Journal of Economics and Sociology* 16 (October): 1–23.

——. 1957. "The Entrepreneur as Cultural Hero." *Southwestern Social Science Journal* 38 (3): 248–56.

Lincoln, W. Bruce. 1983. *In War's Dark Shadows*. New York: The Dial Press.

Newman, William J. 1961. *The Futiliarian Society*. New York: George Braziller.

Routh, Guy. 1977. *The Origin of Economic Ideas*. New York: Vintage Books.

Tool, Marc. 1979. *The Discretionary Economy*. Santa Monica, Calif.: Goodyear.

24 Rickshaws, treadmills, galley slaves, and Chernobyl

Journal of Economic Issues, vol. 26 (June 1992), pp. 477–83

COMMENTARY BY WILLIAM M. DUGGER

Hamilton focuses this essay on a fundamental distinction emphasized by many institutionalists in the Veblen–Dewey–Ayres line. Hamilton points out that although all human behavior is a whole, much can be learned by distinguishing between two different aspects of the whole: the instrumental and the ceremonial. The ceremonial has to do with status, charisma, power, money – getting the reward for a job well done. Market behavior is ceremonial. The instrumental has to do with planting, harvesting, manufacturing – getting the job done in a skillful manner. Technological behavior is instrumental. Institutionalists downplay the significance of the ceremonial and up-play the significance of the instrumental.

So far, so good, explains Hamilton. However, technology is often taken as institutionalists' shining knight and the market as their *bête noire*. If such is truly the case, institutionalists should have a very hard time dealing with the current situation in which technology is often blamed for much human degradation (rickshaws), meaninglessness (treadmills), and exploitation (galley slaves). The institutionalist plight would seem to be made even worse by the nuclear devastation caused by Chernobyl. Hamilton addresses these technological issues using his ample wit and wisdom.

RICKSHAWS, TREADMILLS, GALLEY SLAVES, AND CHERNOBYL

About forty years ago, Harry Estill Moore, a prominent sociologist of the time, wrote that institutionalism was "that branch of economic thought which attacks institutions, as it defines them, as the brakes on progress and hails technology as the shining knight in armor who leads us forward in spite of our worst efforts" (1953). Although written presumably in a spirit of goodwill, the statement bears a cutting edge. Belief in "shining knights," while perhaps not necessarily in the same league with the belief of those who followed James Jones to Jonestown, smacks of sycophancy and mesmerism. We do know, for sure, that shining knights are the stuff of dreams and that, in actuality, all of them bear tarnished armor.

But Harry Moore's slightly veiled accusation against institutionalism was made forty years ago. Has not greater understanding among institutionalists at least been achieved in the meantime? One might conclude from some of the uneasiness in some of the more recent institutionalist writings that the same kind of doubtful cynicism is still very much alive. Certainly, Moore had it half right; institutionalism does emphasize technology as the dynamic force within the industrial economy and all of those forms of economy that preceded it, for that matter.

But just what kind of dynamic force is it? There is, after all, Chernobyl! No longer designating a place and specific event (for the specific event has never been made that specific in the Western world), Chernobyl has become a generic name for the disaster that modern technology represents. How, then, can one take seriously an economics that emphasizes those very cultural forces that produce the Chernobyls? Surely, institutionalism must at least reexamine that older position and perhaps bring about a neoinstitutional synthesis. If technology is all that Chernobyl stands for as a name, then perhaps the orthodox brethren were more right than we once thought. Who will be our Samuelson? Who will develop a bastard institutionalism?

Such questions may at first seem to be contrived. However, I think not. Fundamental to institutional economics is the distinction between the price system and the machine industry, between investment for a profit and the manufacture of goods, and between the ceremonial of economic life and the instrumental by virtue of which we place butter on the table and satellites in space. It is fundamental in the same manner that the concepts of supply and demand are to conventional economics, from which perception all of the economic activities of humankind can supposedly be engrossed. So persistent is this latter persuasion that the breakup of the monolithic political system of the Soviet Union is construed by George Will (1991: A6) as a victory of the Chicago School of Economics over the wickedness that once prevailed. And during times when it is not very clear just what "the market" refers to in our economy, we are sure that those fortuitous, or perhaps calamitous, events beyond what proved to be not such an iron curtain are merely way stations to a new market equilibrium. One might even declare Schumpeter's "creative destruction" at work under the aegis of a swarm of newly liberated former commissars acting as Schumpeterian innovators.

With such stirring events in the former Soviet Union, now the Commonwealth of Independent States (CIS), an economics that downplays the significance of the market and emphasizes the technological process could, to those with weak intellectual knees, call for a reassessment, perhaps to be known as neo-neoinstitutionalism.

For the classical economist, technology is secondary, and the market is primary. The dramatic part of the culture – the buying and selling signifying ownership transfer in the village bazaar – is viewed as the driving force, and all of the grubbing, painstaking, socially organized effort that brings forth that which is the object of the frenzied buying and selling is taken for granted as mere technology. Just as in our own economy, the classicist would urge the Soviets to adopt the market system whereupon nitty-gritty technological problems – the Chernobyls – will disappear. Wheat will grow in abundance, queuing will become a memory, and life will be a thing of beauty. The people of the Commonwealth of Independent States (CIS) are being offered the same recipes that were served at home as Reaganomics and now Bushenomics.

It seems to me that what the citizens of the CIS have an opportunity to get rid of is a shining knight, even though in their case the reflection may have a reddish glow. And it is clear that what the West has to offer is our shining knight (the free market) in exchange for the fallen red horseman.

Is technology, then, also a tarnished knight? After all, there is Chernobyl and before that all of those galley slaves, rickshaws, and treadmills. If so, then the institutional analysis stands condemned.

What, I believe unfortunately, has become known as THE dichotomy sometimes is viewed as two separate and diverse patterns of human behavior. At one time we are ceremonial and at other times technological. This may be almost unavoidable, given those marked events such as the marriage rite, in which the major focus of attention is upon the conveyancing of mystic stuff that gives authenticity to two individuals in subsequent roles. But lying behind the whole thing is that activity often deprecatingly referred to as "mere technology." It is what follows the wedding ceremony to the success of which the wedding pretends. Weddings are not mere occasions to drink champagne and eat cake. They pretend to the alleged competence of the parties involved to perform the grubbing, nitty-gritty tasks involved in "perpetuating the species." Families are often almost exclusively conceived in terms of those events when, supposedly, feelings of social solidarity are rekindled (or, perhaps, diminished). However, families have a technological meaning that is far more overriding. The skill and dexterity with which the family skills are employed is one of those matters that determine the wealth of a nation.

Sometimes, the institutionalist recognizes all of this when noting that ceremonialism overlies some other kind of activity referred to by Veblen as matter-of-fact. This vertical bifurcation, however, is also troublesome. All social behavior must be taken as a whole. Every aspect has an element of ceremonialism and matter-of-fact, in varying combinations. And even this kind of analysis, I think, confuses matters, for behavior comes in wholes neither bifurcated nor layered – when we are behaving. That is to say, no one states, or could state, that now I am being ceremonial, now I am being technological. In one sense we have two ways of viewing one whole process. From the ceremonial perspective, the mundane matter-of-factness by which we secure a livelihood is dramatized by assigning mystic responsibility to particular roles and hence to particular individuals occupying those roles. Heroes do great things, and it is by virtue of a differential holding of the tribal mystic life-force, be that *mana, orenda, wakan,* capital, or labor, that the world putatively does its work. On the other hand, when one examines the means by which cakes are baked and satellites put into space, it almost seems that anyone could do it. Imagine, for the moment, a matter-of-fact job description for the president of the United States, or of Zimbabwe, or of General Motors. As a matter of fact, a caveat will be found in every job description manual or how-to-do-it book to the effect that above a certain level in the job hierarchy, job descriptions cannot be done. The job has such esoteric requirements that no simple prosaic description is possible. That is where *mana* alone will do the job; writing a job description would expose the fraud.

But this mundane example itself reveals much. We are obviously into that esoteric world of status in which heroic individuals manhandle the stuff of this world that is impossible for mere mortals. And it is to that instituted hierarchy and its preservation that we owe civilization. So strong is this kind of belief that people will annihilate one another in order to preserve that perspective and ordering of affairs. No people ever went to war to preserve the hammer and sickle other than as symbols of some mystic stuff called labor.

Systems of economic thought have generally consisted of an account of the economy drawn in terms of mystic forces and social hierarchies differentially charged with the life-force of the group. Within modern times (i.e. the last four hundred years) those life-forces, at one time or another, have been represented by land, capital, and labor, and all with a hierarchical social system based on a differential endowment of that mystic stuff. It was through the beneficence of the lord of the land that crops and flocks flourished; through the foresight, initiative, and enterprise of the capitalist that goods were plentiful; and through the intercession of the commissars, those paragons of labor, that well-being was assured. And the supporting theory, or ideology, testified to the certainty of the outcome. Failure occurred not within the system, but by neglecting to adhere rigidly to the mores and taboos that defined the status hierarchy that supported them.

With such a long history of practice and belief, it is indeed daunting for a group of economists identified as institutionalists to defy eons of wisdom and to state that well-being is to be found in digging sticks and their manipulation and the knowledge secured from their manipulation.

What the institutionalism (without the ism) of C. E. Ayres and Veblen seems to have been doing is demystifying just how we do in fact secure a livelihood. Most of us concede the necessity for rolling, forging, and slitting mills to procure steel and steel products. But those necessities represent mere technology. To the conventional mind, those are not social processes by which we secure steel, just as the digging sticks, the lack toys, and the fishhooks of the Trobrianders are mere technology. We seem to be unable to understand that these objects which we refer to as "mere" technology are integral parts of socially learned behavior. We do not first learn to speak and then invent a language with which to do it. We do not first learn how to capture fish and then invent the instruments with which we put our knowledge into practice. We do not first learn how to control pollution and then invent the instruments with which to control it. Instruments and social action are integral parts of a whole social pattern of behavior.

Nor is the opposite true. Even though within the individual experience of each of us, the world may seem to be inhabited by items called technology that we must somehow master, that is not true for the group as a whole. Although those fiberglass sticks may be meaningless to us, someone already has the skill to employ them on the ski slopes. In fact, we learn their meaning as we learn to use them in the process of skiing. Surely no one could, on sufficient contemplation, view technology as inert stuff that somehow had a prior existence to socially organized human beings.

But what about Chernobyl? And what about those demeaning rickshaws and enslaving treadmills and galleys? About the rickshaws, treadmills, and galleys, we can perhaps be a bit flippant. Would anyone declare that oars are responsible for the tyranny of the coxswain in the Harvard shell any more than for the slavery in the Mediterranean galley? And what about the health nut on the home treadmill being demeaned with every step? And the ignominy of the macho male spouse pushing the baby carriage? But let us be more serious.

What Dewey, Ayres, Malinowski, and Leslie White have been saying is that the real source of human well-being is our ongoing stream of tool-oriented behavior. This is an impersonal, nonheroic, prosaic, matter-of-fact process within which human beings come and go, but which has a continuity and momentum all its own. It is not heroes who make technology; technology makes heroes. It would, of course, be preposterous to say that technology would have any meaning without participating individuals; it would be equally preposterous to assume that individuals would have meaning in the absence of V. G. Childe's phrase concerning "man making himself."

But within the technological process, how are choices made? How is the meritorious separated from the meretricious? How do we deal with Chernobyls? On what outside standard can we rely? These are large, but not very helpful questions, and, no matter how tempting and conference- and symposia-provoking, perhaps they will remain unanswerable. The real questions come in more specific, matter-of-fact, and temporal form. How do we choose an appropriate wrench? How do we decide to use a crosscut saw rather than a ripsaw? Why do we insist that we all adhere to driving consistently on one side of a two-way highway? Why now is there wide consensus on the inadvisability of smoking cigarettes or using tobacco in general? Or questions about a specific event at a specific time and a specific place called Chernobyl?

The answers to these questions seem quite straightforward. They are given in terms of the ongoing technological process within which, at the moment, each is germane. Valuation is a temporal matter, not one of arranging valued things by some mystic significance. Which are better – wrenches or ripsaws; music or literature; ice cream or penicillin; automobiles or boats; bananas or rutabagas; toilet plungers or push brooms? Such questions make no sense outside the context within which each of these items and skills would, for the moment, be relevant.

It seems to me that what Dewey and Ayres were doing was demystifying and depersonalizing the process by which we secure our livelihood. If we desire more potatoes, then we had best devote our attention to potato raising and not to some instituted hierarchy honored by ritual that reinforces a belief in differential personal possession of mystic potencies. Apparently, this matter-of-fact point is up against such long-established social precedent as to be almost insurmountable. But even individuals sympathetic to the point of view of Ayres, Dewey, and Veblen seem to have trouble understanding that there is nothing more social nor more human than technology. This is, however, no shining knight. It is the life process: rust, warts, and all.

References

Moore, Harry Estill. Preface to *Newtonian Classicism and Darwinian Institutionalism*, by David Hamilton. 1953. Reprint. Westport, Conn.: Greenwood Press, 1975.
Will, George. "Wit and Wisdom Gave Economist Powerful Voice." *Albuquerque Tribune*, 9 December 1991, p. A6.

25 Technology and institutions are neither

Journal of Economic Issues, vol. 20 (June 1986), pp. 525–32

COMMENTARY BY WILLIAM M. DUGGER

Hamilton puts another enigmatic title on another significant article. He startles his readers into pondering a non-traditional position. David Hamilton's prose reminds me of Mark Twain. Few economists share Hamilton's masterly use of language. Veblen did, and often used it in the same way. All three – Twain, Hamilton, and Veblen – have used language in this peculiar way to teach their readers unconventional thoughts. It is the unconventional that is so hard to learn. So first, these great teachers startle us into a condition conducive to unconventional thought.

In this article, Hamilton argues that "technology" and "institution" mean something very different in institutionalism than they do in conventional usage: In institutionalism, technology refers to the process of manipulating tools to achieve ends-in-view while institution refers to the process of propitiating spiritual forces to achieve ends-in-view. On the other hand, in conventional usage, institution refers to an aspect of social organization while technology refers to physical instruments (shovels, hammers, typewriters, computers).

Hamilton's unconventional meanings of institution and technology are used to great advantage by a significant number of institutionalists, particularly by most followers of Clarence E. Ayres and his Texas School. Nevertheless, it is my editorial duty to point out that not all institutionalists use "institution" and "ceremonial" in exactly the same way. In particular, radical institutionalists do not use these terms to mean the propitiation of spiritual forces, but instead to mean the legitimization of the unequal distribution of income, power, and status in contemporary society. The radicals claim, rightly or wrongly, to be going back to the more fundamental institutionalism of Veblen. The difference does not represent a break with other institutionalists. Rather, the significance of the difference lies in the fact that in their critiques of institutions, the radicals emphasize the legitimation of social stratification while the Ayresians emphasize the propitiation of spiritual forces.

TECHNOLOGY AND INSTITUTIONS ARE NEITHER

One, but only one, of the reasons conventional economics in its formal market glorification form has such staying power is that those who come to it for the first time for formal instruction come predisposed to believe. All of our young lives we heard of the laws of supply and demand, much as we took in the notion of an all-abiding divine protector. It is part of the cultural fabric, part of the perspective from which all of us learn early on to perceive the universe. All of our young lives we heard how the economy is under the suzerainty of the law of supply and demand. If prices for the moment are troublesome because they are either going up too fast or going down too fast for the comfort of all, but perhaps for the betterment of some, we are assured that it is merely supply and demand on its way to reestablishing a new equilibrium in which economic justice will once again prevail.

We come similarly predisposed to view institutions as social organization, and technology as things similar to rocks and trees on the landscape. We do know that the social fabric is not fragile and that social practices seem quite rigid and tough. And most certainly there are physical objects in which our technology is most manifest. But common usage holds that institutions are synonymous with socially organized behavior patterns and that technology refers to shovels, hammers, typewriters, and now computers, in their physical manifestation.

This common meaning is one familiar in general social analysis. In the early decades of the twentieth century, the "cultural" lag thesis was quite widely used to define social problems from just such a perspective. Technology, viewed as a material force that traveled at an untamed, accelerating speed in the modern industrial economy, constantly raced ahead of our ability to devise the social organization essential to its domestication. The lag inherent in the definition of institutions is subject to only slow change, and technology subject to accelerating rates of growth is what caused social problems.[1]

One example often referred to in illustrating this lag was the persistence of old forms of driving on roadways, left over from the days of horse-drawn vehicles, in a time when the automobile had become ubiquitous. The patterns of driving were viewed as institutions and the horse-drawn vehicles and their successors, the automobiles, as technology. The problem was provoked by the inability of automobiles traveling at sixty miles an hour to pass one another consistently in opposite directions with no more than three feet between. This was a trick that presumably posed no problem in the days of horse-drawn vehicles with their more modest speeds. The lagged institutional arrangements were causing carnage on the highways. Hence, the problem was to develop more modern driving institutions to conform to the needs of automobiles.

The persistence of supply and demand theory is in no way endangered by the fact that those who come to learn its intricate details come pre-programmed. The fixation of belief among those predisposed to that belief is all to the advantage of those determined to inculcate in the young its nuances and its more sophisticated versions. Predisposition favors perpetuation of the conventional wisdom.

Unfortunately, the predisposition of those who come to institutional analysis to view institutions as social organizations, and technology as things, is apt to leave the learner with a sense of understanding when in fact there is none. Instructor and instructee are very apt to think right past one another, with the instructor thinking that learning has taken place and with the instructee believing that understanding has taken place. Actually neither has been communicating with the other. To use the words "institutions" and "technology" does not an institutionalist make, nor does their use in economic analysis make an institutional analysis.

Unfortunately, more than misunderstanding takes place. Since everyone possesses the notion that the word "institution" refers to socially organized structures (socially sanctioned ways of doing things and behaving) and "technology" refers to material things that are manipulated, a person of conventional economic persuasion cannot be faulted if he/she wonders what all the shouting is about. Even the most erudite and sterile conventional economic exposition will at least pay heed to the "institutional" structure in which choices are being made and things called "resources" are being arranged. Who can possibly say that they are not cognizant of the importance of institutions and technology? Now let's get on with the game of allocating scarce resources among an infinity of wants. The institutionalist seems to be a needlessly bothersome busybody who wants to make a fuss where none need be made.

In view of these conditions, it would seem a worthy effort to see what the shouting was and is all about. I feel that the most significant contribution that institutionalism has to make to economic analysis is the use of the dichotomy of institutions/technology to analyze economic phenomena. Without it there is no such thing as institutional economics. The orthodox brethren are perfectly correct when they say that conventional economics has always taken into account institutions – meaning social structures, of course. Therein lies more than just a semantic problem.

The notion of institutions and technology is as seminal to institutional economics as is that of supply and demand to conventional economics. It is presumably through the forces of supply and demand that new states of equilibrium are secured, each presumably at an enlarged state of output. To the institutionalist, the cultural processes of technology and institutions are the forces through the interaction of which we achieve economic progress, the first being a dynamic cultural force and the other being a permissive force at best and a retardant at worst. This being the case, it is mandatory that the meaning of these cultural forces be clear, most certainly among institutionalists.

In the opening paragraphs of *The Quest for Certainty*, John Dewey stated that we live in a world of uncertainty but are "compelled to seek for security."[2] That quest for security has taken two directions. We attempt to "propitiate the powers that environ" us by "supplication, sacrifice, ceremonial rite and magical cult." The second approach is to develop arts to manipulate the forces of nature and turn them to our own advantage. The first of these approaches, of course, promises certainty of outcome. Adhere rigidly to some prescribed ritual and belief and the desired outcome will be achieved. If it is not achieved, it is not because of the inefficacy of the ritual or belief, but because of failure to adhere to all of the prescribed canons for proper manipulation.

The second approach is always uncertain in outcome and has only a probable success. Yet it is by virtue of the latter social process that the human enterprise has succeeded as well as it has to the present. There is no certainty, but at least uncertainty can be reduced.

These two facets of human behavior are quite manifest in the reports of so-called primitive cultures on which anthropologists spent their time when such peoples were still available for study. One that always readily comes to mind is Bronislaw Malinowski's work in which he detailed canoe constructing and taro gardening among the Melanesians of the Trobriand Islands.[3] There the matter-of-fact work of canoe construction was punctuated by an elaborate ritual at each stage, from tree selection to launching of finished canoe. There was a mixture of the two phenomena of which Dewey wrote. Matter-of-fact adzing took place in conjunction with bull-roaring, which gave to the matter-of-fact activity, ceremonial authenticity.

Taro gardening proceeded with the same dichotomous association of ritual and incantation and matter-of-fact grubbing work. The kumkola was erected at the periphery of each garden plot, before which mystic forces were propitiated almost simultaneously with the matter-of-fact tilling of the soil essential to successful taro raising.

To the participant observer the distinct nature of these two social processes is readily apparent. As a matter of fact, by the very manner in which we verbally address these practices, it is apparent that we have no doubt that taros can be secured by slighting the ritual. We refer to that aspect of the culture of the Trobrianders or any other people being similarly observed as "ceremonial." The very word indicates that it is dispensable, that in the case of the Trobrianders, taros can be secured without it. So can seaworthy canoes be constructed without the ceremonial activities centered on bull-roaring?

Although the two aspects of behavior may be apparent to the observer, to the culturally conditioned participant, canoe making and taro cultivation make up one whole social process, no part of which can be avoided if canoes are to be sailed and taro harvested successfully. In the belief system that authenticates all of these activities we can similarly make distinction between that which is a function of mythopoeic imagination and that which is based on pragmatic experience. When the ceremonial bull-roaring is performed and explained by the belief that evil forces will stand in the way of a successful sail to Dobu unless warded off by proper ritual, we know that this is a different type of knowledge than that which explains why the outrigger must bear a certain proportion to the hull to facilitate sailing.

These two cultural processes were applied by Thorstein Veblen to an analysis of the industrial economy. To some readers of Veblen this application left them in the same state of consternation as the Trobrianders would have been in had they been able to comprehend what Malinowski was reporting. Certainly it is possible to make such an analytic distinction in the social processes of so-called primitive peoples, but is not our "advanced" technology and science sufficient evidence that we have been emancipated from such superstition? To this question Veblen was responding with a very strong "no."

His use of institutions and technology, however, was in no way related to the rather common association of the term "institution" with social organization, and "technology" with instruments in their physical embodiment. Unfortunately, he never did set down a precise definition, but it is clear from the context in which he wrote that when he referred to "imbecile institutions" and to "ceremonial adequacy" and to "use and wont" and to "magical and superstitious practice" he was referring not to social structure, but to a social process by virtue of which alleged spiritual forces were manipulated and propitiated.[4]

When he referred to technology, or to matter-of-fact activity, or matter-of-fact thought, or to workmanship, he was referring to tool-oriented behavior equally socially organized and socially learned. It was to on-going social processes that he was referring. His vision is of a people caught up in securing a livelihood, in the course of which they manipulate tools and engage in propitiatory activities; in doing so, no great distinction is made over the necessity of both to achieving their ends-in-view. Veblen frequently referred to the life-process, a concept I find similar to that of Dewey when he referred to the continuity of life or to the continuum as a series of ends–means and means–ends relationships in which ends become means to what is subsequent.[5]

From an analysis of the institutional and technological cultural processes, it becomes apparent that human well-being is related to the technological process. That is where problem solving and innovation take place. The institutional or ceremonial process is mandated by past events and hence is past bound. "As it was in the beginning, 'tis now and ever shall be" is the doxology of the institutional process.

All of this, of course, has been pointed out before, but apparently to no avail. Among conventional economists the pre-natal meanings of institutions and technology constitute an impermeable membrane that prevents understanding these as social processes. Looked at in the conventional manner, it is easy to perceive that the institutionalist is saying nothing more than that it is necessary to accommodate to technological change. Who would fault that? If that is what the institutionalist is saying, it is something with which we have never been in disagreement. As a matter of fact, it is on the same high level as endorsing apple pie.

But among some who are professional institutionalists, the same preconception concerning these terms is apparent. When we begin to sort out institutions into those that are ceremonial and those that are instrumental, we reveal our predilection to view institutional structures rather than institutional processes. And when we state that there are institutions, some of which are ceremonial and some of which are instrumental, and that then there is technology, we are viewing institutions as socially organized behavior and technology as just things like the rocks and trees. And then it is easy to view institutions as "encapsulating" technology and technology institutionally encapsulated as a force detrimental to the human enterprise.

By making these observations I am not attempting to split hairs or to pick fights. There are enough people mad at one another in this world without adding to the acrimony. What I am trying to do is to clarify some concepts that I feel have become rather muddled in the past decade or so; and to point out that the muddle does have consequences.

I also respect the concern of those who are uneasy with the interpretation of Clarence Ayres's use of the ceremonial/instrumental dichotomy as one in which a new theology is being developed with technology as a primal force or first cause. Long ago, in a preface written for my *Newtonian Classicism and Darwinian Institutionalism*, Professor Harry Moore of the University of Texas wrote: "This book is written from the 'Institutional' point of view – that branch of economic thought which attacks institutions, as it defines them, as the brakes on progress and hails technology as the shining knight in armor who leads us forward in spite of our worst efforts."[6] Today some individuals, including some professed institutionalists, would applaud that statement with great enthusiasm. After all, there is the shining knight sitting on Three Mile Island, more than tarnished; the residue of pesticides on our dried fruit; the failed ground-nut project in Africa; and a whole laundry list that can be pointed to with great glee by the present followers of William Morris and Matthew Arnold.

However, no one, least of all Ayres and Dewey, ever insisted there was any absolute certainty about the technological process. The outcome of technological activity is problematic. There will be *Titanic*s. The virtue of the technological process is that it is self-correcting. The test of truth is an operational one. If we employ this tool (technology) in this socially organized manner, then ... If the "then" immediately or subsequently has undesirable consequences (that is, disrupting, thwarting, inhibiting the continuity of living), which it may well have, we reassess its value to the human enterprise. It seems to me that is what is involved in our relatively recent reassessment of the employment of atomic energy. And we will undoubtedly reassess those reassessments if the recent successes with Sandia Lab's Particle Beam Fusion Accelerator prove more than illusory. The technological process is an irreverent one and a liberating one, in that it focuses on problem solving rather than on adherence to ideology and ancient prescriptive.

The other route to security, that of the institutional process, is the realm of certainty. No adversity can be so great as to challenge abiding faith. The nostrums and prescriptives are guaranteed to deliver certainty. When the security sought is not achieved, it cannot be the fault of the process employed because it, by definition, is infallible. Either the correct ritual was not employed, some error crept into its execution, or there were counterforces at work.

It seems to me that this institutional analysis has never been more applicable than it is today. We were beset during the 1970s with an assortment of economic problems, some niggling, some significant, and some imagined. They consisted of persistent unemployment, of trade balances that seemed to get unbalanced, inflation, energy shortages, accelerating food prices, falls in productivity, and you name it. Some of these, when we think about it, are perennials. But in any event, a technological approach would attack each in its own. Some might be of such magnitude and geographic dimension that we alone could do little about it. And some might not be worth a whole lot of effort. But a technological approach would address each in turn.

On the other hand, we have been told that if we would but return to faith in the free market, to the ways of the ancestors, all of our troubles would disappear. The results in the United States, as well as in England, have not been ones to sustain the faith. But under such circumstances the system is not self-correcting. What are called for are more faith and more time for the lazy fairy to bring on untroubled times. The present suffering is but the storm before the light. But it is warranted, for it is the sins of the arrogance of the New Deal, of the New Frontier, and of the Great Society visited upon subsequent generations. This route is analogous to resorting to bull-roaring alone to secure seaworthy canoes.

What differentiates the present climate of opinion from that of the decades of the 1930s through the 1960s is an unwillingness to experiment, to attack operationally defined problems with tentative solutions. At no time has an analysis centering on institutions and technology been more appropriate to understanding what is being experienced. We see a tribe that, we hope only temporarily, has lost its head.

Notes

1 The original and most influential formulation of this thesis appeared in W. F. Ogburn, *Social Change* (New York: B. W. Huebsch, 1922).
2 John Dewey, *The Quest for Certainty* (New York: Minton, Bach, 1929).
3 Bronislaw Malinowski, *Argonauts of the Western Pacific* (New York; Dutton, 1961); *Coral Gardens and Their Magic* (Bloomington: Indiana University Press, 1965); *Magic, Science and Religion* (Glencoe, Ill.: Free Press, 1948). For the economist unfamiliar with such concepts, excellent treatments are to be found in Walter Goldschmidt, *Man's Way: A Preface to the Understanding of Human Society* (New York: Holt, Rinehart & Winston, 1959) and Lucy Mair, *An Introduction to Social Anthropology* (New York: Oxford University Press, 1972).
4 Thorstein Veblen, *Imperial Germany and the Industrial Revolution* (New York: Viking Press, 1939). In the second chapter of this book, Veblen is at his best in distinguishing these two aspects of human behavior.
5 John Dewey, *The Theory of Valuation* (University of Chicago Press, 1939). This is the clearest and briefest presentation of Dewey's instrumental theory of value. An excellent contemporary treatment is to be found in Thomas R. DeGregori, *A Theory of Technology: Continuity and Change in Human Development* (Ames, Iowa: Iowa State University Press, 1985). In this volume the topic is treated specifically in chapter II, "Technological and Valuational Processes." However, in parts of this chapter, when dealing with institutional adjustment, DeGregori sometimes treats technology as the end product of the technological process.
6 Harry Estill Moore. Preface to *Newtonian Classicism and Darwinian Institutionalism*, by David Hamilton. 1953. Reprint, Westport, Conn.: Greenwood Press, 1975.

Index